Old and New New Englanders

Old and New New Englanders

Immigration & Regional Identity in the Gilded Age

Bluford Adams

The University of Michigan Press
Ann Arbor

Published in the United States of America by
The University of Michigan Press
Manufactured in the United States of America
♾ Printed on acid-free paper

2017 2016 2015 2014 4 3 2 1

A CIP catalog record for this book is available from the British Library.

Library of Congress Cataloging-in-Publication Data

Adams, Bluford.
Old and new New Englanders : immigration and regional identity in the Gilded Age / Bluford Adams.
page cm
Includes bibliographical references and index.
ISBN 978-0-472-07208-8 (cloth : acid-free paper) — ISBN 978-0-472-05208-0 (pbk. : acid-free paper) — ISBN 978-0-472-02999-0 (e-book)
1. New England—History—19th century. 2. Group identity—New England. 3. Regionalism—New England. I. Title.
F9.A33 2013
974'.02—dc23

2013034830

To Doris Witt

Acknowledgments

It's a great pleasure to be able to express my gratitude to all the fine folks who have helped me in so many ways over the years I have worked on this book. I will always cherish the memory of your gifts—whether they took the form of a promising research tip or a timely word of encouragement. First, thanks to Tom Dwyer, Andrea Olson, and Christopher Dreyer at the University of Michigan Press for the unfailing good humor with which they have shepherded me through the publication process. I am also grateful to the University of Iowa for the support it provided me during this project. The Provost's Office granted me two career development awards that enabled me to focus on my research, and the Office of the Vice President for Research generously provided funds to help pay for a research assistant, an indexer, and the illustrations. Thanks as well to everyone in the Interlibrary Loan Office and the Special Collections Department of the University of Iowa Libraries who helped me track down sources.

I am deeply grateful to my research assistants from the University of Iowa English and American Studies departments: Joann Quiñones-Perdomo, Tim Bryant, Ray Mescallado, Jennifer McGovern, Kevin Wyne, Andy Clinton, Greg Bales, Jodi Byrd, Amy Lilly, Kim Cohen, Josh Raulerson, Katie Gubbels, Gyorgy Toth, Eric Johnson, Amy Hezel, Ashley Brewer Gill, Matt Lavin, Steven Williams, and Nate Titman. Many of these folks helped me back in the predigital era, when doing research meant scanning texts with one's eyes. I have a mountain of photocopies that attest to their hard work!

A million thanks to my chairs in the English and American Studies departments, Dee Morris, John Raeburn, Brooks Landon, Lauren Rabinovitz, Kim Marra, Susan Birrell, Horace Porter, Jon Wilcox, and Claire Sponsler, who have supported my career, fostered my research, and lifted my spirits on many occasions. I am also indebted to my other terrific colleagues at Iowa, who have taken an interest in my research and nurtured it in myriad ways. Thanks in particular to Ed Folsom and Kathleen Diffley, who have come to my aid more times than I can remember. I am also deeply indebted to the generous Iowa colleagues who have read and commented on earlier versions of my chapters. Claire Fox, Laura Rigal, and Harry Stecopoulos all provided me with thoughtful and stimulating responses to my work, not to mention a thousand words of encouragement to keep me writing. Thanks so much!

I have also received crucial support from colleagues at other institutions, including Bruce McConachie, Dale Knobel, and Tom Lutz. I am especially indebted to Joseph Conforti, who over the years has emerged as my ideal of scholarly achievement and intellectual generosity. He powerfully influenced this book not only through his own excellent scholarship on New England regional identity but also through his thoughtful and supportive responses to my work.

I would like to thank Michèle Schoenfeld for providing me with elegant translations of French texts and for all the warmth and loving kindness she has shown my daughters. Merci beaucoup, Michèle!

I could not have written this book without the love and encouragement I received from my family. My deepest gratitude to Faye and Eldon Smith for all the good times, hilarious stories, and cherished memories and to all the Conrads, Christensens, and Adamses for making trips home so magical. I am truly humbled when I consider my debts to my parents, L. B. Adams Jr. and Margaret W. Adams. They have calmed my nerves and kept me writing through the years with a steady stream of sympathy, sage advice, and loving kindness. I honestly can't express my gratitude. Thanks to Binh and Mai for making life so rich and exciting every day. I am so proud of both of you! Most of all, thanks to Doris Witt for two dazzling decades—for all the wisdom, all the generosity, and all the love. Here's to the next twenty!

The first chapter was originally published as "World Conquerors or a Dying People? Racial Theory, Regional Anxiety, and the Brahmin Anglo-Saxonists," by Bluford Adams, *The Journal of the Gilded Age and Progressive Era,* Volume 08, Issue 02 (April 2009), pp. 189–215. Copyright © 2009 Society for Historians of the Gilded Age and Progressive Era. Reprinted with the permission of Cambridge University Press.

An earlier version of the second chapter previously was published as Bluford Adams, "New Ireland: The Place of Immigrants in American Regionalism," *Journal of American Ethnic History* 24, no. 2 (Winter 2005): 3–33. Copyright by the Immigration and Ethnic History Society. Reprinted by permission.

Contents

Introduction

Regional Identity in an Age of Immigration

Of all the social categories that have shaped the lives of Americans, regional identity is surely one of the most complex and poorly understood. Though seemingly transparent at first glance—most of us can probably conjure up a mental image of a southerner or a midwesterner—regional identity proves, on further scrutiny, to be a very slippery customer, unstable, ambiguous, and often passing itself off as something else. Like raced or gendered ones, regional identities are constantly being formed and deformed by the social and political pressures bearing down on them. Regional identities seem particularly susceptible to those pressures because of the sheer variety of things that go to make them up. Think of the range of associations that a regional identity can carry today. A cautious list might include not only accents, foodways, and musical tastes, but also religious preferences and political tendencies. That list was much longer in the period this book covers, the era between the end of the Civil War and start of the twentieth century, the so-called Gilded Age. In those days, Americans confidently ascribed to regional identity a host of physical, intellectual, and even spiritual traits. Many thought regional background determined a person's attitudes toward work, consumption, and class, her views on education, culture, and morality, and her response to reform movements and political institutions. Some Americans believed regionalism went to the very core of a person's character, determining her degree of sociability, self-interestedness, and optimism. Yankees were shrewd and self-interested, westerners sunny and openhanded, southerners hot-tempered and gracious. These were stereotypes to be sure, and numerous commentators dismissed them as such. But their very existence speaks to the widely assumed power of regional background to explain human thought and behavior in the era.

The capaciousness of regional identity in the nineteenth century was at least partly a function of the various theories that attempted to account for it. The oldest of those theories were based on climate. For centuries European and American commentators had attributed to environmental factors such as heat and humidity the power to shape the bodies and minds of the inhabitants of a given place. The best-known and most controversial of these theories—associated with the followers of the French naturalist Georges-Louis Leclerc, Count of Buffon—claimed that European settlers and their descendants degenerated in the New World. Along with these hemispherical differences, many observers assumed that climate also created regional differences among the Americans themselves. They ascribed perceived regional variations in birthrates, health, and temperament to environmental effects. Many thought, for example, that it was climate that explained why Kentuckians and Tennesseans had so many babies or why western farmwives were so enervated.[1] While most commentators agreed that the effects of climate waned as people became acclimatized, they believed that this process took anywhere from several years to several generations. This meant that most Americans, even native-born ones, were still feeling the climatic effects of their regions.

Closely related to climate as a source of regional identity was the countryside. Most nineteenth-century Americans took for granted that the essence of an American region was to be found not in its cities but in its remote villages and farmsteads. They looked to rural Americans for the distinctive ways of working, playing, worshiping, and socializing that typified a regional identity. It was agriculturalists in particular—the southern planter, the Yankee farmer, the western homesteader—who seemed to embody the traits of their respective regions. Some observers, particularly urban ones, romanticized rural dwellers as simple folk untouched by the social and economic forces that were remaking the nation's cities. Others rightly pointed out that rural Americans were as affected by, and aware of, those modernizing forces as their urban cousins were. But even the most tough-minded commentators thought a region needed its rural districts as a repository of distinctive values, history, and cultural continuity. Summing up the received wisdom, Bowdoin College president William D. Hyde declared that "the country is the fountain of the nation's life. Sociologists tell us that 'only the agricultural class possesses permanent vitality; from its overflow the city population is formed, displaced, renewed.'"[2] Without cities a region might lack wealth and cultural amenities, but without a countryside it lacked a soul.

A third major source of regional identity in the nineteenth century was race. At a time when Americans took seriously the differences among the so-called white races, many believed the regional variations among Euro-Americans could be traced to their diverse Old World ancestries.[3] The most famous example of this emerged in the 1830s, when southern partisans invoked race to justify their escalating conflict with white northerners. The former claimed descent from the seventeenth-century Cavaliers, and beyond them, the Norman rulers of medieval England. In contrast they saw northerners as the scions of the seventeenth-century Puritans and ultimately the Anglo-Saxon commoners of medieval England. As would-be Normans, the southerners considered themselves a dashing and aristocratic people, born to conquer and rule, while they deemed the northern "Anglo-Saxons" a plodding, materialistic race. Proslavery ideologue George Fitzhugh explained, "The former are a master-race—the latter a slave race, the descendants of Saxon serfs. . . . The Saxons and Angles, ancestors of the Yankees, came from the cold and marshy regions of the North, where man is little more than a cold-blooded, amphibious biped."[4] Not surprisingly, many northerners, particularly in New England, rejected the Cavalier-Norman thesis, not because it was patently false (just as most northerners actually were not Puritan scions, most southerners were not descended from the Cavaliers) but because of its unflattering portrait of their alleged Anglo-Saxon ancestors.[5] On the other hand, many northerners did accept the fundamental premise that regional identity flowed from race. That idea would become especially popular in the heyday of Anglo-Saxonism that followed the Civil War. By that point even some prominent southerners had started to celebrate their region as a pure product of the Anglo-Saxon race.[6]

A fourth basis of regional identity, and one at least acknowledged by most nineteenth-century commentators, was history. Many observers argued that two centuries of life on this continent had left a deep imprint on Euro-Americans in every part of the country, distinguishing them not only from their kinsmen across the Atlantic but also from their countrymen in other regions. They particularly emphasized the shaping influences of a region's political and social institutions. Over time those institutions could create marked differences even among the members of the same race. For example, many Gilded Age historians argued that, by the time of the Revolution, two hundred years' experience with local self-government had made the Yankee patriots better republicans than their fellow Anglo-Saxons in the British army. Some of those historians maintained that the Yankees had been further transformed in the years after the Revolution when they migrated to the Old Northwest, where progressive political and social institutions broadened their minds and liberalized their politics. Over time, it seemed, even the most entrenched regional character was subject to change.

A fifth source of regional identity for nineteenth-century theorists was economics. Anticipating the centrality of economic determinants to present-day regional identities—apparent in terms like *Rust Belt* and *Breadbasket*—nineteenth-century Americans tended to associate each of the nation's regions with a dominant industry: the West stood for grain farming, the South meant cotton production, and New England symbolized manufacturing. To a greater extent than today, nineteenth-century theorists believed the economic differences between the nation's regions produced contrasting class relations. There was good reason for this in the antebellum period, when the contrast between the class structures of the slaveholding South and the free North far exceeded anything we know today. Yet the class differences between North and South would continue to shape Americans' notions of regional identity long after emancipation. Consider the disparity in regional attitudes toward manual labor. After the Civil War, native-born whites in various parts of the country viewed manual labor as stigmatized and rejected it for other occupations, even lower-paying ones. What motivated them in many cases was their refusal to work alongside racial or ethnic groups they considered inferior. Thus, white agricultural laborers in parts of the post–Civil War South where blacks were present disdained manual labor as "nigger work," and Yankees in New England eschewed jobs in domestic service and farm labor as "Irish work."[7] Yet, while the white southerners had two centuries of regional economic history on their side, their Yankee counterparts did not. To the contrary, numerous New England authorities tried to shame Yankees back into manual occupations by affirming universal manual labor as a New England tradition. Native-born whites in New England may have been just as unwilling to do manual labor as their counterparts down south, but they were far more likely to be told that their ancestors had done so—and therefore they should too.

The final, and to many nineteenth-century observers the most important, source of regional identity was culture. Anticipating contemporary scholars who theorize regions as "culture areas," nineteenth-century commentators believed the nation's regions were distinguished by deeply rooted cultural differences. In the antebellum period, antislavery northerners and their southern opponents made much of those differences, with the former insisting that slavery left most southerners—black and white alike—illiterate and ignorant and the latter countering that northern capitalist society lacked the leisure class essential to a truly advanced civilization. After the

Civil War, regional cultural differences lost some of their political urgency, but they remained of intense interest for Americans. Perhaps the best sign of that interest is the proliferation of regional fiction in the period, showcasing the accents, folkways, lifestyles, and spiritual lives of people—usually native-born rural people—living in every corner of the country, from the mine camps of California to the coulees of Wisconsin to the coastal villages of Maine. That body of fiction varies greatly in quality, as well as its degree of empathy with its rural characters, but one thing it commonly features is a claim (sometimes baseless) to accurately represent the nation's regional cultures in all their rich variety.

Climate, the countryside, race, history, economics, and culture would continue to dominate theories of regional identity well into the twentieth century. But, in the years after the Civil War, those theories were already coming under strain from a series of seismic changes to US society. Topping the list were urbanization, industrialization, and immigration. The growth of the nation's cities threatened treasured icons of regional culture, as historic homes and churches gave way to factories and tenements. Meanwhile, the migration of native-born young people from the countryside seeking jobs and adventure in the industrial city left many rural communities feeling depopulated and stagnant. Commentators warned of moral and economic decline in those former strongholds of regional culture. But it was immigration that posed the most fundamental challenges to Americans' cherished beliefs about regional identity. The arrival of millions of newcomers with no ties to the culture, history, or political institutions of their new home was bound to set native-born Americans searching for the things they had in common, and what they arrived at, in many cases, was regionalism. Some Americans responded to mass immigration by hunkering down behind their regional identities. Nativists invoked the racial roots of their regions to justify excluding the foreign born: if New England (and, as some were now saying, the South) truly was Anglo-Saxon territory, wasn't it right to keep out other races? Regionalism—albeit with a historical rather than a racial emphasis—was also a favorite tool of native-born Americans who favored assimilating immigrants instead of excluding them. Through public educational programs, historic preservation campaigns, and heroic statuary, they sought to instill in the foreign born a proper reverence for the histories of their adopted regions. From there, the assimilationists hoped, the immigrants would naturally come to identify with the history of the nation as a whole. This was regionalism as a stepping-stone to Americanization.

Nowhere were the challenges and opportunities that immigration posed for regionalism more visible than in Gilded Age New England. There a Yankee community that was itself internally divided over what it meant to be a New Englander encountered an immigrant population with its own diverse notions about the meanings and uses of regional identity. Scholars disagree on the Yankees' attitudes toward immigration, with some emphasizing the group's nativism and others finding a more accommodating response. Representing the former camp are Dona Brown, Roger Stein, William Truettner, and Thomas Andrew Denenberg. Brown demonstrates the centrality of nativism to the region's nascent vacation industry, which invited Yankees to flee their increasingly "foreign" cities to a romanticized old New England of sleepy port towns and farm communities, where Anglo-Saxon bloodlines and Puritan values purportedly still reigned.[8] Stein, Truettner, and Denenberg argue that the same nativist sentiments structured Yankee visual culture from the late nineteenth and early twentieth centuries. Stein sees the rampant Anglo-Saxonism of Yankee historical painters and sculptors of the period as a not so subtle response to the rise of non-Anglo-Saxons in New England. In contrast Truettner and Denenberg are struck by the relative absence of the foreign born from the era's Yankee iconography.[9] But, while they might disagree about whether the Yankee visual artists wanted to wage war on immigrants or wish them away, Stein, Truettner, and Denenberg agree that Yankee anxieties about the region's changing population left their mark across a wide swath of New England's visual culture.

Yet, as Barbara Solomon, Joseph Conforti, and James Lindgren point out, not all Yankees dreamed of fleeing or fighting the foreign born. In her classic study *Ancestors and Immigrants: A Changing New England Tradition,* Solomon writes of the New England patricians who in the 1880s launched educational projects—such as the public lectures on civics sponsored by the Massachusetts Society for Promoting Good Citizenship and the historical tours of the North End that editor Edwin D. Mead organized for the Old South Meeting House—that sought to inculcate in the foreign born a proper reverence for the political and historical traditions of their adopted region.[10] Similarly, Conforti describes the Americanizing projects of turn-of-the-century colonial revivalists like Caroline Emmerton, who bought and restored Salem's House of the Seven Gables to support the educational programs of her adjacent settlement house.[11] James Lindgren argues that the same Americanizing agenda motivated Emmerton's fellow patricians in the Society for the Preservation of New England Antiquities and similar organizations. Challenging those who see the early preservationist movement as motivated by escapism, Lingren insists, "Historic preservation was anything but a retreat by a dispossessed elite from the chaos of the fin de siècle, as some have charged."[12] Instead it was a paternalistic effort to instill in the immigrant lower classes—whose crumbling neighborhoods often surrounded the historic structures the preservationists wanted to save—a respect for the region's Anglo-Saxon founders and the values they stood for. The preservationists believed a monument like Paul Revere's house (the focus of much early preservationist energy) had powerful lessons to teach immigrants about "patriotism, philanthropy, civic virtue, and pride."[13]

Like their colleagues who targeted the immigrant poor with civics lessons and settlement houses, the Yankee preservationists saw the foreign born as passive recipients of New England culture. They were unable to conceive of the newcomers as making their own cultural contributions to the region. As Americanizers, they believed the role of the immigrants was to learn from New England's traditions rather than to change them. Yet, while that paternalistic attitude was typical of many old stock liberals, I discuss other Yankees who took a more welcoming and sometimes even egalitarian view of the foreign born. They include conservatives disturbed at what they saw as the betrayal of regional ideals by their fellow Yankees, particularly those of the younger generation. Frustrated at their kinsmen's refusal to follow in the footsteps of their grandparents, Yankee agricultural writers, domesticity experts, and physicians began celebrating immigrants as the true upholders of traditional New England lifestyles and values. Sometimes their praise for the foreign born rings hollow, as it was obviously calculated to shame Yankee backsliders into the paths of virtue, but in many instances the Yankee conservatives seemed honestly to believe that their own group, not the immigrants, posed the real threat to New England ideals. They present us with the bizarre spectacle of old stock Americans from what was arguably the nation's most nativist region seeking traces of their ancestors among the foreign born.

A more open-minded view of the immigrants' contributions to the region came from Yankees who critiqued their own group's influence on it. Convinced that their fellow Puritan descendants were too conservative, elitist, and dour, these critics called for a countervailing influence from abroad, perhaps a dose of Celtic gaiety and imagination or a dollop of liberal Catholic social commitment. Many thought the Yankees themselves would be changed for the better through their contact with the foreign born; others emphasized the immigrants' ameliorating influence on the region's culture and political institutions. Regardless of how they imagined the immigrant contribution, these self-critical Yankees welcomed it as a major improvement to a region that had stultified under the sway of their own people. What was needed, they insisted, was a New England that incorporated the best of both its native-born and immigrant peoples.

If we have underestimated the degree to which Yankees accepted the immigrant contribution to New England, we have largely ignored the regionalism of the foreign born themselves—the *American* regionalism, that is. To be sure, many scholars have discussed the Old World regional identities European immigrants brought with them. Immigration historians generally agree that most nineteenth-century immigrants lacked strong national identities on arriving in this country; instead their primary identification was with their native village, province, or region. It was only in the United States, the argument goes, that newcomers learned to think of themselves as Irishmen rather than Connachtmen or Italians rather than Neapolitans.[14] But at the same time that the United States taught the immigrants to set aside their Old World regionalisms, it also introduced them to New World ones. How did immigrants respond? Did their familiarity with the concept of regional identity make the idea of becoming southerners or westerners appealing to them? Or did they see American regionalism as irrelevant to them—a concern only for native-born people? On these questions, immigration history has been mostly silent.

I argue that many immigrants in Gilded Age New England eagerly embraced the idea of regional identity. Representatives of various ethnic groups argued that their contributions to the region's culture, economy, and spiritual life—not to mention their growing prominence in its population—gave them as much right to call themselves New Englanders as the Yankees. True, the foreign born often disagreed about what it meant to be a New Englander. For example, while some viewed themselves as proud inheritors of the political and cultural legacy of the Puritans, others saw nothing worth saving in that tradition. For the latter the whole point of making a home in the land of the Yankees was to make it over into something that better reflected their own culture and ideals: New Ireland or New France, maybe, but certainly not New England.

As the following summaries suggest, my chapters are on diverse topics, but they are all preoccupied with the relation of the foreign born to New England regionalism. Contemporaries often charted the rise of the foreign born in the region as a pageant of dramatic events: the Ursuline Convent Riots of 1834; the dedication of a Catholic church in Plymouth in 1879; the election of Boston's first Irish Catholic mayor, Hugh O'Brien, in 1884. I do not deny the symbolic importance of these and other milestones. Yet we must not allow them to overshadow the myriad subtler ways in which the foreign born made their presence felt in the region's culture—as, for example, when they debated whether to appropriate the region's colonial history for their own communities or when they forced the Yankees to reflect on their vexed relation to their own ancestors. Ultimately, I believe these less conspicuous interactions of the foreign born with New England culture have the most to tell us about the far-reaching effects of immigration on regional identity.

My first chapter explores how some of New England's most prominent intellectuals, the Brahmin Anglo-Saxonists Henry Cabot Lodge, James K. Hosmer, and John Fiske, struggled with the tension between their racial and regional identities. Proud New Englanders all of them, these men were also committed racialists. The Brahmin Anglo-Saxonists had little trouble reconciling their racial and regional allegiances in their popular writings on New England history. To the contrary, they believed that history was a testament—perhaps the ultimate testament—to the unique gifts of their race: its genius for self-government, its boundless restlessness and enterprise, and its bottomless capacity to assimilate other peoples without losing its own purity. Yet, when the Brahmin Anglo-Saxonists turned from the past to the present, the harmony between their race and region seemed to dissolve. The Anglo-Saxons might have been marching to triumph in the far corners of the globe, but in New England they were enduring a string of humiliating defeats. I argue that this tension between their racial and regional identities helps explain the Brahmins' contradictory attitude toward other groups, particularly immigrants. Speaking from the heights of Anglo-Saxon power, the Brahmins looked kindly on the foreign born and spoke confidently of absorbing them. But one thought of contemporary New England was all it took to silence the Brahmins' brag. As they contemplated their own weakened condition in their native region, the Brahmins came to see the foreign born not as candidates for absorption but as formidable enemies of their cultural traditions and political institutions.

My second chapter contextualizes the Brahmin Anglo-Saxonists in a larger debate about race and regionalism that divided both New England's Yankee and immigrant communities. On one side were those I call racial regionalists. They saw their regional identities as products of, and buttresses to, their racial ones. The racial regionalists all dreamed of turning New England into a stronghold of their race. This led them to minimize the influence of other peoples both on their own group and on the culture of the region as a whole. They included leading members of the American-Irish Historical Society and their Anglo-Saxonist rivals, the Brahmin historians John Fiske and Henry Cabot Lodge. A third prominent group of racial regionalists were the French Canadian imperialists, who brashly called for a peaceful conquest of New England that would transform it into a center of French and Catholic power. But not all New Englanders shared the racial regionalists' chauvinism and racial essentialism. Also present in both the Yankee and immigrant communities were those I call regional pluralists, who believed that, along with race, regional identities were shaped by religion, culture, and history. The regional pluralists viewed regional identity as a dynamic, hybrid affair, the product of interactions among all the inhabitants of a place. They contended that immigration kept the regional identity in flux, as new arrivals exchanged influences with those already here, in the process changing New England in ways no one could predict.

My third chapter explores the relation of immigrants to one of the oldest and most familiar symbols of New England, the delicate female body. I trace the origins of the stereotype to eighteenth-century debates between the opponents and defenders of American colonization, who disagreed about the effects of the New World climate on European bodies. By the early nineteenth century, the delicate New England body—particularly the delicate Yankee *female* body—had emerged for many European commentators as exhibit A in their case for the degenerative effects of the New World climate. That negative assessment would be challenged in the antebellum years, when the cult of True Womanhood taught middle-class Americans to see female delicacy as a sign not of ill health but of moral refinement. Many New England writers responded by juxtaposing the ethereal beauty of the Yankee mistress against the coarseness and immorality of her Irish servants. During the Gilded Age, however, that opposition was called into question by conservative Yankee physicians, who insisted that female delicacy actually signified poor health, rather than moral purity. They warned the Yankee female that she was undermining her physical and reproductive health by overindulging in fashion and education. Some conservative medical men urged the Yankee female to take a cue from her immigrant counterpart, who in their view embodied the best traditions of New England womanhood with her sturdy physique, large family, and devotion to manual labor. Yet the conservative physicians' praise for the immigrant female was itself challenged by the region's feminists, who argued that education was actually making the Yankee female much healthier than her "foreign" rival. In particular the feminists warned of the poor health of second-generation Irish American women, who were widely reported to be suffering from bad living and working conditions, as well as the rigors of adjusting to a new climate. As the century turned, it seemed that the dubious distinction of New England's most delicate women was passing to a new ethnic group.

My fourth chapter discusses the role of immigrants in what many observers considered New England's greatest social and economic crisis—the one centered on its countryside. During the century's last decades, the region's farmers confronted a variety of economic challenges—including high taxes, declining prices for wool and small grains, and labor shortages—as well as a torrent of dire commentary about the moral, cultural, and political decadence of their communities. I focus on the two groups that took the lead in debating what had gone wrong in the countryside and what should be done to fix it. Those I call traditionalists embraced the rural republican ideals of thrift, egalitarianism, universal manual labor, and a deep and abiding love for the soil. They blamed the city for undermining those ideals among the rising generation of rural New Englanders, and they offered a variety of suggestions for fortifying them. In contrast the progressive farmers had a different understanding of the challenges facing rural New England, as well as a different strategy for addressing them. They too called for a return to the region's core values, but they defined those values diametrically opposite from the traditionalists. The progressive farmers believed rural New England had always stood for an aggressive and entrepreneurial style of agriculture. This meant expanding profits, higher living standards, closer ties to the city, and the strategic abandonment of some farmland. Yet, despite their vast differences, there was one way in which the traditionalists and progressive farmers strongly resembled each other. Both groups were led by Yankees, though they both relied heavily on the figure of the immigrant to define what it meant, and did not mean, to be a rural New Englander. Some members of both groups were nativists, who constructed immigrants as derided Others to their cherished regional ideals. But, in a surprising number of cases, both traditionalists and progressive farmers hailed the foreign born as better embodiments of rural New England values than the Yankee farmers themselves.

My fifth chapter explores the relationship between New England and the Old Northwest, or, more precisely, the swath of the Old Northwest stretching from northeastern Ohio to southern Wisconsin that was settled over several generations by Yankee migrants and their descendants, whom I dub Yankee Westerners. This western zone of Yankee settlement had always stood in uncertain relation to New England proper, and that was particularly true in the Gilded Age, when immigration tested Yankee hegemony in both places. I focus on three groups that were especially prominent in the debate over the relationship between the two regions. The first, which I call Greater New Englanders, was comprised of Yankee Westerners with Anglo-Saxonist racial views. The Greater New Englanders celebrated the Yankee settlement of the Old Northwest as the latest chapter in the triumphant westward march of their race. They viewed New England as an expanding empire that thoroughly dominated the Old Northwest, though in reality the Yankee Westerners had long struggled with Upland Southerners and immigrants over issues that included temperance, education, and black civil rights. Yet the Greater New Englanders ignored those battles, painting rival groups as assimilating into Yankee culture rather than challenging it. A second set of commentators, whom I dub the preservationists, saw New England as not an expanding empire but a dwindling tradition whose chief symbol was the Yankee village. Convinced that urbanization, industrialization, and immigration had obliterated traditional Yankee culture in New England, the preservationists sought it in the Old Northwest. They found what they were looking for in the villages of Ohio's Western Reserve, which the preservationists romanticized as homogeneous communities of thrifty, hardworking Puritans. That image tells us little about the demographic reality of the Western Reserve, which was more ethnically diverse than the preservationists let on, but it does speak to the depth of their discontent with New England, where they were convinced such villages no longer existed. My final group of commentators, whom I call nationalists, wasted no tears on the decline of traditional Yankee culture in New England. To the contrary, they were heartily glad to see it disappear, inasmuch as they blamed it for making the Yankees narrow-minded, conservative, elitist, and provincial. The nationalists thought the best way to rid the Yankees of those flaws was to send them west, where they encountered people and places that broadened their minds, liberalized their politics, and nationalized their identities. The nationalists credited much of the Yankee migrants' transformation to their immigrant neighbors. They believed "give and take" with the foreign born over issues like education and temperance was chiefly responsible for turning provincial Yankees into broad-minded Americans.

I close with a short coda that considers the place of immigrants and their histories in the present-day New England regional consciousness. While much has changed in the region since the Gilded Age, much has not. That is particularly true of the ambiguous, even contradictory, relation of the foreign born to the region's self-presentation. Traveling around New England today, one sees plenty of evidence of the insertion of immigrant histories into the overarching regional narrative. Memorials to Irish famine victims, statues of ethnic politicians, and efforts to preserve three-decker tenements give one the strong sense that New England is, and always has been, immigrant territory. But, in an era of virulent anti-immigrant sentiment, it is not surprising to see nativists resorting to some of the same regionalist strategies as their Gilded Age predecessors. I discuss the Minuteman Project as a prime example of a contemporary organization that wields New England's Revolutionary heritage as a weapon against immigrants.

ONE

World Conquerors or a Dying People?

Racial Theory, Regional Anxiety, and the Brahmin Anglo-Saxonists

Although he was best known in his time as a politician and popular historian, Massachusetts senator Henry Cabot Lodge also occasionally weighed in on cultural matters, particularly when they touched on his abiding concerns of race, nation, and New England history. In an essay from the 1890s titled "Shakespeare's Americanisms," he argued that one measure of the power and mobility of a people was the feasibility of standardizing its language:

> It is quite possible to have Tuscan Italian or Castilian Spanish or Parisian French as the standard of correctness, but no one ever heard of "London English" used in that sense. The reason is simple. These nations have ceased to spread and colonize or to grow as nations. They are practically stationary. But English is the language of a conquering, colonizing race, which in the last three centuries has subdued and possessed ancient civilizations and virgin continents alike, and whose speech is now heard in the remotest corners of the earth.
>
> It is not the least of the many glories of the English tongue that it has proved equal to the task which its possessors have imposed upon it. Like the race, it has shown itself capable of assimilating new elements without degeneration. It has met new conditions, adapted itself to them, and prevailed over them. It has proved itself flexible without weakness, and strong without rigidity. With all its vast spread, it still remains unchanged in essence and in all its great qualities.[1]

Lodge's distinction between stagnant and growing races—as well as his classification of his own race among the latter—sprang from his background as an Anglo-Saxonist. In an era that saw Anglo-Saxon chauvinism pervade the upper reaches of American scholarly and political life, Lodge was one of his race's most energetic and influential champions. Like most Anglo-Saxonists, he believed he belonged to the world's dominant race, one with a special capacity for absorbing other peoples and cultures without losing its purity. Lodge also joined many other Anglo-Saxonists in the belief that the traits of his race extended to its language. He presented English as a tongue uniquely capable of absorbing other languages and adapting to local conditions while remaining "unchanged in essence." The idea of measuring all the speakers of such a language by the standards of one place (e.g., "London English") was ludicrous. Lodge insisted that the "only possible standard for English speech" was the "usage of the best writers" and "best educated and most highly trained" speakers throughout Anglo-Saxondom.[2]

On the other hand, Lodge believed languages such as Italian, Spanish, and French were subject to a different set of racial and cultural forces. He embraced the Anglo-Saxonist view that the Latin race—to which the speakers of those three tongues belonged—was characterized by decadence and lassitude. They were "practically stationary" peoples who lacked the vigor and suppleness to absorb other races and cultures. Lodge believed the inertness of the Latin nations manifested itself in their languages, whose "stiffness and narrowness" was a sure sign that their speakers had "ceased to march, and that expansion for people and speech alike is at an end."[3] At that point it became feasible to hold everyone to the linguistic standard of a single place.

Despite his contempt for Latin senescence, Lodge also knew what it felt like to belong to a "practically stationary" people, one whose days of conquest and absorption were long since over. I refer, of course, to the Anglo-Saxons of New England, in particular members of the patrician class to which Lodge belonged, whom Oliver Wendell Holmes had famously christened Brahmins. It was they, not the Castilian Spanish, Tuscan Italians, or Parisian French, who were best known among American ethnic groups for "stiffness and narrowness," for condemning cultural innovations by inherited standards, and for failing to assimilate new people and ideas. In this chapter I explore how this tension between their racial and regional identities shaped the thinking of Lodge and the other Gilded Age Brahmin Anglo-Saxonists.

I will be discussing the Brahmin Anglo-Saxonists as a group, but they had professional and ideological differences that must not be overlooked. Although most of them were Mugwumps, they included the stalwart Republican Lodge; although most of them were academicians, they also included the politician Lodge and the sometime public servant Francis Amasa Walker. The Brahmin Anglo-Saxonists also differed in the methods they adopted to promote their racial views, with some joining organizations such as the Massachusetts Society for Promoting Good Citizenship and the Immigration Restriction League and others remaining aloof from them.[4] But what they all shared—aside from their patrician status—was the enormous pride they took in their dual identities as Anglo-Saxons and New Englanders and their belief that those identities were mutually defining. Wherever they looked in New England's history—from the Pilgrims and Puritans to the patriots at Lexington and Concord to the Yankees who died at Gettysburg—the Brahmin Anglo-Saxonists saw proof that to be a New Englander was to be an Anglo-Saxon. But not just any Anglo-Saxon. The Brahmins believed that settling New England and building its institutions had enhanced the racial characteristics of their ancestors, turning them into the finest members of their race—the most pure-blooded, independent, inventive, and self-governing Anglo-Saxons—not just in America but on earth. Thus, to study New England's history was to appreciate not only the past triumphs of the Anglo-Saxon race but also its potential for even greater accomplishments in the future.

Yet, when the Gilded Age Brahmins turned from their region's past to its present, they felt an increasing incompatibility between their identities as Anglo-Saxons and New Englanders. All of them had reached adulthood at a time when the New England Yankees—particularly those of the elite class—were becoming notorious for their decadence. Commentators both inside and outside the group blamed its decline on an array of social and demographic forces, including overcivilization, falling birthrates, poor diets, declining maternal instincts, and out-migration. Confronted on all sides by signs of their demise in New England, many Brahmins longed for the good old days when their region was the heartland of Anglo-Saxondom. Others gave themselves up to despair. Among the most despondent was literary scholar Barrett Wendell, who lamented that "we Yankees are as much things of the past as any race can be. America has swept from our grasp. The future is beyond us."[5]

But outside New England the prospects for the Anglo-Saxons looked considerably brighter. Indeed, many Brahmins believed their race was embarked on a mission of conquest that would not end until it ruled most of the earth. Dazzled by that fantasy, the Brahmins sometimes managed to forget how badly they were faring in New England. Even Barrett Wendell could sound remarkably muscular as he argued that the future belonged to "the domination of that race which in the struggles of the ages proves most worthy to survive. And that race, I hope and believe, is the race of which we form a part and in a certain sense the advance guard."[6] Not surprisingly, most Brahmins preferred to focus on the victories of their race in the far corners of the globe rather than its defeats in their corner of the United States. But the historical identification between the Anglo-Saxons and New England made it impossible for them to keep their racial and regional identities separate.

Granted, at times the Brahmins could swagger with the boldest Anglo-Saxonists, but just as often regional worries made a mockery of their racial brag. The results are the unique mixture of power and impotence, arrogance and despair, expansionism and defensiveness that characterizes their writings about race and distinguishes them from their counterparts in other parts of the country. The Brahmin Anglo-Saxonists were particularly contradictory when it came to their relations to other peoples. When they succeeded in setting their regional worries aside, they spoke confidently of enlarging and strengthening their race by incorporating outsiders, particularly those from the "best" non-Anglo-Saxon peoples. But, when the shadow of New England fell over them, the Brahmins saw those same outsiders as menacing invaders whose fecundity and vigor contrasted painfully with their own sterility and decay. This contradictory attitude toward other groups is most evident in the Brahmins' response to immigration, an area where they wielded an outsized influence over national policy.

The case of the Brahmin Anglo-Saxonists thus prompts us to attend more carefully to the power of regional identities to shape how we theorize and live racial ones. That power is particularly evident when we compare the Brahmins to their Anglo-Saxonist allies in other parts of the country. In this chapter I argue that regional influences help explain why the Brahmins responded to immigrants so differently than a prominent group of their Anglo-Saxonist contemporaries from the Mid-Atlantic region. The latter shared the Brahmins' concern about the arrival of millions of non-Anglo-Saxon immigrants, but they were able to allay their racial fears by mythologizing the West as a site of Anglo-Saxon supremacy. That was not an option for the Brahmins, however, whose racial fortunes were tied to the one part of the country, indeed the one place in the world, where the Anglo-Saxons seemed to be faring worst.

Anglo-Saxon Cowboys

To be sure, the Anglo-Saxons of New England were not the only members of their race in the late nineteenth century to be suspected of racial decay. Many leading Anglo-Saxonists feared that their entire race was at risk. They were convinced that modern civilization threatened the moral fiber, physical strength, and mental health of all the "advanced" peoples, and they anxiously scanned the globe for signs that their race was deteriorating. Particularly worrisome were the struggles of the British army in its wars against the Boers, the falling birthrates of the Australians, and the growing taste for luxury among the upper classes everywhere. While these symptoms were anything but definitive, taken together they suggested the need for vigilance lest the Anglo-Saxons join the Latins among the world's decadent races.[7]

According to many commentators, the one place in the world where the decadence of the Anglo-Saxons had already passed the tipping point was New England. There they identified signs of degeneration among Anglo-Saxons of all social classes in both rural and urban areas. The region that had long prided itself as the chief stronghold of the Anglo-Saxon race in America was now being taken over by more vigorous and prolific races. Things had gotten so bad for the Yankees that the *Boston Pilot,* the leading Irish Catholic journal, joked that the last descendant of the Puritans should be placed in a glass case and put on display as a national curiosity.[8] New *England?* Many suggested that the region should rechristen itself "New Ireland" or "New France."

The decay of New England's Anglo-Saxons was widely discussed by natives and outsiders alike, and in much the same terms. There is little to separate the portrayals of New England decadence by outsiders such as William Dean Howells and Brahmins like Henry Adams and Barrett Wendell.[9] But the outsiders and insiders did disagree about what the decay of the Anglo-Saxons in New England meant for the race as a whole. Anglo-Saxonists outside the region certainly worried about what was happening there, but they did not believe it spoke to the overall health of the race. To the contrary, some of them constructed an image of Anglo-Saxon strength over against the weakness of the Yankees. Those who did so included a group of mid-Atlantic Anglo-Saxonists who romanticized the West as the place where their race still retained the vigor it had given up in the homeland of the Puritans.

Gilded Age elites outside New England routinely idealized the West as a stronghold of Anglo-Saxon power. This was particularly true of three friends, Theodore Roosevelt, Frederic Remington, and Owen Wister. They saw the history of the West as the second great Anglo-Saxon invasion, one that replicated the mythic conquest of Britain by the Angles and Saxons.[10] They celebrated the Anglo-Saxon settlers of the West for killing and driving out the Indians in the same manner that their ancestors allegedly had exterminated the original inhabitants of Britain.[11] Granted, race war between Anglo-Saxons and Indians was already becoming a thing of the past by the 1880s, when Roosevelt, Remington, and Wister began visiting the West and representing it for the American public. Nevertheless, their personal experiences of rejuvenation in the region taught them to cherish its powers of renewal for their race as a whole. They believed that in the West the Anglo-Saxons could recover the youth, courage, and aggression that had been stripped from them back east, particularly in that epicenter of overcivilization, New England.

Roosevelt, Wister, and Remington all portrayed the settlement of the West as the latest chapter in a larger narrative of Anglo-Saxon world conquest. All saw the American settlers as a predominantly Teutonic group that had continued on this continent the inexorable sweep across lands and peoples that had begun on the coastal plains of ancient Germany. Moreover, all celebrated their western heroes for preserving undimmed the traits of courage, restlessness, and violence that had distinguished their Anglo-Saxon ancestors. Thus, Roosevelt began his four-volume history, *The Winning of the West,* with an account of the birth and spread of the "English race" or "English-speaking peoples" (the terms that he, like many of his colleagues, preferred to *Anglo-Saxon*) that paints them as ruthless destroyers of their racial enemies.[12] As historians Gail Bederman and Sarah Watts have pointed out, these are precisely the qualities that Roosevelt celebrates in the American frontiersmen.[13] In one lurid episode after another, Roosevelt shows how the pioneers wrested the continent from savage Indians, just as their Anglo-Saxon forebears had relentlessly overrun the original Britons. Wister and Remington likewise portrayed their western heroes as reincarnations of their Anglo-Saxon forefathers. In his *Harper's New Monthly* essay "The Evolution of the Cow-Puncher," Wister traces a genealogy for the cowboy that includes the Anglo-Saxons who fought at Hastings, defeated the Spanish armada, and defended the Reformation.

> Thus, late in the nineteenth century, was the race once again subjected to battles and darkness, rain and shine, to the fierceness and generosity of the desert. Destiny tried her latest experiment upon

> the Saxon, and plucking him from the library, the haystack, and the gutter, set him upon his horse; then it was that, face to face with the eternal simplicity of death, his modern guise fell away and showed once again the medieval man. It was no new type, no product of the frontier, but just the original kernel of the nut with the shell broken.[14]

As Ben Merchant Vorpahl points out, what Wister is describing here is not the "evolution" promised by his essay's title but repetition. No matter whether he is writing of eleventh-century England or nineteenth-century America, Wister believes sufficiently harsh conditions always bring out the same rugged traits in the Anglo-Saxon. Remington underscored that point in one of his five illustrations for Wister's essay. Titled "The Last Cavalier," it depicts a mounted, pistol-wearing cowboy surrounded by a vast, ghostly crowd of armored knights, plumed swordsmen, and buckskinned frontiersmen. The Anglo-Saxon's external trappings might change, but his essential traits of mobility, virility, and violence were constant through the ages.[15]

Yet, despite their faith in the West's powers of racial rejuvenation, Roosevelt, Wister, and Remington believed that most of the Anglo-Saxons of New England were too far gone to be saved. Granted, they sometimes acknowledged that New England had contributed its share to the cowboy population, but more commonly they attacked it as the breeding ground of their race's most overcivilized members. If the West was where the Anglo-Saxons were recovering their fighting spirit, New England was where they had first lost it.

Remington saw the Yankees of New England as the epitome of the urban industrial civilization that he sought to escape in the West. But by the mid-1890s he conceded that the Yankees had tainted even that last haven of rugged Anglo-Saxonism. He sent Wister some rough notes for "The Evolution of the Cow-Puncher" that wistfully recalled the cattle boom of the late 1860s and 1870s, when "adventurous young men from all parts" got "rich" on the $75 a month they earned as cowboys: "Cheyenne saddles—fine chaps—$15 hats fringed gloves—$25 boots &c. With the crash of the boom—Yankee ingenuity killed the cattle business as much as anything."[16] No place, it seemed, was entirely safe from the Yankee capitalist.

For Roosevelt it was the issue of birthrates that highlighted how badly the Anglo-Saxons of New England had diverged from the heroic example of their western cousins. Beginning in the mid-1890s, Roosevelt regularly warned that the low birthrate of the Yankees would soon spell their demise: "When a people gets to the position . . . where the death-rate surpasses the birth-rate, then that race is not only fated to extinction but it deserves extinction."[17] Roosevelt would eventually come to see low birthrates as the foremost threat to his race, and he would spend much of his energy in the new century railing against "race suicide" wherever he spotted it.[18] Yet he always reserved a special contempt for the Anglo-Saxons of New England, whose early and enthusiastic embrace of family limitation contrasted in his mind with the fertile Anglo-Saxon families of the West.[19] As we shall see in chapter 3, many experts believed the Yankees' low birthrate had physiological causes, but Roosevelt insisted, "It is due to moral, and not physiological, shortcomings. It is due to coldness, to selfishness, to love of ease, to shrinking from risk, to an utter and pitiful failure in sense of perspective and in power of weighing what really makes the highest joy." By 1911 Roosevelt was forced to admit that birthrates were dropping not only in New England but also "throughout the North and West."[20] Nevertheless, he clung to the image of the West as a land of fighting, breeding Anglo-Saxons: "Our forefathers were the heroes of the tremendous epic that tells of the conquest of a continent. The conquerors, the men who dared and did, with hearts of steel and thews of iron, looked fearlessly into the eyes of the future, and quailed before no task and no danger; are their sons and daughters, in love of effortless ease and fear of all work and risk, to let the blood of the pioneers die out of the land because they shrink from the most elemental duties of manhood and womanhood?"[21] The Anglo-Saxons of America needed to reject the example of the effete New Englanders and look to their moral forebears in the West in forming their ideas about family.

Although he lacked Roosevelt's special disdain for the New England members of his race, Owen Wister also saw them as polar opposites of their counterparts out west. Wister underscored this contrast in his celebrated novel *The Virginian* (1902), which pairs its rugged, western Anglo-Saxon protagonist with the native Vermonter, Molly Stark Wood.[22] Wood is the granddaughter of New Hampshire Revolutionary hero John Stark. She is named for, and is said to resemble, Stark's wife, whose portrait she brings west with her. But things have declined for the Starks and the rest of the Yankees since the Revolution. As Molly's great-aunt observes, the region has been badly hurt by out-migration: "New Hampshire was full of fine young men in those days. But nowadays most of them have gone away to seek their fortunes in the West."[23] Molly's family suffers an additional loss when the mills that have supported it fail. Although she gamely goes to work to help her mother, the experience leaves her looking pale and tired. She is also somewhat anemic as a lover. For much of the book, she struggles to resist her desire for the Virginian, whose bluff, unschooled western style shocks her genteel New England sensibility. As the narrator explains, "[T]he pale decadence of New England had somewhat watered her good old Revolutionary blood . . . and she was inclined to think under glass and to live underdone—when there were no Indians to shoot!"[24] As the final qualifying phrase suggests, albeit in Indian-hating terms, Molly still has some of the fighting spirit of the Starks. The same cannot be said for her family back in Vermont. When Molly writes home with the news of her engagement, her family is scandalized. Thus, we are not surprised to learn in the final chapter that Molly and the Virginian settle in Wyoming to raise a family and build a fortune. Neither the newlyweds nor the rest of their race appear to have much of a future in New England.

The Brahmin Teutonists

Yet, in the years that Wister, Roosevelt, and Remington were constructing the West as the heartland of Anglo-Saxonism, the Brahmins consistently refused to join them. Even Lodge, who shared so many enthusiasms—both political and personal—with his close friend Roosevelt, could muster no affection for the far West. For Lodge, one contemporary observed, "Pittsfield, Mass., represented the Farthest West except . . . when he was willing to cross the state boundary to attend a Republican National Convention at Cleveland, at Chicago, or at St. Louis."[25] The Brahmins' loyalty to New England was partly a matter of uncritical regional chauvinism. Thomas Jefferson's famous complaint about New Englanders—they think they are God's chosen people—certainly applied to the Brahmin Anglo-Saxonists. But their identification with their native region also sprang from their faith in its crucial role in the history of their race. Most of the Brahmins believed that New England had long been one of, if not the, world centers of Anglo-Saxondom, and though they conceded that it was losing that status, they continued to insist on the inextricable ties between their race and region. As a result they were unwilling, and perhaps even unable, to imagine an Anglo-Saxon identity that was separate from their New Englandness.

The Brahmins' sense of the historical importance of New England to the Anglo-Saxon race largely derived from the Teutonic origins (aka Teutonic germ) theory. This theory traced the political and legal institutions of Britain and the United States to the Anglo-Saxons and beyond them to their ancestors, the ancient Germanic tribes described by Tacitus. Many Teutonists believed their race had originated not only local self-government but also the concepts of representation and the nation-state. They maintained that the Teutonic peoples had dispersed these political ideas among other northern and western European peoples through a long history of conquest, migration, and intermarriage.[26]

Although the British and American Teutonists were convinced of the racial superiority of all German-descended peoples—whether they lived in Holland, Britain, or Scandinavia—most thought the Anglo-Saxons reigned supreme. They insisted that of all the European nations founded by the ancient Germans, Britain boasted the purest Teutonic institutions. The doyen of US Teutonists, British historian Edward Augustus Freeman, argued, "It is . . . in our land that the old Teutonic institutions have really had the freest play, that they have grown and developed with the most unbroken continuity down to our own day. Nowhere else have both liberty and national unity received so few checks."[27] Elsewhere in Europe, Freeman maintained, Teutonic self-government had been undermined by the centralizing force of the Roman Empire or, in the case of Scandinavia, despotism and oligarchy. Only the Anglo-Saxons had a continuous history of self-rule stretching from ancient Germany down to the present.[28]

With a strong boost from Freeman, who toured the United States in 1881–82, the Teutonic origins theory became the dominant paradigm of the nation's first generation of professional historians. That group included Albert Bushnell Hart at Harvard, Andrew D. White and Moses Coit Tyler at Cornell, and Roosevelt's mentor, John W. Burgess, at Columbia. Beginning in 1882, the Teutonists boasted a prestigious venue for their work in the *Johns Hopkins University Studies in Historical and Political Science,* founded by Brahmin Anglo-Saxonist Herbert Baxter Adams. In its first years, that journal published essays, including several by Adams himself, comparing the political, economic, and legal institutions of the Anglo-Saxons in America, Britain, and ancient Germany. Yet, despite its popularity in the 1880s, Teutonism enjoyed only a brief reign among professional historians. By the early 1890s, scholars such as Charles McLean Andrews, Edward Channing, Herbert Levi Osgood, and Frederick Jackson Turner had raised serious objections to the Teutonic origins theory. Andrews questioned whether the self-governing village community of medieval Germany had been reproduced in seventeenth-century New England, and Channing doubted that the self-governing Teutonic village community had ever even existed.[29] Such attacks soon spelled the demise of Teutonism among historians, but nonspecialists would keep the theory alive for decades. That was particularly true in New

England, where in 1897 one could still hear a Brahmin Anglo-Saxonist drawing distinctions between "British, German, and Scandinavian stock, historically free, energetic, progressive" and "Slav, Latin, and Asiatic races, historically down-trodden, atavistic, and stagnant."[30] For some people Teutonism was simply too convenient an untruth to give up.

One reason for the Brahmins' special attraction to Teutonist theory was the proud place it accorded their region in the history of their race. The Brahmins contended that New England had played a crucial role in the westward migration of the Anglo-Saxons and their institutions. They believed the arrival on these shores of the Pilgrims and Puritans was an event no less significant to the race than the landing in Britain of those legendary Teutonic heroes Hengest and Horsa.[31] Using the comparative method that British Teutonist Henry Maine had originated and Freeman had popularized, Brahmin historians traced the legal and political institutions of colonial New England to their supposed origins in Anglo-Saxon England and ancient Germany. They also followed Maine in focusing most of their attention on the village community. The Brahmins explored the supposed Teutonic roots of various aspects of colonial New England village life, including communal landholding patterns, defensive palisades, and democratic town governments. The goal of those studies was to prove not only that colonial New England had been essentially Anglo-Saxon but also that it had been more Anglo-Saxon than any other place in America, if not the world.[32]

Exhibit A in such arguments was the town meeting, which the Brahmin Teutonists hailed as the direct descendant of the ancient German local assembly and the primary ancestor of the entire American political system. The Brahmins believed that when the Puritans adopted the town meeting, they were rejecting the select vestry form of local government they had known in England. The Brahmins contrasted the elitism of the select vestry with the direct democracy of the town meeting, which they saw as a "revival of a most ancient thing," a return to the primitive democracy of the ancient Teutons.[33] They distinguished their ancestors from the aristocratic colonists of Virginia, who adopted the select vestry.[34] In taking the more democratic path, the Brahmins reasoned, the Puritans proved themselves better Anglo-Saxons than the Virginians, better even than their own English fathers.

Yet the stark contrast that the Brahmins drew between local government in old and New England is not supported by recent scholarship. First, colonial New England was by no means a paradise of direct democracy, even for the males eligible to vote. In some communities, the power of the town meeting was rivaled or even surpassed by that of elected boards of selectmen.[35] Second, local democracy was alive and well in many agricultural villages in seventeenth-century England, where, as David Grayson Allen points out, inhabitants held parish offices and met in assembly to vote on agricultural bylaws. Allen maintains that the Puritans did not abandon the forms of local government they had known in the old country; instead, they adapted those institutions to the new social and economic conditions of America.[36] But the Brahmins tended to ignore these continuities between village life in old and New England, arguing instead that the Puritans had voyaged all the way back to their Teutonic past when they crossed the Atlantic.

Although the Brahmins focused much of their attention on the colonial period, they believed New England had remained a world center of the Anglo-Saxon race well into the nineteenth century. As proof they cited key moments in American history when their ancestors had emerged as race leaders. Historian James Hosmer believed one such moment was the Revolution, when the Anglo-Saxons of New England had supposedly taken the lead among the colonists. Moreover, he argued that a century and a half of tutelage in the town meeting had made the New Englanders better Anglo-Saxons than the British: "What influence had surrounded lord and commoner across the water to develop in them a capacity to cope with the child of the Puritan, schooled thoroughly in the town-meeting!"[37] Henry Cabot Lodge believed the descendants of the Puritans had continued to lead their race during the Civil War. He elevated slain New Englanders Robert Gould Shaw and Charles Russell Lowell into a pantheon of Anglo-Saxon heroes that also included Oliver Cromwell and John Hampden.[38] Although Lodge's political ambitions prevented him from saying so explicitly, he implied that the racial purity of the New Englanders had contributed to the North's victory in the war.

Rampant Anglo-Saxons, Dying Yankees

Yet, when the Brahmins turned from the past to the present, they confronted a growing disjuncture between their racial and regional identities. The Anglo-Saxons of New England may have led their race in earlier eras, but by the Gilded Age they seemed bent on undermining it. According to their harshest critics, the Yankees suffered from overcivilization, cowardice, and race suicide, and even their staunchest defenders acknowledged that they were no match for the waves of immigrants pouring in on them. Only the enemies of the Anglo-Saxons now saw the descendants of the Puritans as fitting representatives of their race.

Significantly, the dismal fate of their race in their region did not dim the

Brahmins' Anglo-Saxonism. To the contrary, they took as much pride as anyone else in belonging to a "conquering and colonizing" people, and they loved to spin gaudy fantasies about the might and spread of their race in fifty or a hundred years when, they predicted, it would have colonized much of the globe and grown to six hundred million or even a billion people. In embracing muscular Anglo-Saxonism, the Brahmins may well have been seeking to compensate for their weakened regional identity. They obviously would have been attracted to a racial ideology that portrayed them as powerful, young, expanding, and fecund—in short, everything the Yankees notoriously were not. But the Brahmins finally were unable to separate their high hopes for their race from their worries about their region. Priding themselves on New England's historic centrality to the Anglo-Saxons, they could not cast off their region now that it had become a liability to their race. The results are visible in their writings, where their bold ambitions for their race in distant lands are steadily compromised by their anxieties about its fate in New England.

To sense how the Brahmins' decayed regional identity could undermine their muscular Anglo-Saxonism, consider historian John Fiske's *American Political Ideas Viewed from the Standpoint of Universal History* (1885). Originating as a three-lecture series that Fiske delivered—all or in part—many times in the United States and Britain, the book frequently is cited as an early statement of the expansionist sentiments that would flourish among the turn-of-the-century Anglo-Saxonists.[39] In the final speech, "'Manifest Destiny,'" Fiske boldly predicts that the "English race" would dominate the globe in the next century: "By that time all the elements of military predominance on the earth, including that of simple numerical superiority, will have been gathered into the hands . . . of the offspring of the Teutonic tribes who conquered Britain in the fifth century."[40] Fiske maintains that his race will be led to world dominance by an American nation boasting six to seven hundred million Anglo-Saxons and the largest concentration of power in world history.[41] Starting with an inflated estimate of his race's presence in America, he arrives at an eye-popping prediction of its coming world supremacy: "The day is at hand when four-fifths of the human race will trace its pedigree to English forefathers, as four-fifths of the white people in the United States trace their pedigree to-day." Eventually, every land that is not already home to an "old civilization" will be colonized by the "English race."[42]

Although Fiske does not specify what will happen to the native peoples colonized by his race, he implies that some of them will be absorbed and the rest wiped out. Their fate would depend on their proximity to the "English

Fig. 1. John Fiske. (Courtesy of the Library of Congress.)

race." In the case of "the barbarous races," Fiske questions whether they will be able "to maintain their foothold upon the earth at all."[43] He can see no future for the "negro fetich-worshippers [*sic*]" of Africa and the "irredeemable savages" of Australia.[44] But, when it comes to non-Teutonic Europeans, Fiske offers some hope. Echoing Freeman, he believes they will benefit from his race's "rare capacity for absorbing slightly foreign elements and moulding them into conformity with a political type that was first wrought out through centuries of effort on British soil." His example, again, is the "American," who "has absorbed considerable quantities of closely kindred European blood, but he is rapidly assimilating it all," while remaining "thoroughly English." Fiske imagines an "English race" supple enough to engulf non-Teutonic immigrants without impairing its purity.[45]

Fiske believes that the primary source of his race's power lies in its Teutonic tradition of local self-government. In the first lecture in the series, "The Town-Meeting," he cites that tradition as the key to the success of the British Empire: "It is to the self-government of England, and to no lesser cause, that we are to look for the secret of that boundless vitality which has given to men of English speech the uttermost parts of the earth for an inheritance." Fiske supports this thesis with the example of colonial America, where, he maintains, Britain's commitment to local self-government gave it an enormous advantage over the centralized French in the race for empire: "The town-meeting pitted against the bureaucracy was like a Titan overthrowing a cripple."[46] The self-ruling New Englanders and their allies from New York and Virginia proved too much for the tyrannized French colonials.

Yet, when Fiske turns to contemporary New England, he is struck not by the strength of his race but by its weakness. In "The Town-Meeting," he laments the decay of the "English race" in its former stronghold, the New England village community. In deeply nostalgic tones, Fiske memorializes the rapidly disappearing world of the Yankee village, where—he claims—literacy, manual labor, and moral purity once were universal and poverty, vice, and crime unheard of. Some residents did not even bother to lock their doors.[47] In orthodox Teutonist fashion, Fiske traces the democratic spirit of such villages to the Puritan founders and beyond them to the ancient Teutons, whose legacy is visible in such Yankee institutions as the town meeting and the common.

But Fiske believes that New England's day as the heartland of his race is coming to an end. He introduces his account of the Yankee village by warning, "[W]e are unwillingly forced to contemplate the possibility of a deterioration in the character of the most perfect democracy the world has ever seen."[48] The problem is population turnover. As the children of the Yankees leave the villages to go to college or the city, "There is a visible tendency for farms to pass into the hands of proprietors of an inferior type to that of the former owners,—men who are content with a lower standard of comfort and culture."[49] Even more worrisome is the arrival of factories, which deface the New England landscape and "introduce into the community a class of people very different from the landholding descendants of the Puritans. When once a factory is established near a village, one no longer feels free to sleep with doors unbolted."[50] Although Fiske is vague about the ethnic background of these newcomers (i.e., are they non-Anglo-Saxon immigrants or merely Yankees of an inferior sort?), he leaves no doubt that they are badly diluting the strength of the "English race" in the region. To gauge how badly, one might compare these passages with the one from "'Manifest Destiny'" where he boasts of his race's ability to absorb other groups while still remaining "thoroughly English." Fiske's Yankee villagers display none of that assimilative power as they greet the newcomers by retreating behind locked doors. Despite Fiske's insistence that the rural Yankees still "operate like a powerful leaven upon the whole of American society," they do not even leaven their own neighbors.[51] The group that once symbolized the imperial might of the "English race" now suggests its liability to decay.

The weakness of the Yankees also undermined the muscular Anglo-Saxonism of Brahmin historian James Hosmer. In *A Short History of Anglo-Saxon Freedom* (1890), Hosmer traces the spread of his race and its institutions from the coastal plains of ancient Germany to the far reaches of the British Empire. It is a story of steadily expanding numbers and ever-increasing power. By the final chapters, Hosmer is quoting British predictions that in the next century the Anglo-Saxon race will "occupy the fairest portions of the earth" and boast over a billion members.[52] Hosmer claims that all of this is good news for anyone who believes in freedom and democracy, inasmuch as the Anglo-Saxon stands alone as the guardian of those ideals. He maintains that the race that "has preserved for two thousand years the connected tradition of ordered constitutional freedom" is uniquely qualified to extend liberty and self-government to the world's oppressed peoples.[53]

New England occupies a prominent but contradictory place in Hosmer's study. He believes the region once played a leading role in the spread of Anglo-Saxon people and institutions. He celebrates the seventeenth-century Puritans who supposedly revived the Teutonic local assembly after it had died out in England, the eighteenth-century Yankees who led the struggle for freedom and self-rule against Britain, and the nineteenth-century migrants who carried the town meeting from New England to the Midwest.[54] Yet, when Hosmer turns to contemporary New England, he is struck not by the expansion of the Anglo-Saxons and their institutions but by their contraction. Indeed, New England seems to be the one place in the world where the race is in retreat. He depicts the Yankees as diluted by out-migration and overwhelmed by the arrival of two imposing groups of newcomers. First came the "Celtic race, energetic and prolific, whose teeming families throng city and village, threatening to outnumber the Yankee element, depleted as it has been by the emigration of so many of its most vigorous children." Next arrived the French Canadians, "following the track of their warlike ancestors down the river-valleys . . . an industrious but unprogressive race, good hands in the mills and marvelously dexterous at wielding the axe." Hosmer believes these two groups have badly eroded the political power of the Yankees and undermined the town meeting: "The institution is uncongenial to any but Teutonic men; the Irishman and Frenchman are not at home in it." He clings to the hope that the children of the newcomers will eventually take on the political genius of the Yankees, but for now he can only sigh at the thought of town meetings packed with immigrants who passively follow demagogues and whippers-in.[55]

The helplessness and fear with which Hosmer regards New England's immigrants contrasts with the air of superiority he takes toward them outside the region. When he considers the nation as a whole, Hosmer either welcomes or condemns non-Anglo-Saxon newcomers depending on their racial backgrounds, but he always views them from a position of strength. He is enthusiastic about immigrants of the right sort, arguing, "The Anglo-Saxon stock has been made rich and strong by a score of crossings with the most vigorous and intellectual of modern races, but it remains, nevertheless, Anglo-Saxon."[56] Hosmer explains how his race has managed this with a quote from Edward Freeman: "In a nation there commonly is a certain element which is more than an element, something which is its real kernel, its real essence; something which attracts and absorbs all other elements, so that other elements are not co-ordinate elements, but mere infusions into a whole which is already in being."[57] Hosmer argues that in America, as in England, the essential "element" is the Anglo-Saxon. He wants his race to continue to incorporate immigrant groups: "Invigorate the stock as you please with blood from Scandinavian, German, Irish, French, Russian,—from whatever good source,—but let it remain Anglo-Saxon still."[58] Provided the immigrants are of "good" blood, they can actually strengthen the Anglo-Saxon.

On the other hand, Hosmer warns that immigration will only benefit the Anglo-Saxons if "it comes from sources not too remote, and is without morbid taint." From his perspective those two conditions are equivalent, since morbidity among races increases the farther one gets from the Anglo-Saxon. He supports this assumption by quoting Peter Bayne that "you cannot have the growth of the living creature, plant, animal, man, nation, seriously injured in the growing time and then set right in subsequent years." Since Anglo-Saxons are the only people never to have been "at some time crushed and become spirit-broken," it is crucial that the race not weaken itself by absorbing immigrants from subjugated races.[59] To avoid that, Hosmer joins those Brahmin Anglo-Saxonists who were beginning to urge the nation to restrict immigration: "What dikes can be erected against the undesirable foreign flood, which . . . seems likely so far to dilute our blood as to make it unequal to the task of sustaining Anglo-Saxon freedom?"[60]

At first glance there seems to be little to separate Hosmer's attacks on immigrants in New England and the nation as a whole. After all, he sees the newcomers as a threat to his race in both contexts. Yet I would argue that the nature of the threat differs categorically in the two cases. At the national level, Hosmer fears only immigrants from "undesirable" races (i.e., those farthest removed from the Anglo-Saxon). He calls for restriction to prevent them from passing on their weakness his race. But in New England Hosmer fears *all* immigrants, even those from "good" races such as Irish and French Canadians. There it is the strength, rather than the weakness, of the newcomers that frightens him. Speaking from the perspective of a "depleted" Yankee population, he seems overawed by the vigor and aggression of the "energetic and prolific" Irish and the ax-wielding French Canadians. Rather than absorbing either group, the Yankees seem more likely to be absorbed by them. It is quite a comedown for a region that, according to Hosmer, has served as an Anglo-Saxon stronghold for the past three centuries.

In the years after Hosmer published *A Short History of Anglo-Saxon Freedom,* his call for restriction would be taken up by many other Brahmins, including, most notably, the members of the Immigration Restriction League (IRL), a national organization with New England leadership founded in Boston in 1894 by three recent Harvard graduates.[61] The IRL and its allies often justified their calls for restriction in the same racial terms that Hosmer had employed. Most saw America as an Anglo-Saxon country that had the right and moral obligation to protect its superior bloodlines from weaker races. They particularly wanted to restrict the "new" immigrants from southern and eastern Europe, whom Brahmin Anglo-Saxonist Francis Amasa Walker (an IRL vice president) memorably termed "beaten men from beaten races; representing the worst failures in the struggle for existence."[62] Abandoning the traditional view of European immigration as a winnowing process that brought only the most ambitious and talented to these shores, the IRL insisted that the "new" immigrants were too inert and dependent to come to America on their own; instead, they were being dumped here by greedy labor contractors and steamship companies. Members of the IRL often attacked the "new" immigrants in explicitly Teutonist terms, complaining, for example, that they lacked the talents for self-government "such as belong to those who are descended from the tribes that met under the oak-trees of old Germany to make laws and choose chieftains."[63] Even more ominously, some restrictionists warned that if the Anglo-Saxons intermarried with the "new" immigrants, they would become tainted with their weakness. The only way to preserve the strength of their race was to bar the door against the southern and eastern Europeans.

But, as we have seen, New England was in many ways an unsuitable home for an organization founded on the idea of Anglo-Saxon supremacy. To any objective observer, it was the Yankees, rather than the "new" immigrants, who were the beaten men. One can sense the tension between the Brahmin restrictionists' Anglo-Saxon strength and their New England vulnerability in the writings of their chief legislator, Senator Henry Cabot Lodge. Beginning in 1895, Lodge aided the IRL by regularly sponsoring legislation—finally passed in 1917—that would require all immigrants to pass a literacy test. The test was designed to restrict the "new" immigrants, since, as Lodge openly acknowledged, they were far more likely to be illiterate than their counterparts from northern and western Europe. Lodge primarily justified his call for restricting the "new" immigrants in racial terms, warning that the southern and eastern Europeans would undermine the strength of the "English-speaking race." New England played a contradictory role in this argument. On the one hand, Lodge cited the history of his race in his native region as proof of its unmatched aggression and strength. Yet, in Lodge's commentary on contemporary New England, the "English-speaking race" looked anything but overpowering. Indeed, in his later years, the senator would concede that "armies" of non-Anglo-Saxon newcomers had broken his race's hold over the region.

Lodge often began his restrictionist speeches and essays by sketching the history of the "English-speaking race" from its origins in ancient Germany to its settlement of America.[64] In orthodox Anglo-Saxonist fashion, he argued that his race was the product of intermarriages between the various Teutonic peoples that had invaded England and exterminated the original Celtic inhabitants. He contended that the members of the "English-speaking race" who had migrated to America had received further Teutonic infusions by way of immigrants from Holland, Germany, and Scandinavia. The result was a people that epitomized the Teutonic gifts for making nations, conquering vast territories, and absorbing closely related peoples. Lodge believed that the only real threat to such a masterful race was intermarriage with inferior groups, such as the "new" immigrants. He spelled out that danger in an 1896 speech to the Senate advocating the literacy test: "[I]t is on the moral qualities of the English-speaking race that our history, our victories, and all our future rest. There is only one way in which you can lower those qualities or weaken those characteristics, and that is by breeding them out. If a lower race mixes with a higher in sufficient numbers, history teaches us that the lower race will prevail." Lodge feared that his race's chief source of strength—its capacity for absorption—would finally prove

Fig. 2. Henry Cabot Lodge. (Courtesy of the Library of Congress.)

its undoing. Rather than swallowing the "new" immigrants, the "English-speaking race" would be swallowed itself: "The lower race will absorb the higher, not the higher the lower, when the two strains approach equality in numbers." The only way to avoid this nightmare, Lodge contended, was for the "English-speaking race" to restrict the immigration of inferior races, such as those from southern and eastern Europe. He attributed its failure to do so to an attitude of "careless strength."[65] While Lodge cherished the strength of his people as deeply as anyone, he believed that even the world's most powerful race sometimes needed to protect itself from weaklings.

New England played two opposing roles in Lodge's writings about immigration. On the one hand, he frequently cited the history of the Anglo-Saxons in New England as proof that they possessed masterful traits worthy of protection from weaker peoples. He believed that the Pilgrims and Puritans had embodied to the full their race's aggression and strength. Rejecting the popular view of the Pilgrims as men of peace, Lodge insisted, "Whatever else they were, or were not, the Pilgrim Fathers were pre-eminently conquerors." He saw them as the vanguard of a race that would eventually drive out the Indians and defeat the French and Mexicans in a relentless march across North America.[66] Lodge also believed the early New Englanders had exemplified their race's capacity to absorb other groups without losing its purity. He acknowledged that non-Anglo-Saxon immigrants to the region had been relatively few during colonial times—he usually only mentioned the French Huguenots and Scotch Irish—but he credited his ancestors with absorbing them while preserving their region's status as the most purely Anglo-Saxon place in America.[67]

Yet, when Lodge considered contemporary New England, he saw an Anglo-Saxon population that was no longer capable of conquering or absorbing other groups. At times Lodge tried to make a virtue of this, as in his history *Boston* (1891), where he argued that the Yankees' hostility to immigrants had preserved their metropolis from "some of the worst evils which have been the misfortune of other great cities of the United States."[68] But, as the years passed, Lodge increasingly acknowledged that his people had lost their conquering spirit. He sometimes tried to stiffen their backbones. Addressing Harvard's Phi Beta Kappa Society in 1894, Lodge complained that collegians—particularly those at Harvard—were being educated "to become critics of other men, instead of doers of deeds themselves." He urged his listeners to give up criticism for "the spirit, the faith, the courage, the determination of men. . . . These are the qualities which have carried the dominion of the English-speaking people across continents and over wide oceans to the very ends of the earth."[69] But, by the time he penned his memoir, *Early Memories* (1913), Lodge seemed reconciled to a more modest role for his race in New England. He conceded that his region had become more multiethnic since the days when its culture was "essentially English" in everything from its "modes of thought" to "trivial customs of the dinner-table."[70] Lodge attributed the change to the "huge increase of immigration, drawing its armies no longer from the British Isles alone, but from all Europe."[71] Perhaps even more striking was Lodge's revised view of Boston. Rather than the bastion of Yankee strength he had described in *Boston,* he now acknowledged that the city was, and had long been, immigrant territory. In *Early Memories* he recalled the epic snowball fights he and other Brahmin boys had waged against their rivals from the South Cove and North End, the chief neighborhoods of the city's Irish lower class. With mingled pride and sadness, Lodge concluded, "we made gallant fights, but were in the end, as a rule, outnumbered and driven back. What was more serious, the ever-increasing number of our opponents gradually by sheer weight pushed us, and still more our successors, from the Common hills and the Frog Pond to seek coasting and skating in the country."[72] Lodge's childhood experience of being driven out of the city obviously cast an ironic shadow over his subsequent career as a militant Anglo-Saxonist. Yet it was only when he spoke as a New Englander that he was forced to acknowledge that the Anglo-Saxon was not only—to cite one of his favorite phrases—"a conquering, colonizing race" but also, sometimes, a conquered one.

Cowboys and Immigrants

To appreciate how the decay of their race in New England complicated and undermined the Brahmins' Anglo-Saxonism, it is useful to compare them to their mid-Atlantic contemporaries Owen Wister, Frederic Remington, and Theodore Roosevelt. This trio, we recall, resembled the Brahmins in associating their Anglo-Saxonness with a particular American region, though in the case of Wister, Remington, and Roosevelt that region was the vital West rather than decayed New England. The effects of that regional difference are evident in the two groups' contrasting responses to immigration. If the weakness of the Anglo-Saxons in New England made the Brahmins fear immigrants, the strength of their race in the West helped allay those fears in the mid-Atlantic trio. The latter group regularly invoked the power and aggression of Anglo-Saxon westerners as proof that their race was superior to the newcomers arriving from southern and eastern Europe.

Although the mid-Atlantic trio differed greatly in their attitudes toward the "new" immigrants, they all viewed the newcomers as inferior to their western Anglo-Saxon hero. On the more tolerant end of the spectrum was Roosevelt, who celebrated the West as a key site where non-Anglo-Saxon immigrants were absorbed into the new branch of the "English-speaking race" taking shape there. He believed this process of incorporation began in colonial times and had continued right up to the present. Granted, Roosevelt would eventually come to doubt his race's capacity to absorb all comers. By the mid-1890s, he was calling for the restriction of "races which do not assimilate readily with our own."[73] But his fears were largely focused on the cities, where he believed large concentrations of immigrants slowed the process of absorption. Long after many Anglo-Saxons had given up hope of assimilating the "new" immigrants, Roosevelt remained confident that the race that had conquered a continent was up to the challenge of incorporating the southern and eastern Europeans.[74]

Wister and Remington did not share their politician friend's optimism about absorbing the "new" immigrants, but they did share his faith in the West as a symbol of their racial superiority to the southern and eastern Europeans. Both of them invoked the power of the Anglo-Saxon westerner to counter their fears of the newcomers from southern and eastern Europe. In "The Evolution of the Cow-Puncher," Wister imaginatively flees westward from the specter of an urbanized, immigrant-infested East: "No rood of modern ground is more debased and mongrel with its hordes of encroaching alien vermin, that turn our cities to Babels and our citizenship to a hybrid farce, who degrade our commonwealth from a nation into something half pawn-shop, half broker's office. But to survive in the clean cattle country requires spirit of adventure, courage, and self-sufficiency; you will not find many Poles or Huns or Russian Jews in that district."[75] Wister consoles himself with the thought that there is still a place in America where the Anglo-Saxon's rugged manhood reigns supreme, a place where the only immigrants are the "cheap foreigners" the Virginian spies working on the railroad.[76]

Remington also took solace in the masterful figure of the Anglo-Saxon westerner when threatened by the "new" immigrants. He faced that threat in 1894, when *Harper's Weekly* sent him to cover the Chicago railroad strikes. Remington presented the labor struggle as a battle between immigrant protesters and native-born forces of law and order. As scholars have pointed out, the artist makes his sympathies clear by vilifying the strikers as beery, violent anarchists and valorizing the soldiers as pure-minded, self-disciplined patriots.[77] Remington also distinguishes between the two sides in racial terms, as when he brutally fantasizes about a typical soldier's response to the strikers: "The soldier idea would be to create about eleven cords of compost out of the material at hand. And, again, the soldier mind doesn't understand this Hungarian or Polack, or whatever the stuff is." Remington imagines his soldier exclaiming, "Say, do you know them things ain't human?—before God I don't think they are men."[78] In contrast, the artist sees the soldiers as the embodiments of Anglo-Saxon manhood, "tall, bronzed young athletes." Although he does not name their race, he makes it clear enough by identifying them with the West, the region he, Wister, and Roosevelt had long associated with the Anglo-Saxons. He gushes over the "gallant" Seventh Cavalry, which had arrived in Chicago fresh from fighting with Indians in the West: "The regiment was born on the Platte River, pretty far up stream, and it has never been far enough East until the last few years to buy a fine-tooth comb or hear a hand-organ; but it is East now, and right in the middle of civilization." Only a die-hard opponent of industrial, multiethnic urban America like Remington would identify Chicago as the "East." He would obviously prefer to be up the Platte himself, but in the company of the Seventh he can at least stop worrying about the strikers: "[I]f you want the recreated spirit of Homer you ought to hear a Seventh Calvary trooper tell what he thinks of Chicago's mob."[79] Hungarians and "Polacks" stood no chance against these Anglo-Saxon warriors.

Roosevelt, Wister, and Remington were not unusual among Gilded Age Americans in turning to the region to work out their complex feelings about immigration. In New England, especially, population turnover seems to have heightened many people's awareness of regional identity. They asked themselves what it meant to identify with a region at a time when its ethnic profile—and everything that profile connoted in terms of institutions, culture, religion, and politics—seemed to be changing on a daily basis. Some joined the Brahmin Anglo-Saxonists in seeking clues to the future of their region and their nation in ideologies of race. Among those racialists were immigrant spokesmen who dreamed of displacing the Anglo-Saxons, just as the latter had driven out the Native Americans. Irish Catholic and French Canadian racialists talked confidently of turning New England into New Ireland or New France. But other New Englanders saw the region as less a battleground than a common ground of its many peoples. These pluralists called for a more open and capacious conception of regional identity, one that recognized the contributions of *all* New Englanders, Yankee and non-Yankee alike. As I argue in the following chapter, the conflict between the racialists and pluralists over the meaning of New England would be waged throughout the century's final decades. Before it was over, many of the region's most sacred symbols and heroes—including the Puritans, Pilgrims, and Plymouth Rock—would become objects of struggle between those who claimed the region for a single people and those who dreamed of sharing it with all peoples.

TWO

New Ireland, New France, New England

The Place of Immigrants in American Regionalism

Most scholars of American regionalism have treated it as the exclusive province of the native born, assuming that only those born in this country could have a particular identification with, or interest in, one of its regions. Many of those scholars contend that regionalism is not merely native born, but nativist. They read the regionalist's investment in the history, culture, and folkways of a particular place as a form of hunkering down in the presence of aliens.[1] Some have suggested that nativism is the driving force behind most, if not all, regionalist movements.[2] But few scholars go this far, with most focusing instead on the nativism of specific regional cultures. One of the regional cultures most frequently cited for its overt hostility to immigrants is Gilded Age New England. There waves of newcomers encountered a Yankee community that prided itself on its Pilgrim, Puritan, and Revolutionary heroes, its republican ideals, and its cultural attainments. The result, in many cases, was a virulent nativism that left its mark on an array of Yankee regionalist cultural productions, including fiction, town restorations, local and regional histories, Puritan statuary, Old Home Week celebrations, and the colonial revival movement. The scholars who have studied these phenomena (they include Dona Brown, Joseph Conforti, and John Seelye) do not always agree in their conceptualizations of regionalism.[3] For example, whereas some see New England regionalism as a recovery project, others stress its reliance on invented traditions. But all of them view nativism as a primary motivator of regionalist sentiment and cultural expression in the post–Civil War period.

Yet, while fear of the immigrant has certainly been a driving force behind regionalism—in Gilded Age New England and elsewhere—there is another side to the story. Our tendency to associate regional identities with the native born has blinded us to the participation of immigrants in regionalist sentiment and expression. Accordingly, regionalism should be viewed less as a tool of nativist hegemony and more as an object of contestation and sometimes even collaboration between natives and newcomers. Some signs suggest that this is beginning to happen. A growing number of scholars have explored the regional histories of particular immigrant groups.[4] But we still do not know much about how or why immigrants came to identify with American regions. What benefits did they see in calling themselves westerners or southerners? Did claiming a regional home in America strengthen or break down the boundaries that separated them from other groups? Did it help or hinder their struggles for nationhood back in the old country? And finally, how did immigrant regionalists view their native-born counterparts?

In this chapter I argue that regional identity became a contested idea in Gilded Age New England, not only for the region's Yankees but also for two of its largest immigrant groups, the Irish and French Canadians. I show that all three groups were similarly divided on the question of the relationship between race and regionalism. On one side were those I call racial regionalists, who viewed regional identities as a function of, and buttress to, racial ones. Among the most energetic advocates of this position were the region's leading Irish and Brahmin historians. The two groups were bitter rivals, as is evident in the conflicts between the founding members of the American-Irish Historical Society (AIHS) and the Brahmin historians Henry Cabot Lodge and John Fiske. During the early years of the AIHS, it clashed with the Brahmin historians over issues ranging from the use of the term *Scotch-Irish* to the legacy of the Puritans. But their main object of struggle was New England's past. The Irish historians rightly complained that the Brahmins' work on the region was filled with filiopietism, regional exceptionalism, and racial chauvinism. But, as I will argue, the same biases characterized much of the AIHS's work on New England. Indeed, in their basic assumptions about regional and racial identities, the Irish and Brahmin historians were more alike than they cared to admit. Both groups of scholars saw New England as merely one battleground in a worldwide struggle among the races. Their preoccupation with that larger conflict prompted the Brahmin and Irish historians alike to claim for their race the lion's share of the credit for New England's greatness, while downplaying the contributions of rival groups.

The third set of racial regionalists I discuss were the French Canadian imperialists, who boldly called for a conquest of New England by immigrants from Quebec. Inspired by the mass influx of their countrymen into the region after the Civil War, these men predicted that New England would soon emerge as a bastion of the French people and the Catholic faith, and many of them hoped to unite New England with Quebec, either as an independent nation or, after the annexation of Quebec, as part of the United States. It was precisely their prospective orientation that distinguished the French Canadian imperialists from the Irish and Brahmin historians. Readily conceding New England's past to other groups, the French Canadian imperialists laid claim to its future.

Other New Englanders resisted the racial regionalists' efforts to subordinate regional identity to race. Leading the opposition was a motley crew of Yankee, French Canadian, and Irish commentators whom I term *regional pluralists*—*regional* to signify their belief that New England identities were a product not only of race but also of climate, culture, history, and religion—and *pluralists* to convey their ethnically inclusive social vision. Rejecting the racial regionalists' chauvinism, the regional pluralists saw New England's culture as a storehouse to which many ethnic groups were contributing and on which all could draw. They also rejected the racial regionalists' emphasis on purity within groups and conflict between them. Whereas the racial regionalists viewed the characteristics of all of New England's peoples as permanently fixed, the regional pluralists believed mutual influences were so transforming the region's natives and immigrants as to make them unrecognizable to their ancestors.

The Historians

To argue that the AIHS in its early years was largely motivated by regional concerns is to read against the grain of its founding documents, which frame its mission through the rhetoric of American nationalism. The fifty or so distinguished men who met at Boston's Revere House on January 20, 1897, made clear that they were launching an organization with a national focus, membership, and leadership. They approved a constitution that listed among its "objects and purposes":

(1) The study of American history generally.
(2) To investigate, specially, the immigration of the people of Ireland to this country, determine its numbers, examine the sources, learn the places of its settlement. . . .
(3) To examine records of every character, wherever found, calculated to throw light on the work of the Irish element in this broad land.[5]

The founders further emphasized their society's national scope by electing a native New Yorker, Admiral Richard W. Meade, as president and by recruiting vice presidents from states as far-flung as South Carolina and Minnesota. At one of the society's first meetings, founding member Dennis Harvey Sheahan would urge that its ranks be filled with people from "every state in the country."[6]

In defining its goals and membership in all-American terms, the AIHS resembled other ethnic historical societies of the period, such as the Scotch-Irish Society of America (1889), the American Jewish Historical Society (1892), and the German American Historical Society (1901). Differences in the structure, size, and level of professionalization of these organizations make them difficult to compare. In the case of the Irish and Scotch-Irish societies, those differences were compounded by a fierce dispute over the very existence of the ethnic group the latter society claimed to represent. But one thing the early ethnic historical societies did share was the goal of demonstrating the essential Americanness of their respective peoples, whether they were fresh off the boat or many generations removed from it.[7] The chief tools at the societies' disposal were what Orm Øverland has called "homemaking myths," the standard narratives and arguments through which turn-of-the-century ethnic groups claimed a place in the American nation. Øverland groups these myths in three main categories: "myths of foundation ('we were here first or at least as early as you were'), myths of blood sacrifice ('we fought and gave our lives for our chosen homeland'), and myths of ideological gifts or an ideological relationship ('the ideas we brought with us are American ideas')."[8] To one degree or another, all of the ethnic historical societies employed these myths, though some (the AIHS among them) were more willing to abandon scholarly rigor for homemaking rhetoric than others.

John Higham argues that the American nationalism of the early ethnic historical societies distinguished them from their predecessors, the local historical societies of the mid–nineteenth century. He contends that the latter were run by Anglo-Protestant elites who were out to demonstrate the continuity of their leadership in a single community since the time of settlement, while the former were led by ethnic elites bent on documenting their groups' long-standing presence in the nation.[9] Yet, while the quest for a place in the American home may have been the overriding motivation of other turn-of-the-century ethnic historical societies, it was but *one* of the goals of the AIHS. At least as important to many of the group's founders was the desire to stake a claim to New England. There are a number of possible reasons why the Irish historical society displayed such a strong regional animus during what Higham has called "the era of *ethnic Americanism.*"[10] Perhaps most important was its status as the only ethnic historical society founded by New Englanders. Living among the Yankees had taught the founders of the AIHS—immigrant and native born alike—the prestige that went with a long New England pedigree. Kenneth Moynihan is surely right when he argues that the group's intense interest in colonial New England history was largely a response to Yankee ancestor worship: "The *Mayflower* rubbed sores in Irish hides."[11] The Irish historians also may have been inspired by the success of the New England Societies, those state and local associations of relocated Yankees and their offspring in such cities as New York, Cincinnati, and St. Louis. The New England Societies were perhaps best known for hosting self-congratulatory banquets enlivened by luminaries like Mark Twain.[12] But perhaps the primary reason for the Irish historians' regional focus was their oft-stated desire to rebut the work of the "New England historians" who, they argued, had misrepresented the history of the Irish not only in their region but across the nation.

As John J. Appel has demonstrated, the New England roots of the AIHS went back to the 1880s, when a number of Irishmen in the region began calling for a society devoted to the history of their ethnic group.[13] In *The Story of the Irish in Boston. . . .* (1889), a collection of historical and biographical sketches of the region's Hibernians, Boston printer and author James B. Cullen argued that his people needed a historical society in his city to continue the work he had begun.[14] The call was renewed in 1894, when the nativist American Protective Association attacked the service of the Irish in the Civil War. The region's leading Irish Catholic organ, the *Boston Pilot,* lamented that it lacked the historical data needed to refute the charges and urged the formation of a Catholic historical society in New England to fill the gap.[15] At this point, the *Pilot* seems to have had in mind a New England version of the American Catholic Historical Society, which had been founded in

Philadelphia in 1884. But the paper also cited as a promising model the secular research of amateur historian Thomas Hamilton Murray.[16] Murray was a journalist (and former *Pilot* staff writer) who, along with another tireless amateur, New Hampshire state insurance commissioner John C. Linehan, was recognized as the leading expert on the history of the Irish in colonial New England. Ultimately, it was the secular approach of these two men (both of whom would be among the society's officers and most active members in its first years) that would dominate the AIHS. From the start, the society was nonsectarian in its membership and research. The founders vowed, "The work of our projected society will be influenced by no religious or political divisions, for with us the race stands first, its qualifying incidents afterwards."[17] The members kept this promise by downplaying sectarian conflicts among the Irish, while focusing relentlessly on the commonalities shared by the Irish "race."

The work of Murray and Linehan also prefigured the AIHS's regional orientation. Although both men wrote about the Irish in other parts of the country, their overriding interest was New England. The years leading up to the society's birth saw the appearance of Linehan's *Pilot* articles on the Irish settlers of Massachusetts and New Hampshire and Murray's lectures and essays on such subjects as the Irish in King Philip's War and "David O'Kelly, the Irishman, a Settler at Yarmouth, Mass., 1657."[18] This concentration on New England topics also would characterize the AIHS until 1901 when, with the election of John D. Crimmins as president, "its meetings, activities, and strength gravitated to New York."[19] Until that point, the society's meetings and publications devoted far more attention to New England than any other region.

The Irish historians' preoccupation with the history of colonial and Revolutionary New England was driven largely by a desire to meet their rivals, the Brahmin historians, on their own ground. Chief among those rivals were Henry Cabot Lodge and John Fiske. The Irish historians were at an extreme disadvantage in this conflict. Although, like most members of the AIHS, Lodge and Fiske were, in the strictest sense, amateurs, they had far closer connections to professional historiography. They could draw on the institutions—particularly Harvard—where they had studied and many of their friends taught. Their essays appeared in the most prestigious general circulation magazines; their books were published by the foremost presses. Fiske was a celebrity lecturer; Lodge was first a congressman and later a US senator. The Irish historians, by contrast, operated on a much more modest scale. For the most part, they were journalists, lawyers, doctors, and state government officials who published the bulk of their work with the AIHS or in the Catholic press.[20] Their reputation among professional scholars was so slight that most simply ignored them. Yet, despite the long odds against them, the Irish historians entered the fray against the Brahmins charged with a high sense of moral purpose. They were on a mission to vindicate the many generations of New England Irish who had been ignored, misrepresented, and worst of all, classified as Anglo-Saxon by a set of Puritan-worshiping bigots. Moreover, the stakes were not entirely scholarly. The Irish historians were convinced that their Yankee rivals were fomenting prejudice against living Irish Americans. In an 1893 *Pilot* piece, Joseph Smith (later credited as the chief founder of the AIHS) refuted the popular belief that most of America's "lunatics, idiots, criminals and paupers" were Irish.[21] Smith blamed the English colonists for originating this stereotype and the Brahmin historians for keeping it alive. He cited Henry Cabot Lodge's *A Short History of the English Colonies in America* (1882) as the source of

> a corollary . . . of this historic fiction—the doctrine that the "Anglo-Saxon" alone was responsible for all the achievement of America. The Senator holds that New England did everything for America, Massachusetts for New England, the district in and around Boston for Massachusetts, Nahant for this location, and of course the sires of the Lodges glorified Nahant.

Smith drew a direct connection between the biases of Lodge's historical scholarship and his contemporaries' prejudices against the Irish. By "fighting and disproving this hoary-headed slander," he hoped to protect the living members of his race while honoring their dead.[22]

Smith blamed Lodge for the three forms of bias—racial, regional, and filial—that most commonly appear in the Irish historians' critique of their Yankee patrician rivals. Those forms of bias also have been cited by the Brahmin historians' latter-day critics, who generally echo the critique of Smith and his colleagues.[23] One aspect of the Irish historians' critique that has not been noted, however, is its applicability to their own work, which is just as filiopietistic, regionally biased, and ethnically chauvinist as that of the Brahmins. The Irish historians' backfiring criticisms point to a series of assumptions they shared with their Yankee patrician rivals concerning the relationship between regionalism and race. Both groups agreed that New Englanders boasted a set of traits that distinguished them from other Americans. They also generally agreed that those traits had originated mainly in the settlers of a single race. But the two groups of historians clashed over the identity of that founding race, with the Brahmins giving all credit to the Pilgrims and Puritans and the Irish awarding the palm to the forgotten Irish "pilgrim fathers." In their struggle over the bragging rights to New England, the Irish and Brahmin historians revealed a final assumption they shared: that dominance in New England mattered mostly insofar as it provided an advantage in the global struggle for hegemony being waged by Anglo-Saxons, Celts, and other races.

The Irish historians repeatedly charged their rivals with a bias toward New England. They argued (rightly, later scholars would say) that the Brahmin historians displayed an unfair preference for their region, overestimating its importance to the nation while belittling the contributions of other parts of the country. The primary target of these criticisms was Henry Cabot Lodge, whom they accused of looking through national regionalist glasses that made New England appear to be the primary founder and defender of America.[24] Joseph Smith, for example, charged Lodge with exaggerating the importance of New Englanders in the Revolutionary War. Citing the senator's claim that Washington began and ended the war with an army composed mainly of New England men, Smith pointed out that this begged the question of what had happened in the intervening years, when the patriot effort was sustained by the contributions of the other regions and France (including its famous Irish Brigade).[25]

Occasionally, the Irish historians' attack on Yankee regional bias expanded into a sweeping assault on the New England character. The Irish historians usually were careful to restrict their criticisms to the Brahmins' Puritan heroes, whom the Hibernians presented as intolerant, theocratic, and narrow-minded. But in a few instances, the target broadened to include all New Englanders, past and present. Smith followed one critique of the Puritans with the dismissal, "New England in colonial days produced some shrewd and level-headed men, but if she ever produced a great one, I have failed to catch his name."[26] These are strange words from a leader of an organization that, in those days, was largely devoted to celebrating the Irish heroes of colonial and Revolutionary New England. Yet Smith was not the only Irish historian whose hostility to the Puritans sometimes betrayed him into general attacks on the regional character. Thomas Hamilton Murray concluded one critique of the Puritans with the observation, "Typical New Englanders they were; honest, but deplorably mistaken in their views; relentless in their persecutions as any zealot."[27]

But such broadsides against New England and its people were uncommon among the Irish historians. In fact the group was far more likely to celebrate the region than critique it. Although they twitted their Brahmin rivals for their New England bias, the Irish historians generally shared it.[28] They, too, devoted the region disproportionate space in their scholarship and mental map of America. They, too, were sometimes guilty of equating New England with the nation. Finally, they, too, placed the region's colonial history at the center of their narrative of national origins.

Among the Irish historians, the temptation of New England exceptionalism could overcome even the most determined opponents of regionalist thinking. In a *Boston Pilot* article titled "The Passing of New England," Thomas Hamilton Murray set out to deconstruct the very notion of the region. He opens by declaring, "The term 'New England' is today a tottering shibboleth. . . . a huge misnomer—a thing of the crude, formative past. The term has no real status or significance today. It can have none tomorrow."[29] Murray mounts the case for the region's demise in geopolitical, cultural, and historical terms, respectively. First, he insists that there are "no sectional issues, no grievances and no desires" that unite the six states and distinguish them from the rest of the nation. Next, he denies that there is anything distinctive about the region's culture now that the pharisaical spirit of the Puritan has finally evaporated. Finally, he dismisses as legend some of the Yankees' most sacred historical traditions: "Where the traditions are constructed on the idea that this nation owes its conception solely to Plymouth Rock, or the Bay, they must be tumbled down. So, also, the idea that the people of these six States are overwhelmingly of English descent must likewise be demolished. Why? Because it isn't true."[30] Murray grants that there was a day when the term *New England* had a certain validity, but that day ended with the Puritans.

Yet, when he turns his attention to the groups that have been overshadowed by the Puritans, Murray seems much less willing to abandon the idea of region. Foremost among them is the Irish, who, he notes, have been coming to these shores since the era of Winthrop and Endecott. Murray blames the Brahmin historians for ignoring and deliberately obscuring the region's Irish: "The New England juggernaut has been driven over the neck of New Ireland."[31] Murray's use of the term *New Ireland* is arresting in an ostensibly antiregionalist essay. *New Ireland* was a term with a long history and multiple associations on both sides of the Atlantic. Among other uses, in the seventeenth century it had served as an alternative to *Nova Scotia,* while in 1877 Irish politician A. M. Sullivan had employed it to celebrate the modernization of the rural Irish.[32] In Gilded Age New England, however, *New Ireland* carried strong regionalist overtones. It was used by both Yankees and Irish to convey the startling demographic, cultural, and political shifts whereby a region long dominated by descendants of the English had come increasingly under the sway of the Irish. That Murray has these regional associations in mind is evident at the end of the essay, when he gestures toward the other ethnic groups, besides the Yankees and Irish, that had contributed "to the up-building of these six prosperous States." He foresees the writing of a "history of these six States" that will give all the groups their due.[33] This vision is notable not only for its pluralism (Murray usually keeps his eye squarely on the Irish) but also for its overt regionalism. Although he is careful not to use the term *New England* or even *New Ireland,* Murray clearly thinks "these six States" have enough in common to warrant a single history. This may seem a blatant contradiction of the beginning of the essay, but we must consider the shift in Murray's ethnic focus. Whereas regionalism is a tool of domination in the hands of the Yankees, it is a wellspring of resistance for the Irish and other non-Anglo-Saxons. Far from rejecting regionalism per se, Murray is simply trying to wrest it out of the hands of the Yankees.

For the Irish historians, laying claim to New England did not mean turning one's back on the struggle for freedom in Ireland. To the contrary, AIHS members insisted that their ties to the region actually enhanced their commitment to Irish independence. James F. Brennan culminated his account of "The Irish Pioneers and Founders of Peterborough, New Hampshire" by declaring, "If there is a town or city in this broad land owing a greater debt of gratitude to that green isle over the sea than does this town, I know it not. If there is a place which should extend more earnest and loving sympathy to Ireland in her struggles, I know not where it is."[34] For some Irish historians, to delve into New England's history was to be constantly reminded of their ancestors' long history of suffering and resistance in the old country. Thus, disputes over land proprietorship in colonial New Hampshire seemed, to John C. Linehan, "strangely like a page from Ireland's annals describing landlord rule."[35] The Reverend S. Banks Nelson also was struck by the similarity between the histories of British tyranny in New England and Ireland. Addressing the society on April 19, 1899, the anniversary of the battles at Lexington and Concord, the Presbyterian minister and Belfast native challenged his audience not to forget their Irish revolutionary forefathers and the cause for which they died: "It is impossible for Irishmen to think of Lexington without the associated thought of the United Irishmen, 'Who fears to speak of '98?'"[36] Several of Nelson's fellow speakers displayed their fearlessness by interspersing praise for the heroes of 1775 (particularly the Irish ones) with protests against the movement for a closer alliance between America and Britain, which was then being promoted by political and intellectual elites on both sides of the Atlantic. Their yoking together of New England's Revolutionary history and Ireland's past and present independence movements gave the lie to Yankees who insisted that schooling immigrants and their offspring in their region's history would assimilate them.[37] For the Irish historians, the more closely one identified with New England the harder one fought for Irish freedom.[38]

A strong regional identification was not the only thing the Irish historians shared with their Brahmin rivals. The two groups also resembled each other in their laudatory treatment of their forebears. Filiopietism was one of the Irish historians' favorite charges against the Brahmins. Murray accused them both of "[a]n intense bias, willing to chronicle nothing unless it reflected, or could be twisted to reflect, credit on the Pilgrims of the Mayflower" and of an "extreme partiality for the Puritans which has not hesitated to claim for them well-nigh every virtue under Heaven."[39] While the Brahmin historians actually did sometimes criticize their Puritan ancestors, they were careful to do so in muted terms, often emphasizing the good that came out of the Puritans' worst deeds. John Fiske, for example, readily acknowledged their intolerance but still managed to see them as unwitting contributors to religious liberty.[40] Thus, the Irish historians were on solid ground in attacking their Brahmin rivals for their filiopietism. But, as recent scholars have pointed out, the same charge justly can be made of the Irish historians. John J. Appel characterizes their research as "too polemical, laudatory and insufficiently documented to have value for the specialist."[41] That is not how it was supposed to be. At the founding meeting of the AIHS, Joseph Smith urged, "We cannot deal in hurrah business. . . . We must produce the cold documents and facts that no one can dispute, and eliminate from history its imaginary and fictitious bluffs."[42] This mandate was put even more bluntly in a letter to the society from Massachusetts Senator George Hoar. He celebrated the contributions of the Irish to America before noting that "they have had, have now, and will continue to have for a good while to come, grave faults. To say this is only to say that they are human. Do not be afraid to record their faults as well as their virtues."[43]

But no such evenhandedness characterizes the work of the Irish historians. Instead, the story they tell of the Irish in New England is one long praise song. Whether they are writing about unknowns such as the "brave, honest, manly men" who founded Peterborough, New Hampshire, or luminaries such as General John Sullivan, the Irish historians consistently emphasize their subjects' sterling qualities and defend them against critics.[44] Even more so than their Brahmin rivals, the Irish historians present a whitewashed view of their forebears. For example, in telling the story of New England's Irish in the Civil War, the AIHS members inevitably stress the group's valor and self-sacrifice, while leaving unmentioned their widespread hostility to the antislavery movement.[45]

Much of the myth making of the Irish historians was a conscious retort to the racial chauvinism of their Brahmin rivals. That bias displayed itself most obviously in the significance Lodge and Fiske attached to the Anglo-Saxon origins of the Puritans and Pilgrims. The Brahmin historians were far from alone in mythologizing colonial New England as "purely and exclusively English."[46] This inaccurate view of their region's settlers was shared by many, if not most, New Englanders. Yet, whereas most people in the region believed that race was merely one of several key determinants of New England identity, the Brahmin historians believed it far outweighed all others. The racialism of the Brahmin historians is particularly obvious in their effort to account for the republicanism of the Yankees. Most New Englanders saw that prized Yankee regional trait as the product of an array of historical, institutional, environmental, and racial factors, but the Brahmin historians thought it all came down to race. Thus, John Fiske's *The Beginnings of New England* opens after the fall of the Roman Empire when "wave after wave of Germanic colonization poured over romanized Europe . . . setting up in every quarter baronies, dukedoms, and kingdoms fermenting with vigorous political life."[47] As subscribers to the Teutonic origins theory, the Yankee historians believed that the descendants of the ancient Germans had carried the seeds of democracy everywhere they went. Where the Teutonic population was purest, they reasoned, republicanism was strongest. Lodge repeated the common Teutonist claim that "[t]he Puritan emigrants, reproduced in the New World, unconsciously, of course, but in all essential features the village community which the Saxons, Angles, and Jutes brought to England more than a thousand years before from the forests of Germany."[48] According to Lodge, that same Teutonic inheritance also explained such proud moments in the region's history as the signing of the Mayflower Compact, the spread of the town meeting, the formation of the New England Confederation, and the passage of the US Constitution.

The Irish historians strongly resisted their Brahmin rivals' effort to claim New England in the name of the Anglo-Saxons. They challenged the Teutonic origins hypothesis—Joseph Smith argued that the misgovernment of Germany and Ireland rendered ludicrous the idea of Teutonic political genius—as well as the Brahmins' portrayal of colonial New England as purely English.[49] As we have seen, the Irish historians sometimes called instead for a history of the region that would give proper credit to all of its peoples. More commonly, however, the Irish historians countered Brahmin Teutonism with their own racially motivated narratives of the region. Echoing the Yankee patricians' assumption that one race was chiefly responsible for New England's regional character, they claimed that honor for the Celt.

A major obstacle to the Irish historians' search for a usable past for their race in New England was the growing popularity of Scotch-Irishness. After the Civil War, increasing numbers of Protestant Irish Americans—including many with no Scottish ancestry—identified as Scotch-Irish, a term that, as the Irish historians tirelessly pointed out, was practically unknown in Ireland. Yet by the end of the nineteenth century Scotch-Irishness had been established as a force to be reckoned with in the United States through the work of the national and state Scotch-Irish Societies and their many political and religious allies. These partisans wove a "Scotch-Irish myth," which lauded the history and racial traits of the descendants of the Scottish Presbyterians transplanted to Ulster by James I. The Scotch-Irish Societies and their supporters celebrated the courage, enterprise, self-reliance, piety, and individualism of the Scotch-Irish both in Ulster and in America.[50] Among their many purported achievements, the Scotch-Irish were credited with contributing the core of the patriot army and the principles of the Constitution.[51] Many of the group's champions also hailed them for keeping their distance from Irish Catholics, whom they stigmatized as lazy, irresponsible, impetuous, immoral, and impious.[52] Although some Scotch-Irish partisans conceded that substantial numbers of Ulster Scots had intermarried with Irish Catholics, most insisted that contact between the two groups had been minimal.[53]

All of this was too much for the Irish historians, who devoted much of their energy to exposing the Scotch-Irish "humbug." Contradicting their own assumptions about the permanence of racial categories, they sometimes argued that the transplanted Scots had become Irish in Ireland. More commonly, they insisted that the Scots were already Irish before they arrived, since Scotland was originally peopled by Irish Gaels.[54] The Irish historians also cited evidence from the history of the Ulster Presbyterians in America to prove that the group always considered itself Irish, not Scotch-Irish. Favorite examples from that history included the Ulster Presbyterians who in 1737 named their new Boston organization the Charitable Irish Society; those serving under New Hampshire's General Stark during the Revolution who requested an extra liquor ration to celebrate St. Patrick's day; and those who christened a Portsmouth, New Hampshire, Masonic lodge after Ireland's patron saint.[55]

As these examples would suggest, the Irish historians concentrated their critique of Scotch-Irishness on New England. No doubt this was partly a function of their superior knowledge of the region. They were simply less well-equipped to debate the history of the Ulster Presbyterians in Pennsylvania or North Carolina. But at least some of the New England focus is attributable to the Irish historians' larger goal of establishing the centrality of their race in the region. If, as many people were now claiming, most of colonial New England's Irish were actually Scotch-Irish, that would make the Irish historians' task nearly impossible. Even more worrisome, Henry Cabot Lodge was insisting that the Scotch-Irish were actually "Scotch *and English* in blood."[56] Scotch-Irishness threatened not only to wipe Irishness from the map of New England but also to help secure the region for the Anglo-Saxon. Hence the relentless energy with which the Irish historians attacked it.

Along with their assault on Scotch-Irishness, the Irish also asserted the centrality of their race to New England by claiming credit for the region's core republican values. The Brahmin historians may have defined New England's reputation for independence as a Teutonic legacy, but the Irish historians insisted it was Celtic. Speaking both as a native Irishman and "an adopted son of New Hampshire," John C. Linehan proclaimed, "I glory in the spirit of independence displayed by the people of that state from the very first, and believe that it is largely due to the liberal strain of Irish blood running in the veins of her sons."[57] Linehan cited as proof the services of those sons—under Irish commanders—in the wars against the French, British, and Confederates. According to the Reverend John J. McCoy, the Irish roots of New England liberty also were evident during the Spanish-American War. McCoy called attention to the predominantly Irish cast of the Massachusetts troops, including the Second Volunteers, which "is spoken of by press and people as the ideal Massachusetts regiment, and as made up from the best blood of liberty-loving New England. This is true; and it is the best blood because most of it is Irish blood."[58] If the Brahmin historians could claim New England's most cherished regional traits for their race, then so could the Irish.

To beat the Brahmin racial chauvinists at their own game, the Irish historians constructed a countermyth of Celtic New England settlement.

They even went so far as to christen their Hibernian forebears "Irish Pilgrim Fathers" and "Irish Puritans" (the latter a particularly ironic name, given the Puritans' notorious hostility to the Irish Catholics). Granted, the Irish historians occasionally used those terms to challenge the Yankee "Anglo-maniacs" with the reality of ethnic mixing in colonial New England. New York physician Thomas Addis Emmet wrote of intermarriage between Puritan men and the Irishwomen sent as slaves by English commissioners to New England: "[I]t would seem not improbable that these two hundred and fifty young Irish women, with many others sent over from Ireland about the same time, must have all eventually been transformed at least into Irish Puritans. If so their progeny must in time have given quite a Hibernian tint to the blue blood of the descendants from the *Mayflower.* I have not found that the New England writers have noted these facts."[59] Yet in most cases the Irish historians used terms like *Irish Pilgrim* and *Irish Puritan* to signify not the kinship between their forebears and Puritans but their ineffaceable differences. John C. Linehan cited evidence that the "Puritan Irish" kept up the customs of their homeland—and their ethnic distinctions from the Yankees—for more than a generation after arriving in New Hampshire.[60] Thomas Hamilton Murray also underscored the ethnic differences between New England's early settlers by appropriating another term sacred to Yankees:

> They were heroic men, these Irish pilgrim fathers! Unlike another pilgrim element, upon which the changes have been rung unceasingly, they did not deny to others that liberty they so dearly prized themselves. Their influence on the future of the colonies was incalculable. To them, and to the broad spirit of tolerance, charity, and patriotism which they inculcated, this nation owes far more than to any influence proceeding from Plymouth Rock.[61]

By critiquing the intolerance of the Pilgrims, Murray questions their legitimacy as the founders of New England and by extension the nation. The rightful claimants to those titles are the Irish, whom Murray mythologizes with a national regionalist flourish worthy of the Brahmin historians. In a period that saw the Yankees celebrate the national importance of the Pilgrims and Puritans through statuary, paintings, popular histories, fiction, poetry, and public celebrations, it took courage to knock them from their pedestal.[62] Murray clearly expects an outcry: "This is said, not through a gratuitous desire to be argumentative or controversial, but as a plain statement of fact."[63]

A *New* New France

The Irish American historians were not the only group that dreamed of wresting New England from the Yankees. Beginning in the 1880s, a number of prominent French Canadians on both sides of the national border also saw dominating New England as the key to advancing the political and cultural fortunes of their race. While they remained a minority among French Canadian elites, these *Canadien* imperialists won wide favor among their compatriots and struck fear in the hearts of Yankees with their bold talk of Gallicizing and Catholicizing New England. They celebrated the French Canadians of New England—long derided as traitors by their nationalist compatriots in Quebec—as the vanguard of an army that would eventually conquer the region. Like the Irish American and Brahmin historians, the French Canadian imperialists were racial regionalists. The New England of their dreams might include many peoples, but it would be the stronghold of just one. Yet, unlike the historians, the French Canadian imperialists based their claims to the region not on its past but on its future. They pointed to the rising numbers of their countrymen in New England, as well as their successful resistance to assimilationist pressures, as proof that New England's future belonged to them. Convinced that outmigration, moral decay, and declining birthrates were rapidly undermining the strength and numbers of the Yankees, the French Canadian imperialists eagerly awaited the day when New England would become the new New France.

Before the 1880s most French Canadian elites in Quebec saw their compatriots in New England as anything but conquering heroes. The surge in emigrants from Quebec that began after the Civil War—pushed by difficulties in the province's agricultural and manufacturing sectors and pulled by the demand for factory workers in New England—prompted vociferous protests from French Canadian leaders, who insisted that emigration was a bad thing not only for the departing *Canadiens* themselves but also for their countrymen back in Quebec.[64] Clerics, politicians, and journalists warned that life in New England's factory towns would soon strip the emigrants of their language, culture, faith, nationality, health, and morals. Many condemned the emigrants as lazy, greedy traitors who willingly exposed themselves and their children to the vice and impiety of urban America for a spurious chance at material gain.[65] This critique of emigration was driven not only by genuine concern for the emigrants but also by worries about their effect on French Canadian nationalism. French Canadian leaders feared that continued emigration would eventually turn their people into a minority in

Quebec, thereby sapping their political strength and ending their dreams of nationhood.[66] Seeking ways to keep their countrymen at home and entice back the departed, they embraced the complementary movements for colonization and repatriation. Colonization sought to resettle the surplus agricultural population of the St. Lawrence Valley on virgin lands in Quebec. The repatriation movement was an effort led by the Quebec legislature to lure emigrants back home. In 1875 the legislature passed a measure creating a colony near the US border to receive remigrants from the United States.[67] But neither colonization nor repatriation did much to slow the relocation of French Canadians to New England. Yves Roby estimates that "[f]or each returning emigrant, five or six crossed the border in the opposite direction."[68] From 37,420 in 1860, the number of first- and second-generation French Canadians in New England had climbed to 573,000 by 1900.[69]

Quebec elites would continue to attack the *Canadien* emigrants well into the twentieth century, but by the 1880s the latter could already count on support from a growing number of French Canadian leaders on both sides of the national border. In that decade it became clear that the worst fears of the opponents of emigration were groundless. In fact the emigrants were not rapidly assimilating into New England's dominant Anglo-Protestant culture. To the contrary, most continued to speak their language, practice their faith, and preserve their customs. Many settled in the Little Canadas that sprang up in the region's principal factory towns, where they pursued the goal of *survivance* (cultural survival) with the support of institutions that included francophone newspapers, parochial schools, mutual societies, and national (i.e., French-speaking) parishes. Rather than undermining the ethnic pride of French Canadians, emigration seemed to be strengthening it. As one proponent of emigration put it, "Instead of becoming Americanized, the emigrant remains more patriotic than ever."[70] By the 1880s it was also becoming obvious that emigration did not threaten the political dominance of the French Canadians in Quebec. They comprised 75 percent of the province's population in 1851. Four decades later their share had risen to 79 percent, despite the net loss of over two hundred thousand people.[71] With one of the highest birthrates in the western world, the *Quebecois* women more than made up for the loss of the emigrants.

Confronted with these facts—which were publicized by the emigrants themselves and their supporters in Quebec—many French Canadian elites began taking a more positive view of their New England compatriots.[72] Among the most vocal revisionists were those who believed the emigrants were on a providential mission to convert Protestant America to Catholicism. Men like Monsignor Louis de Goesbriand, bishop of Burlington, Vermont, and attorney Charles Thibault, the future mayor of Pawtucket, Rhode Island, celebrated the emigrants as an army of missionaries sent south to do God's work. Some in this camp hoped to convert all of North America; others limited their ambitions to missionizing New England. In either case they believed that the decline of Protestantism—which they viewed as "plunged in indolence, iniquity, and vice"—was setting the stage for the triumph of their faith.[73] Just as their French ancestors had converted Europe in the Middle Ages, the French Canadian emigrants would bring the Yankees into the true Church in the modern era.[74]

A small, but prominent, minority of French Canadian leaders insisted that the mission of the emigrants was both religious and political in nature. They believed the *Canadiens* were destined not just to proselytize New England but to rule it. The dream of conquering (in some cases reconquering) lands held by the Anglo-Saxon was first popularized in Quebec by the French historian and sociologist Rameau de Saint-Père. In his widely read book *La France aux colonies* (1859), Rameau described the spread of French Canadians in Upper and Lower Canada as a form of reconquest. As Yves Roby points out, Rameau's ideas were taken up by Quebec promoters of colonization led by the *curé* Antoine Labelle, who called for a band of French Canadian colonies stretching from Manitoba to Quebec. But, whereas Rameau and his Quebec followers celebrated the spread of French Canadian colonies within Canada, they condemned their extension to the United States. Roby writes that the Quebec promoters of colonization "vigorously condemned the emigration because it weakened the homeland, by scattering the lifeblood of the French-Canadian nation," and thus weakening the reconquest movement.[75]

By the 1880s, however, some French Canadian elites on both sides of the national border were painting the emigrants as heroes, not villains, in the struggle against the Anglo-Saxon. These imperialists credited the emigrants with expanding Quebec into New England by taking over the lands of the Yankees. Quebec lawyer and politician Joseph-Adolphe Chapleau insisted that the French Canadian emigrant in the United States was "an advanced guard, a scout of the large army of invasion, the victory of which was predicted to us for the next century by M. Rameau."[76] He complimented his compatriots in Salem, Massachusetts, as "the living homeland which moved away from the land of the ancestors."[77] Journalist and lawyer Edmond de Nevers argued that the necessity of defending their institutions in a hostile environment had made the emigrants better nationalists than their countrymen who remained in the friendlier confines of Quebec.[78] The emigrants, he declared, "have not left the homeland, they have extended it."[79] The French Canadian imperialists looked forward to the day when their people would possess demographic and political dominance in New England. According to Charles Thibault, the Yankees were hastening the arrival of that day with their self-destructive practices of family limitation, irreligion, and extravagance. Soon it would be up to the French Canadians and Irish to "rebuild a large and strong Catholic nation on the social and religious ruins of Yankeeism."[80]

Talk of a French Canadian takeover of New England was bitterly ironic for the Yankees, who had long prided themselves on being a colonizing, rather than a colonized, people. As we shall see in chapter 5, the primary focus of their imperial ambitions was the Old Northwest, which since the late eighteenth century had received tens of thousands of Yankee migrants, mainly from the New England countryside. The champions of those migrants believed they had expanded New England by bringing new lands and peoples under the sway of its political institutions, churches, and culture. They were not pleased to discover that while they were busy colonizing the Old Northwest the French Canadians had set their sights on New England. After paying tribute to the rural Yankee migrants who had "New Englandized" the West, Connecticut agricultural writer George Austin Bowen warned that French Canadians were taking their place in the New England countryside: "It is a poor race, low in its instincts and social conditions, yet strong in its vitality, and increasing with great rapidity, both in Canada and the States."[81] Bowen was particularly disturbed to hear that the influx was supported by the Catholic Church: "It is triumphantly declared by their leaders that in less than fifty years they will be in a majority in New England . . . and will have control of its politics, dictate in [*sic*] its religion, and that Boston will be the center of the French-American nation, who will retain their own language and customs."[82] Bowen feared that Boston was being transformed from the center of Yankee imperial power into the capital of French Canada.

Bowen's words seemed prophetic two years later when Father Édouard Hamon published *Les Canadiens-Français de la Nouvelle-Angleterre* (1891), a book that mapped out a *Canadien* conquest of New England that began in the region's countryside. A Brittany-born Jesuit priest, Hamon was a member of the faculty of the Collège Sainte Marie in Montreal who had visited and worked in the French Canadian communities of New England. In *Les Canadiens-Français de la Nouvelle-Angleterre,* he combined short histories of the French Canadian parishes in the region with general remarks on the economic conditions, social life, and political views of his people. But what sparked the most response was the section of the book that lays out a step-by-step plan for peacefully conquering New England. As Robert LeBlanc observes, such detail was unusual at a time when French Canadian nationalists usually contented themselves with vague statements about the mission of their people in North America; in contrast, "Hamon was prepared to consider the practical means by which this objective might be realized."[83] Although Hamon's plan never came close to realization, it seemed plausible to many in the early 1890s, when every advance of the French Canadian community seemed to coincide with a stumble by the Yankees.

Certainly the most striking aspect of Hamon's plan was its focus not on New England's factory towns, where the vast majority of the *Canadiens* were heading, but on its countryside. This was particularly counterintuitive in New England, which boasted not only the nation's largest French Canadian community but also its most urban one. In Massachusetts—home to almost one-third of the nation's *Canadiens*—only seven hundred out of forty-four thousand French Canadian families lived on farms.[84] Nevertheless, Hamon saw this tiny minority as the vanguard of a mighty imperial army. Noting that thousands of *Canadiens* had recently migrated south from the St. Lawrence Valley to Quebec's Eastern Townships, Hamon believed it was only a matter of time before they continued their march across the forty-fifth parallel into the countryside of northern New England, at which point "the great invasion will start."[85]

As the place to launch a French Canadian conquest, the hill country of northern New England had obvious drawbacks, most notably a small *Canadien* population, a dearth of Catholic institutions, and a stagnant economy. On the plus side was an abundance of available farmland. As we shall see in chapter 4, more than half a century of out-migration by the Yankees from the hill country had lowered populations and land prices in many rural townships. This created an opportunity that Hamon was eager to seize. He argued that the French Canadians were the logical choice to take the place of the departing Yankees, since they were primarily an agricultural people. This made them unlike the Irish, who, he claimed, "do not want to farm," preferring to "gather in the large cities."[86] The notion that the *Canadiens* were born farmers had no basis in fact, but, as scholars have shown, it was stubbornly maintained by the group's leaders, who "romanticized the *habitants*' rural way of life and sanctified home and family as vital repositories of the French Canadian cultural heritage."[87] In calling the emigrants to the land, Hamon also capitalized on French Canadian conservatives' persistent worries about the moral dangers of the American city.[88] Of course a countryside with few

Catholic churches, parochial schools, and charities obviously carried moral hazards of its own. Hamon planned to fill the institutional void by relying on the established parishes in Canada's Eastern Townships to take the lead in founding colonies on the New England side of the border, writing that "the old parish must, as much as possible, be used as a base for the new colony, to encourage it, to help it, and to ensure its success."[89] Hamon believed the closer the ties between mother and daughter parish the more likely the new colony was to succeed.[90]

In fixing his sights on rural New England—the hill country in particular—Hamon was assaulting Yankee regional identity at its core. As Dona Brown points out, by the late nineteenth century, the growth of factory towns and immigrant populations in southern New England prompted many Yankees to romanticize the region's north as the "real" New England, the haven of pure Anglo-Saxon bloodlines, Yankee folkways, and rural virtues.[91] To plot a takeover of this subregion was thus to strike Yankee New England where it lived. This may be one reason why Hamon's book received as much attention as it did in the United States despite the absence of an English translation.[92]

Hamon's plan rested on his assumption that an expanding French Canadian population in New England would steadily replace a declining Yankee one. As a racial regionalist, he thought the *Canadiens* were engaged in a winner-take-all struggle, with the victor earning the right to impose its culture, bloodlines, and faith on the entire region. Hamon believed his people were already well on their way to victory, particularly in the factory towns, where "they form the majority of the working population. Quietly, without any fuss, they drive back foreign nationalities and replace them." He depicted the Little Canadas as growing islands of ethnic purity, where the emigrants "tend to become a people distinct with their own religion, race, and customs."[93] As Robert LeBlanc observes, Hamon apparently dreamed of uniting the Little Canadas of eastern New England with the rural colonies of *Canadiens* he hoped to start in the region's rural West.[94] The result would be a solid network of *Canadien* parishes stretching from the St. Lawrence Valley to the New England coast. To naysayers who predicted that the assimilation of the French Canadians would prevent this dream from ever becoming a reality, Hamon replied that linguistic differences and the proximity of Quebec would permanently separate his compatriots from the Yankees.[95] He also thought the two groups would be kept apart by their antithetical racial backgrounds: "The French character is the total opposite of the Anglo-Saxon-American character. As much as the one is merry, extroverted, easy-going, sympathizing with the misfortunes of others, ready for the most generous sacrifices, the other is cold, focused, shrewd and egoist."[96] There seemed little danger that such disparate peoples could ever mingle.

But Hamon thought it was another difference between Yankees and French Canadians—namely, their attitudes toward children and domestic life—that would ultimately determine the fate of New England. As we shall see in chapter 3, like many other commentators on the declining Yankee birthrate, he took it as a sign of moral decay. He warned that selfishness and sensualism were tempting the Yankees into an "open revolt against the providential laws which guarantee the conservation and the propagation of family." By "revolt," Hamon apparently meant abortion and contraception. Echoing other opponents of both practices, he believed that their prevalence among the Yankees was leading to health problems, including sterility, which in turn caused rural depopulation: "[T]he natural course of things is avenging the ignored divine law. Already a third, at least, of the farms of New England are abandoned."[97] Through their immoral embrace of family limitation, the Yankees were rapidly driving themselves toward extinction.

Conversely, Hamon believed moral reproductive practices and continued immigration guaranteed a steadily rising French Canadian population in New England. The *Canadiens* were "faithful to the laws of God, especially those which ensure the stability of marriage and the fecundity of families."[98] Scholars have confirmed that New England's French Canadians were more prolific than the Yankees, but the gap was not as big as Hamon believed. Emigration significantly lowered the birthrates of French Canadian women. Enjoying the independence that came with factory work, *Canadiennes* in New England were more likely to delay marriage than were their counterparts in Quebec.[99] Moreover, when the former eventually did get married, they spaced their births at longer intervals than did their married sisters across the border.[100] This resulted in fewer total births among the *Canadiennes* in New England than among those in Quebec. Yet, like most of his contemporaries, Hamon did not notice what life in New England was doing to the French Canadian birthrate. He took for granted that his female compatriots were easily winning the war of the cradles with their Yankee rivals, citing the assessment of the *New York Commercial Advertiser:*

> The victory achieved by the men of the English race, on the plains of Abraham, is avenged by the women from the race of Montcalm. New England is overcome. The detached swarms of the French hive take possession of the land. The descendants of the Pilgrims who multiply

> less quickly than their ancestors become rarefied year by year. . . . The New England of the ancestors is in the process of disappearing.[101]

While Hamon agreed that New England was disappearing, he was unsure what would take its place. He did not doubt that the French Canadians would take over the region or that they would eventually reunite with their brethren in Quebec. But whether they would do so as a sovereign nation or as part of the United States he could not predict. The nationalist in Hamon thrilled at the thought of an independent *Canadien* state, "a young people passionate, fearless, proud to be finally in charge of its destiny."[102] On the other hand, he was by no means totally opposed to the idea of the United States annexing Quebec, a position that put him at odds with *Canadien* conservatives, who opposed annexation as a threat to cultural survival.[103] Hamon countered that French Canadian institutions were strong enough to ensure *survivance* even after annexation. He speculated that if the United States were to acquire Quebec, it would leave his people in control of four or five state legislatures in New England.[104]

A further argument for annexation, Hamon hinted, was that it might well eventuate in an independent French Canadian state. He speculated that annexation could foster the growth of dangerous centrifugal forces within the United States: "Doesn't the United States, which will then count a population well over a hundred million people, run the risk, like any other political agglomeration exceeding certain proportions, of splitting into several independent republics?"[105] Echoing other commentators who talked of the disunion in those years, Hamon speculated that the fragments of the former United States would then become independent nations, each devoted to a single ethnic group.[106] The French Canadian fragment—which would include an annexed Quebec—would emerge as "an independent, Catholic and French people."[107] In short it was possible to be for annexation and French Canadian sovereignty at the same time.

Not surprisingly, Hamon's design for the future of New England did not sit well with the Yankees. A nativist group reportedly reprinted a garbled translation of the first part of *Les Canadiens-Français de la Nouvelle-Angleterre* (i.e., the portion that includes his plan of conquest) as an anti-Catholic tract.[108] Hamon's book also rang alarm bells among more respected commentators, some of whom were themselves racial regionalists. They included Egbert C. Smyth, a Congregational minister and Andover Theological Seminary faculty member, who reviewed *Les Canadiens-Français de la Nouvelle-Angleterre* in the *Proceedings of the American Antiquarian Society.*[109]

Smyth praised the accuracy of Hamon's portrait of French Canadian life in the factory towns of New England. He found alarmingly feasible the priest's proposal to extend a network of parishes across the national border into New England, as well as Hamon's dream of a union of New England and Quebec.[110] Smyth recognized that either of those outcomes would have major consequences for New England: "What possibilities are there of new divisions, new political organizations! In a word, the dream and the vision may at last be fulfilled of a new France."[111]

The thought of a union of Quebec and New England was particularly disturbing to Smyth because he believed French Canadians and Yankees were fundamentally different when it came to their civic life and political ideologies. Like many other Anglo-Saxonists, Smyth contended that a long history of subjugation to crown and church had made the *Canadiens* dependent, slavish, and politically corrupt—in short, the antithesis of the Yankees, whose experience with self-government went back to the Puritans, and ultimately to their Anglo-Saxon and Teutonic ancestors: "The [French Canadian] immigrants who flock to us today . . . have had little or no experience in that method of responsible local government in which we have been trained from the start."[112] Smyth dismissed any hope of bringing the *Canadiens* under the influence of the Yankees, arguing that the former were effectively walled off by language, religion, and parochial schools. What was worse, "They are of a race tenacious of its characteristics, tenacious of a different civilization from the Anglo-Saxon."[113] As Smyth considered the history of the two groups' ancestors in Europe, it seemed more likely the *Canadiens* would absorb the Yankees than vice versa. To avoid that nightmare, he vowed to use "the weapons of truth and light" to defend his people and their institutions.[114]

The Regional Pluralists

Yet not all New Englanders saw their region as a prize in a global racial struggle. Among those who dissented from that perspective were the writers I call *regional pluralists.* They were *regional* in that they viewed their identities as New Englanders as dynamic, multiply determined formations—a product not only of race but also of history, culture, religion, and climate. They were *pluralist* in their willingness to acknowledge the many peoples who had contributed to the region. Rejecting the racial regionalists' emphasis on purity within groups and conflict between them, the regional pluralists stressed the cultural exchanges and collaborations that had brought New England's various peoples together. They saw those ties as beneficial not only for the ethnic groups involved but also for the region as a whole. In their view New England was greater than the sum of its ethnic parts.

The regional pluralists were in a distinct minority among Gilded Age Yankees, most of whom believed immigrants should either be absorbed or kept out. Even some of the staunchest Yankee friends of the foreign born could not imagine them contributing anything to New England's culture. Barbara Solomon explains that this was true even of the leading Brahmin opponents of immigration restriction, including Thomas Wentworth Higginson and Charles W. Eliot. These men resisted the epidemic of nativism that infected so many of their peers at the end of the century, consistently speaking up for the value of immigrants to the economy and affirming their right to settle in the region.[115] But, on the question of who would control New England's culture, the Brahmin antirestrictionists were less open-minded. As Solomon argues, most of them clung to the belief that the main outlines of that culture had been permanently fixed by their own ancestors.[116] Even Charles W. Eliot, who would eventually reject assimilation as a goal for the nation's immigrants, "never considered any reciprocal activity by which the newcomer might contribute to Yankee civilization."[117]

Yet a few old-stock New Englanders did concede that the foreign born had contributions to make, not only to the region's culture but also to the Yankees themselves. Consider Edward Everett Hale, whose *Letters on Irish Emigration* (1852) faulted the Massachusetts and federal governments for offering so little provision to an immigrant group with so much to offer, and gain from, the people of his region and nation. Hale believed the Yankees already had reaped a variety of benefits from the Irish. Invoking what would become a standard defense of immigration, he argued that the arrival of Irish labor had freed the Yankees for "higher and wider uses," such as careers in trade and the arts.[118] He presented Irish workers as the broad economic base that supported such Yankee cultural accomplishments as the Boston Atheneum and the Cambridge Observatory. But Hale's appreciation of the Irish was not limited to their strong backs. To the contrary, he openly admired elements of the Irish character and hoped to appropriate them for his own people. Granted, Hale took a dim view of the "pure Celtic race," concluding that it had "done nothing positive for mankind, and been nothing but a monument of failure." On the other hand, he believed that the race had "proved itself excellent to be absorbed" in countries such as England, France, and Italy (in an appendix Hale suggested that a large proportion of the blood flowing through the veins of Englishmen was Celtic).[119] Hale hoped to "Stimulate the Absorbents" in his country in order to break up the "clannish spirit" of the urban Irish.[120] He proposed a plan for dispersing Boston's Irish to the farms of New England where they would be "surrounded by Americans."[121] Such a scheme would benefit the Irish by removing them from urban "temptations and frauds" and Americanizing them.[122] Yet it would also aid the Yankees, not only by relieving their labor shortage but also by giving them "vivacity and good humor, which we are promised our hard-working population shall receive, from this emigration of an exhausted race."[123] Few people familiar with the long history of complaint about the crabbed Yankee character would deny the need for an infusion of Irish vivacity and humor. To encourage his fellow Yankees to become a little more like Celts, Hale assured them they would easily dominate the Irish: "We are here, well organized, and well trained, masters of the soil, the very race before which they have yielded everywhere besides."[124] The Yankees had everything to gain, and nothing to lose, in taking the Celts into their farms, their homes, even their character.

Seventeen years after Hale's *Letters,* Mrs. C. A. Hopkinson published an essay in the *Atlantic Monthly* that echoed his vision of a mutually beneficial relationship between Irish and Yankees, as well has his scheme for bringing it about. Hopkinson argued that both groups were hurt by the concentration of the Irish in the cities, where they were isolated from potential Yankee employers and subject to the noxious influences of urban life. The solution was to transplant "many hundreds of thousands of impressible Irish men and women" to the New England countryside, where they "might be made into excellent Yankees" through "the unconscious education that would come from daily contact with our own people."[125] All of this was familiar from Hale, but, unlike the minister, Hopkinson did not dream of absorbing the Irish. Despite her talk of remaking the Irish into Yankees, she struck a pluralist note as she considered the effects of bringing the two groups together: "There might be a mutual influence with advantage to both; but the sterner characteristics would be the stronger ones, at least in this bracing climate, and we should see, in the next generation, the vivacious Irish temperament assimilated in outward gravity to that of the Yankee, while he, in his turn, might have possibly borrowed something of the other's hilarity."[126] Hopkinson anticipated her Yankee readers' fears of turning Celt by assuring them that their "sterner" traits—more suited to New England's climate—would dominate the transaction. Moreover, she emphasizes that the acquisition of Celtic traits by the Yankees was no certainty, only something that "might . . .

possibly" occur. Yet, given Hopkinson's investment in nativist stereotypes (e.g., she speaks casually about "the reckless and improvident Hibernians"), the fact that she still dreams of an exchange of traits suggests that she genuinely values the Irish influence.[127] Otherwise, she simply could have joined the many Yankees who called for remaking the Irish in their own image.

In the century's last decades, other Yankees would fully embrace the pluralism that Hopkinson flirts with. Many of them shared her sense that closer relations between New England's Yankees and immigrants would prove mutually beneficial. But unlike Hopkinson the later Yankee pluralists frankly acknowledged that their own group had deficiencies of various sorts that could only be alleviated by the influence of the foreign born. Most imagined a series of cultural exchanges that would leave the Yankees and immigrants looking a lot more like each other. But, while these Yankee pluralists believed the foreign born were eager to enter into such transactions, they sometimes doubted their own people's willingness to do so.

Bowdoin College president William DeWitt Hyde spelled out the potential benefits of a closer relationship between the Yankees and immigrants in his essay "The Transformation of New England: Is It Decay or Development?" He was writing in response to an earlier, similarly titled essay by Albert L. Bartlett, which repeated a number of nativist clichés about the threat of Catholic immigrants to New England's racial homogeneity, as well as its political, cultural, and religious institutions.[128] Hyde countered that those institutions were actually strengthened, not weakened, by the participation of the foreign born; moreover, the immigrants were themselves improved by their participation. Hyde also thought the Yankees stood to gain from closer relations with the newcomers. He critiqued his own people's attitudes toward work, education, and religion and urged them to heed the example of their immigrant neighbors.

Hyde believed New England had been particularly beneficial to the region's foreign-born Catholics. He argued that the Catholic Church was divided between two camps: a "Romanist element . . . which is the bigoted, implacable foe of everything free, everything progressive, everything American" and "a catholic element . . . which is as broad and tolerant and candid and truth-loving and patriotic as any that can be found among Presbyterians or Unitarians or Agnostics."[129] Hyde thought the outcome of this struggle would be determined by external forces, which, in New England, were all on the side of the "catholic elements." He contended that the Church was "already feeling the influence of our free thought and free institutions."[130] In any case, if the "Romanist element" tried to subordinate the state to the

Church, it would "fare no better than did the Puritan theocracy."[131] In short the future of New England's immigrant Catholics looked to be one of toleration and liberalism rather than hierarchy and conservatism.

Hyde argued that the immigrants were also benefiting from New England's political and educational institutions. He dismissed the nativist canard that immigrants were undermining the region's tradition of self-government, countering that the best way to protect its political institutions was through "the intelligent and hearty participation of foreigners in the administration of local government." In an era when nativists schemed to strip power from immigrant-dominated municipal governments, Hyde called for a reversal of that tactic. He insisted that putting the foreign born in control would actually strengthen New England's institutions: "Official responsibility and active participation in political work is the best school of politics." Praising the Irish in particular as "bright and eager learners in that school," Hyde urged that the immigrants be welcomed into the region's political system.[132]

Hyde believed the relationship between the foreign born and New England's educational system was also mutually beneficial. At a time when nativists routinely attacked immigrants as a threat to the common schools, he scoffed at the idea: "The American ideal of free secular education by the State is too deeply rooted in New England to be overthrown."[133] He contended that instead of trying to gain control over the parochial schools, Yankees should simply keep their hands off and "[l]et the public and the parochial school struggle for existence freely and fairly, side by side."[134] If the public schools won, the immigrants would surely flock to them or demand something comparable from their Church. If the parochial schools triumphed, Yankee Protestants would inevitably demand a version of them for their own children. Either way education in New England would be strengthened.

But Hyde doubted that the Yankees would take lessons from the immigrants, on the subject of education or anything else. Not that there were no lessons to be learned. To the contrary, Hyde identified several areas where he thought the Yankees would do well to follow the immigrants' lead. One was religion. He faulted the Yankees for worrying too much about their own souls and not enough "about those objective social institutions and relations on which the salvation or spiritual well-being of society as a whole and of each individual member here and now depends."[135] Hyde clearly thought the Catholic Church was doing a better job addressing those social concerns. He included a lengthy quote from Bishop John Spalding that called for the Church to embrace the truths of science and evolve to meet the changing needs of the people. Hyde declared, "I know no nobler statement of the political and intellectual attitude of the true Christian Church."[136] He held out some hope that the "aristocratic and speculative" Protestant churches would embrace Spalding's vision, but the prospects of that seemed doubtful.[137]

Hyde was even less optimistic that the Yankees would follow the good example of the immigrants in the workplace. Sounding a popular lament of Yankee physiologists, agricultural writers, and domesticity experts, he claimed that "social pride" and "ornamental rather than practical" educational ideals were teaching young Yankees to consider manual labor beneath them.[138] He believed the group's health and fertility were suffering as a result: "Manual labor tends to vigor and reproduction; easy ways of getting a living tend to deterioration and sterility." The foreign born were blissfully free of the bias against manual labor; consequently, they seemed poised to take over many occupations: "Hard work, steady pay, regular savings, and large families are giving to the foreigner the industrial future of New England." Barring some unforeseen change, the "industrial inheritance" of New England would pass from the Yankees to the foreign born.[139]

Other Yankee regional pluralists took a more hopeful view of their group's willingness to learn from its immigrant neighbors. In "The Irish in American Life," attorney and author Henry Childs Merwin contended that mutual influences were transforming New England's Irish and Yankee populations for the better. Like many Yankees, he believed the two groups had inherited complementary sets of traits from their racial ancestors: whereas the Anglo-Saxon Yankees were disciplined, methodical, and rational, the Irish Celts were witty, imaginative, and impetuous. Merwin thought each group's race traits sometimes posed problems in their unadulterated form: Celtic impetuousness made for unscrupulous Irish politicians, and Anglo-Saxon discipline cropped out as Yankee ultraconservativism. Thus, it was "a special Providence" that the two groups had come together in New England to ameliorate each other's excesses.[140] Merwin believed the mutual influences were already at work:

> The Irishman and the American—the Celt from the west coast of Ireland, and the Anglo-Saxon born and brought up in New England—might appear to stand at the very opposite poles of nationality; and yet they tend to come together. On the one hand, the Irishman readily assimilates new ideas and adapts himself to new conditions, so

> that he quickly becomes Americanized; and, on the other hand, the American descendants of the English have become in some important respects less like the English, and more like a Celtic people,—quicker in mind and in body, more sensitive and more impressionable.[141]

Merwin predicted that the interactions between the two groups would pay even bigger dividends in the future. He foresaw great things in literature "when to Celtic fire and imagination there are joined the Anglo-Saxon restraint and sense of form."[142] He was also hopeful that the two groups would moderate each other's political extremes. He speculated that the influence of the Irish might encourage the conservative Yankee to be more aggressive in pursuing political reform at home and humanitarian intervention abroad.[143] Conversely, he counted on the Yankee influence to dampen Irish radicalism, particularly when it came to Great Britain. He ended the essay predicting that, despite the religious differences between the two groups, "the Irish-American will, before many years are past, be lost in the American, and . . . there will be no longer an 'Irish question' or an 'Irish vote,' but a people, one in feeling, and practically one in race."[144] His fear of Hibernian political power apparently led Merwin to conclude with this fantasy of absorbing the Irish rather than exchanging traits with them. But that dream did not cancel out the transactions that, by his own account, already had taken place. If the Irish American was destined to be lost in the Yankee, it was also true that the Yankee already looked suspiciously Celtic.

New England's immigrant communities also produced their share of regional pluralists, who portrayed the region as the site of mutually beneficial cultural exchanges between the Yankees and foreign born. These writers took deep pride in their ethnic heritage, but they were extremely wary of what Rhode Island politician Aram J. Pothier called "the politics of race" and "narrow-minded nationalism."[145] Treasuring New England for its cultural diversity, they opposed both their nationalist compatriots who called for conquest and Yankees who demanded assimilation. Instead, the regional pluralists urged the benefits of harmonious relations between the region's immigrant and old-stock communities by pointing to the long history of productive collaborations between them.

Some Irish and French Canadian regional pluralists presented their ethnic groups as proud heirs of the Pilgrims and Puritans. They divided their praise between the English colonists, who had established the region's free institutions, and their own peoples, who protected and extended that inheritance. According to Michael J. McNeirny, much of the latter work had fallen to the Irish Catholics. Speaking at the silver jubilee celebration of a Gloucester, Massachusetts, priest, McNeirny paid glowing tribute to the Irish Catholic settlers of the area. He likened those "pioneers" to their seventeenth-century predecessors:

> All honor to the men who in the earliest days of our history fled from tyranny to build a nation of the free, but in honoring them it is not necessary to forget these latter-day pilgrims, who came to enlarge, strengthen, beautify, [and] preserve the work only begun by the Puritan founders.

McNeirny did not specify which Puritan "work" the Irish settlers had taken up, but the rest of the speech suggested that it was republicanism. He cited Catholic heroes—including the Irish Americans Charles Carroll and Philip Sheridan—who had helped strengthen and enlarge the nation's free institutions. Dreaming of even greater things for his coreligionists in the future, he urged, "Give the Catholics of America another hundred years and what can they not do for the good of the Republic?"[146] The Irish had already demonstrated themselves worthy inheritors of the Puritans.

Biddeford, Maine, lawyer Godfroy S. Dupré similarly urged his compatriots to take up the mantle of the Pilgrims. Speaking at a French Canadian convention in Springfield, Massachusetts, he declared:

> Emigrants and sons of emigrants, we have become active and respected members of the American society, to such a point that we feel as much American as the passengers of the Mayflower. We have learned to cherish the land they love, their life is ours, their victories like their losses are ours; and because we are here to stay, we want, under the aegis of the American liberties, to take up our part of the duties and responsibilities, the same way we want to take our part of the privileges and rights we are entitled to.[147]

But, if the *Canadiens* felt like *Mayflower* scions, they were not acting like it. Specifically, Dupré faulted his countrymen for failing to naturalize and vote. Like other French Canadian elites after 1880, he worried that the non-participation of his compatriots in the political process was leaving them isolated and powerless in New England. Earlier generations of French Canadian leaders had opposed naturalization in hopes that the emigrants would eventually return to Quebec, but by Dupré's day it was clear that this would never happen.[148] The attorney urged his compatriots to face up to reality and assume the duties and responsibilities of American citizenship.

For Dupré, like other *Canadien* regional pluralists, becoming a US citizen meant setting nationalist goals aside when it came to the American political system. There must be no bloc voting and no talk of forming a French Canadian "state within the state."[149] He condemned nationalism among the emigrants as not only absurd, given the comparatively small number of French Canadians in the United States, but also dangerous, as it was liable to arouse nativist hostility against them. Rather than trying to take over New England, the French Canadians should instead take advantage of their position among its "mixed elements."[150] In a pluralist society, the republican legacy of New England's founders was the common property of all groups, and it was the French Canadians' turn to claim it.

Whereas McNeirny and Dupré emphasized what the immigrants had gained from the Pilgrims and Puritans, other regional pluralists argued that most of the benefits ran in the other direction. In an essay in the Irish Catholic *Donahoe's Magazine,* T. J. Corbett stressed how the immigrants had softened the character and beliefs of the Puritans. He argued that the change had come none too soon: "The nature of the Puritan is cold and narrow and provincial; and he needed contact with the warmer and more impressionable character of the foreigner, to bring out the best in him, and to prevent that *dry rot* which was so surely assailing him from dwelling so long on his own perfections."[151] And who best to perform that service for the Puritan than the proverbially warm and impressionable Irishman? Corbett argued that the Irish and other Catholic immigrants had wielded a positive influence on Puritan spiritual life, as evidenced by the passing of the grim Sabbath, the admission of flowers and music into meeting houses, and the celebration of Easter and Christmas in "evangelical" churches. Others might credit these transformations to the influence of rival Protestant sects, but Corbett considered them a response to the arrival of huge numbers of Catholic immigrants.[152] While stressing what the Puritans had gained from the Irish Catholics, he concluded by acknowledging that the latter had also gained from the relationship. He warned that the declining birthrates of the Puritan descendants pointed to their imminent extinction, though he insisted that their legacy would not be erased: "If it could, we wonder who would do it? Certainly, not one of the children of the Gael, born in New England, who reveres and has profited by all that was good in the Puritan, and who passes lightly over what was false."[153] Ironically, it was New England's immigrants, not the Yankees, who would keep the memory and influence of the Puritans alive.

Plymouth Rock

The differences between the racial regionalists and regional pluralists rarely were acknowledged. They sometimes even regarded each other as allies, citing each other on questions of fact and racial sentiment.[154] Moreover, some Irish Americans, such as Michael J. McNeirny, had ties to both camps.[155] But occasionally the conflicts between the racial regionalists and regional pluralists were exposed for all to see. That was the case in August 1889 at the dedication of the National Monument to the Forefathers at Plymouth, Massachusetts. As John Seelye has shown, the ceremony was a long time coming. The monument was the work of the Pilgrim Society, which laid the cornerstone in 1859, only to be beset by overambitious original designs, fund-raising difficulties, and the Civil War.[156] When the structure—a towering female statue representing Faith above smaller figures of Morality, Education, Law, and Liberty, as well as bas-relief scenes of the Pilgrims' departure, the signing of the Mayflower Compact, the landing, and the treaty with Massasoit—was finally complete, the Pilgrim Society hosted a gala celebration, culminating in a dinner featuring a lengthy roster of orators. The society raised some eyebrows by naming as chief speakers men who were not of *Mayflower* stock. Kentucky congressman William C. P. Breckinridge delivered the main oration, and *Boston Pilot* editor John Boyle O'Reilly read the commemorative poem. With these unlikely choices, the Pilgrim Society obviously was hoping to bridge the divides between North and South, Yankee and immigrant, past and future, but the occasion also exposed the unspannable differences between New England's racial regionalists and regional pluralists. Representatives of both groups seized the chance to leave their mark on New England's most famous icon.

As scholars have demonstrated, the Forefathers monument dedication was but one moment in an ongoing struggle over the meaning of the Pilgrims and Plymouth Rock.[157] Many of the speakers on that rainy August day simply repeated what their predecessors already had said about the fabled stone. What made the 1889 dinner noteworthy was the fact that it brought together, literally under one tent, two competing interpretations of the rock's significance for race and region. On one side were those who saw it as Teutonist symbol, marking the threshold of the Anglo-Saxons in America. The leading advocates of this view were Brahmin historians such as Herbert Baxter Adams, who in 1882 had lauded the Puritans and Pilgrims for blessing New England "with Teutonic village life, strengthened by English parish experience."[158] Against the racial regionalists were pitted the regional pluralists, who viewed Plymouth Rock as the symbol of the many peoples who had come ashore in New England, interacted with those who had preceded them, and in the process steadily remade the region's character. While the Brahmin historians looked to the rock as the enduring symbol of a single race, the regional pluralists celebrated it as an index of New England's ever-increasing diversity.

The ideas of the racial regionalists were well represented at the dinner, most forcefully by William Breckinridge and Henry Cabot Lodge. A former journalist and Jefferson Davis bodyguard, Breckinridge had been invited to participate in the ceremonies in a show of sectional reconciliation.[159] As John Seelye has argued, that plan backfired when Breckinridge appropriated the rock for the cause of states' rights.[160] But, when it came to the question of the rock's racial symbolism, Breckinridge was largely indistinguishable from Lodge. Both men read the Pilgrims as part of a larger migration of Teutonic peoples and institutions from Europe to the New World. To those who saw the Pilgrims as political innovators, Breckinridge insisted they were merely transplanters who brought to America "[t]he Teutonic gift to mankind of delegated power exercised by representatives."[161] Lodge read the landing at Plymouth as a key moment in the global triumph of the Teutons. Scoffing at those who celebrated the Pilgrims as peaceful, he hailed them as shining examples of the "English-speaking race" (the term he, like John Fiske, preferred to "Anglo-Saxon"), "that great conquering race which has built up commonwealths all over the globe."[162]

Opposing the Teutonist reading of Plymouth Rock and the Pilgrims was John Boyle O'Reilly. An Irish Catholic immigrant and former Fenian, he was not the most obvious choice as poet for the occasion. Yet by 1889 O'Reilly had demonstrated a knack for commemorating New England's heroes and ideals through his poems for the Crispus Attucks monument in Boston and the memorial service for Wendell Phillips. Even more to the point, in 1886 he had penned a verse celebrating a Boston yacht named the *Mayflower,* which had won the America's Cup. O'Reilly compared the boat to its namesake:

Sailing the years to us, welcomed for aye;
Cherished for centuries, dearest today.
Every heart throbs for her, every flag dips—
Mayflower! First and last—best of our ships![163]

O'Reilly's reference to the *Mayflower* as the best of "our" ships is not mere poetic license; rather, it speaks to his deep identification with his adopted region. Although he never stopped thinking of himself as an Irishman, he

Fig. 3. John Boyle O'Reilly. Frontispiece from City of Boston, *A Memorial of John Boyle O'Reilly* (1890).

was intensely drawn to New England's legacy of literary achievement, republicanism, and social reform. He certainly would have approved when ex-Governor John Davis Long introduced him at the dedication dinner as "a genuine New England Pilgrim, with all the Pilgrim's love of truth, but he adds to it a certain ecstacy [*sic*] of imagination with a musical note like that of a singing bird."[164]

On the other hand, O'Reilly also had a long history of treating Plymouth Rock and the Pilgrims irreverently. In his early years on the *Boston Pilot,* he routinely lumped the Pilgrims together with the Puritans as Catholic-hating bigots. He crowed over census reports suggesting that the scions of those groups were rapidly being supplanted by Irish Catholics.[165] In 1872 he joked about the day when "the last descendant of the Puritans would be exhibited in a glass case at the United States Patent Office as a national curiosity" and Plymouth Rock would be used as a cornerstone for a Catholic church.[166] When a Catholic church was dedicated in Plymouth in 1879, O'Reilly mused, "How wonderful to look through the centuries and see the Old Church win back its domain, as inevitably as the ocean recovers its plains, despite all artificial barriers. In two hundred years the population of Massachusetts has changed its base."[167] The day of the Pilgrim had ended.

Those familiar with O'Reilly's jibes at the Pilgrims and Plymouth Rock must have been holding their breath when he stood to read his poem "The Pilgrim Fathers." He laid to rest any anxieties on the part of the Pilgrim Society by praising the forefathers in terms that met the immediate approval of Yankees across the region.[168] O'Reilly warmed their hearts by echoing the ideas of the Brahmin historians. He presents the Pilgrims as pious, though somewhat grim, heroes who gave up everything to pursue freedom, equality, and democracy in an unforgiving new land. Downplaying their religious beliefs, which he dismisses as a "gloomy creed," O'Reilly insists that the Pilgrims' real contribution was political: "Their mission was less pastoral than lay— / More Nation-seed than Gospel-seed were they."[169] With a fervor that must have sent a tingle down Henry Cabot Lodge's spine, O'Reilly mythologizes the Pilgrims as the fathers of American democracy through the Mayflower Compact and the town meeting. He even goes so far as to flirt with the Teutonic origins theory, portraying the Pilgrims as the heirs of medieval English ancestors:

> Here centuries sank, and from the hither brink
> A new world reached and raised an old-world link,
> When English hands, by wider vision taught,
> Threw down the feudal bars the Normans brought[170]

Although O'Reilly is careful to refer to the Pilgrims as *English* rather than the inflammatory *Anglo-Saxon,* he clearly has the latter race in mind with his ominous reference to the Norman conquest. O'Reilly presents that event as suppressing a racial genius for democracy that is finally released by the

Pilgrims' arrival in America. It is a remarkable thing to hear from a man who had spent much of his life fighting the myth of Anglo-Saxon supremacy.

But elsewhere in the poem O'Reilly rebuffs the Brahmin historians' attempt to claim Plymouth Rock for the Teutons. He presents such racial chauvinism as counter to the spirit of John Robinson, the Pilgrims' minister in Leiden, who taught that "men are one of blood and one of spirit."[171] Although Robinson never set foot in America, O'Reilly credits him for some of the Pilgrims' (and Puritans') proudest accomplishments:

Thy love won more than force or arts adroit—
It writ and kept the deed with Massasoit;
It earned the welcome Samoset expressed;
It lived again in Eliot's loving breast;
It filled the Compact which the Pilgrims signed—
Immortal scroll! the first where men combined
From one deep lake of common blood to draw
All rulers, rights, and potencies of law.[172]

By selecting Robinson, rather than a more obvious choice—William Bradford or Miles Standish—as the embodiment of the Pilgrims, O'Reilly emphasizes their acceptance of other groups. The poet even suggests that Robinson's commitment to racial tolerance is enshrined in the Mayflower Compact, a document that typically was seen as a symbol of self-government, not the "common blood" uniting all "men" and their institutions.

In his final stanzas, O'Reilly insists that the Pilgrims' legacy belongs both to their American descendants and to oppressed peoples in foreign lands. As he explains what the forefathers mean for each of those constituencies, the poet alternately speaks as a loyal son of the Pilgrims and an Irish immigrant. He establishes his New England credentials by adopting the region's most potent rhetorical form, the jeremiad, to warn the Pilgrims' descendants not to betray the forefathers' beliefs: "The Fathers fled from feudal lords, and made / A freehold state; may we not retrograde / To lucre-lords and hierarchs of trade."[173] Sensing another threat to the region in the decay of town-meeting republicanism, he reminds his audience: "THE STATE IS FREEDOM IF THE TOWN IS FREE."[174] Despite his penchant for cheering Irish Catholic triumphs over the Pilgrim descendants, O'Reilly now offers himself as a *Mayflower* scion, a gesture that recalls Michael J. McNeirny's claim that Irish Catholics are the true defenders of the Pilgrims' republican legacy.

O'Reilly also celebrates the Pilgrims' importance to those living outside New England, even outside America: "In every land wherever might holds sway / The Pilgrims' leaven is at work to-day."[175] He emphasizes that the "Pilgrims' Vision" will be accomplished only when their gifts of freedom and democracy are enjoyed around the globe:

> All living nations, while our eagles shine,
> One after one, shall swing into our line;
> Our freeborn heritage shall be the guide
> And bloodless order of their regicide.[176]

O'Reilly's fantasy of nations swinging into "our line" may strike the modern reader as imperialist, but he probably has in mind a more democratic phenomenon, namely, the guidance, inspiration, and financial support that the American people—often in opposition to their government—have long offered independence movements abroad, particularly those in Ireland. By calling attention to those movements, O'Reilly reminds his audience that his own background is not "freeborn" Yankee but Irish-born subject of Great Britain. Nevertheless, he claims the Pilgrims as his forefathers and invites other immigrants to do the same. That move aligns him with the regional pluralists and against the AIHS members who countered the myth of the Pilgrims with their own racialist myth of the "Irish Pilgrim Fathers." For O'Reilly, in contrast, Plymouth Rock belongs to every person who shares the Pilgrims' dreams of freedom and democracy.

As John Seelye has shown, that theme would be echoed by other ethnic spokespeople over the following decades who compared the nation's newcomers to their more illustrious predecessors of 1620.[177] Mary Antin makes extensive use of that comparison in her book *They Who Knock at Our Gates* (1914), which rebuts the arguments of the immigration restrictionists. Taking on the nativist charge that the "new" immigrants from southern and eastern Europe were inferior to the "old" ones from the continent's north and west, Antin insists that the current arrivals were fully up to the standard of their most exalted predecessors, including the *Mayflower* passengers. She even claims that her fellow Russian Jews are "a little ahead of the Mayflower troop" in their willingness to fight for their faith.[178] Seelye maintains that Antin intends such comparisons to "generaliz[e]" the Pilgrims: "In effect, she is ripping the Pilgrims out of the frames of reference carefully crafted and gilded during the course of the nineteenth century. Instead of standing in a tight little group on Plymouth Rock, they are shoved into line with all the other homeless and tempest-tossed arrivals, indistinguishable from the wretched refuse, those huddled masses waiting at the gate."[179] But, as I have argued, the ethnic spokespeople who compared contemporary immigrants to the Pilgrims often did so to appropriate, rather than discard, the regional frame of reference. Instead of ripping Pilgrims out of their New England setting, Antin more likely wants to place her own ethnic group in it. That would explain why, in arguing for the civic virtue of Jewish immigrants, she cites their commitment to that quintessential New England institution, the town meeting, or why she maintains that "[t]he great New England invention of compulsory education is more eagerly appropriated by the majority of our immigrants than by native Americans."[180] As someone with deep ties to New England, Antin had obvious reasons for seeking a place for her group in the region. Like other immigrant regional pluralists, she understood that a regional identity could help an ethnic group struggling to establish a toehold in an oftentimes hostile American landscape.

On the other hand, Seelye doubtless is correct that some of the ethnic spokespeople who appropriated the Pilgrims had little investment in their original New England context. That was the case for Irish American humorist Finley Peter Dunne, who challenged the New England restrictionists' grip on the *Mayflower* company in the rich brogue of his Chicago bartender persona, Mr. Dooley.[181] In a 1902 sketch titled "Immigration" (published just before Dunne's marriage to the Massachusetts blue blood Margaret Abbott), Mr. Dooley recounts a recent argument with his friend Shaughnessy, who wants a law to keep out "th' offscourin's iv Europe" on the grounds that "they're arnychists" who "don't assymilate with th' counthry."[182] In response Mr. Dooley points out the hypocrisy of such sentiments coming from any European American, whether an immigrant like Shaughnessy or a Brahmin like Lodge: "I ain't so much afraid as ye ar-re. I'm not afraid iv me father an' I'm not afraid iv mesilf. An' I'm not afraid iv Schwartzmeister's father or Hinnery Cabin Lodge's grandfather. We all come over th' same way."[183] In Mr. Dooley's eyes, it is silly for the Brahmin restrictionists to put on airs, given that they are as much immigrant stock as the latest arrivals at Ellis Island. He underscores the point by laying claim to the Pilgrims on behalf of his fellow immigrants. He proposes a meeting of the "Plymouth Rock Assocyation. . . . to discuss th' immygration question . . . I'll sind out a hurry call f'r Schwartzmeister an' Mulcahey an' Ignacio Sbarbaro an' Nels Larsen an' Petrus Gooldvink, an' we 'll gather to-night at Fanneilnoviski Hall at th' corner iv Sheridan an' Sigel streets. All th' pilgrim fathers is rayquested f'r to bring interpreters."[184] Dunne follows Mary Antin's strategy of likening

Fig. 4. Statue of Faith from the National Monument to the Forefathers. (Courtesy of PapaDunesPhotography/Flickr/Getty Images.)

contemporary immigrants to the Pilgrims, but with entirely different intent. Whereas she seeks to win a place in New England for her fellow immigrants by associating them with the region's most iconic heroes, he democratizes the *Mayflower* company by comparing them to his foreign-born friends. By rechristening the Pilgrims with names like Gooldvink and Mulcahey and relocating Faneuil Hall to an intersection in Chicago, Dunne makes clear that New England's heroes and symbols belong not just to restrictionists like Lodge but to anybody in any region who wants to claim them.

Had he been present in 1889 at the dedication of the Forefathers monument, Dunne doubtless would have responded to that Pilgrim love fest with similar irreverence. One wonders, in particular, what he would have made of the statue that topped the monument, the towering figure of Faith, which, to this day, remains the nation's largest solid granite monument (figure 4). Taken by itself, the statue presents us with little to mock. An impressive draped allegorical figure, Faith steps determinedly on a reproduction of Plymouth Rock, while pointing heavenward with one mighty arm and holding her Bible in the other. As Seelye notes, in her symbolism and posture, she closely resembles the Statue of Liberty, which had been dedicated three years earlier.[185] But, while conventional in many respects, the Amazonian figure of Faith would have carried a distinct physiological resonance in Gilded Age New England—thanks to the tireless efforts of some of the region's leading physicians. For years conservative medical men had been warning of the poor health of Yankee women, who allegedly bore little physical resemblance to their robust Pilgrim and Puritan foremothers. Not surprisingly, none of the speakers at the dedication ceremony took the liberty of comparing Faith's physique to those of the female Pilgrim descendants, but the comparison almost surely occurred to some who were present. In Gilded Age New England, people didn't need an eighty-one-foot statue to be reminded that Yankee women were delicate.

THREE

New England Delicacy

Immigration and the Regional Body

If asked to name the one word that best described New England women, a Gilded Age commentator might well choose *delicate.* A profoundly ambiguous term that spoke on multiple registers, it evoked a long history of debates about the health, beauty, morality, and reproductive practices of New England women. The oldest of those debates centered on the issue of climate. For centuries authorities on both sides of the Atlantic had clashed over the effects of the New World climate on Europeans, and New England had always loomed large in that debate. Opponents of colonization routinely pointed to the alleged physical and mental decay of the New Englanders as proof that Europeans degenerated in the New World. From the Great Migration of the 1630s to the Revolution, New Englanders countered that the robust health of their people proved the salubriousness of their climate. By the early nineteenth century, a few Yankee holdouts continued to resist the degeneration thesis, but most admitted that their region's climate was a health risk—especially for women. It was the emergence of the cult of True Womanhood in the 1820s that convinced them to reconsider that view. The champions of True Womanhood argued that the Yankee female's delicacy should be taken as a sign not of physical degeneration but of moral refinement. Many New England writers responded by celebrating the Yankee lady's delicacy over against the coarse strength of her foreign-born Others, Irishwomen in particular. After the Civil War, the willowy body ideal promoted by the cult of True Womanhood came increasingly under attack by a group of conservative physicians whom Carroll Smith-Rosenberg and Charles E. Rosenberg have dubbed medical moralists.[1] In New England the medical moralists contended that Yankee females undermined their own health and fertility when they rejected domestic pursuits for the enticements of education and fashion. The conservative physicians invidiously compared the Yankee daughters of fashion and education with their immigrant rivals, insisting that it with the latter, not the Puritan descendants, who best carried on the New England tradition of large families and robust health. Yet, in the century's last decades, the medical moralists were themselves challenged by New England's feminists, who contended that the educational opportunities of Yankee females were actually making them healthier than their counterparts in other regions. Many feminists also rejected the medical moralists' portrayal of female immigrants as models of good health. They cited reports by medical experts who claimed that female immigrants were in fact quite sickly as a result of their struggles to acclimate to American conditions. A number of those experts identified the second-generation Irish American female as the chief sufferer. As the century ended, they suggested it was she, rather than the Yankee female, who deserved the dubious title of New England's most delicate woman.

Parsing the changing meanings of female delicacy in New England across the decades is made more challenging by the fact that, as new theories about it emerged, the old ones did not simply disappear. Instead, the emergent and residual theories jostled for supremacy in the minds—and writings—of commentators. This accounts for the internal inconsistencies and contradictions that characterize much of the discourse on the subject. Some writers were capable of veering from one theory to another in the span of a few pages or even sentences. In the most extreme cases, the reader is left wondering whether a given writer sees female delicacy as something to be embraced as a point of New England pride or condemned as a betrayal of regional tradition. The ambiguity of female delicacy in New England was further compounded by the sheer variety of debates in which it was implicated. Whether the issue was climate or abortion or domestic labor, people across the political spectrum believed they could read the future of New England on the delicate bodies of its women.

"It Is a Wretched Climate": New England Delicacy as Degeneration

By the early nineteenth century, the question of how New England's climate affected the health of its inhabitants had been bandied about for almost two hundred years—generally as part of a larger debate about the feasibility of transplanting the Anglo-Saxon race to the New World. The stakes of that debate were already becoming clear in the early seventeenth century, when the Puritan supporters of colonization clashed with their opponents over whether the English body would degenerate in the New World climate. But it was the eighteenth-century French naturalist Georges-Louis Leclerc, Count of Buffon, who was chiefly responsible for igniting the transatlantic dispute over New World degeneration, one in which New England would play a prominent role. In his thirty-six-volume work, *Natural History: General and Particular* (1749–88), Buffon famously theorized that the cool, moist climate of the New World stunted the size, strength, and variety of living things. He claimed that the animals of the New World were invariably smaller, weaker, and more timid than those of the Old World (except for reptiles and insects, which were larger and more numerous), and the same was true of the indigenous human populations. Comparing the European man and the American "savage," Buffon argued that the latter was weaker, less sensitive, more cowardly, smaller of genitals, and lacking "ardor for the female of his kind."[2] Significantly, Buffon exempted European colonials from this attack. He argued that European domestic animals transported to America had become weaker and smaller, but that was not the case for transplanted humans.[3] To the contrary, by domesticating the landscape—cutting down the trees, tilling the earth, and controlling the rivers—the Europeans were making the American climate warmer and drier and thus protecting themselves from its harmful effects.

But Buffon's followers insisted that the colonists and their Creole offspring were by no means immune to the degenerative effects of the American climate. Often fueled by a palpable anticolonial bias, writers in several European countries eagerly sought traces of degeneration in the European Americans. The Finnish Swedish scientist Peter Kalm asserted that the colonists aged faster, died younger, and stopped having babies earlier than their European cousins; moreover, the Creoles were even shorter-lived than their parents.[4] Likewise, in early editions of his *A Philosophical and Political History of the Settlements and Trade of the Europeans in the East and West Indies* (which first appeared in 1770 and was revised and republished at least thirty times thereafter), Abbé Guillaume Thomas François Raynal described the Creoles as physical and mental degenerates: "The Creoles, though habituated to the climate since birth, are not as sturdy in their work, or as smart in conflict as the Europeans; that is to say that education has not prepared them, or that nature has made them weak. Under this alien (foreign) sky, their spirit is unnerved like the body."[5]

Given New England's prominence as an intellectual and cultural center, it inevitably became a flashpoint in the debate over New World degeneracy. Raynal insisted that the New England climate had taken a toll on both the bodies and minds of its inhabitants. He blamed the "malignant vapours" of New England for the deaths of early settlers, as well as the Salem witch hysteria.[6] The Dutch-born Prussian clergyman Cornelius de Pauw insisted that the stunting effects of the New World climate were even visible in the graduates of Harvard: "It is not apparent that the professors of the University of Cambridge, in New England, have formed any young Americans to the point where they are able to bring them out into the literary world."[7]

New Englanders responded to these attacks by joining the campaign to refute the degeneracy thesis. The undisputed leader of that effort was Thomas Jefferson, who worked tirelessly to assemble specimens and statistics to challenge Buffon and his disciples.[8] But the New Englanders were not far behind. Connecticut geographer Jedidiah Morse critiqued Buffon and de Pauw for portraying Native Americans as weakened by the New World climate. Noting that the Spanish empire had been built on the backs of indigenous workers, Morse observed, "These labors, in which the Indians are continually employed, certainly, attest [*sic*] their healthiness and strength."[9] The Connecticut (aka Hartford) Wits were equally dismissive of de Pauw and the degeneracy thesis. In 1786–87 four members of that loose group of Federalist poets (Joel Barlow, Lemuel Hopkins, David Humphreys, and John Trumbull) published in the *New-Haven Gazette and Connecticut Magazine* a mock-epic poem titled *The Anarchiad,* which sought to shed a conservative influence on the Constitutional Convention then taking place in Philadelphia. Although the primary targets of the Wits' satire were the alleged enemies of federalism and order—such as the supporters of Shays' Rebellion in western Massachusetts and the advocates of depreciated paper money in Rhode Island—they also lobbed a few shells at their European foes. In one installment, the poem's bard visits an *Inferno*-like underworld where he encounters various groups of European writers who have misrepresented America in their works of natural history, history, and biography. The first group to appear are the Buffon and his followers, who

scan new worlds with philosophic eyes:
Immured at home, in rambling fancy brave,
Explore all lands beyond th' Atlantic wave;
Of laws for unknown realms invent new codes,
Write natural histories for their antipodes;

Tell how th' enfeebled powers of life decay,
Where falling suns defraud the western day;

. . . .

See vegetation, man, and bird, and beast,
Just by the distance' [*sic*] squares in size decreased;

From their distant perch in Europe, Buffon and his followers watch as

Huge mammoth dwindle to a mouse's size—
Columbian turkeys turn European flies;—
Exotic birds, and foreign beasts, grow small,
And man, the lordliest, shrink to least of all. . . . [10]

The Wits single out for special derision "the father of this system . . . the famous *Abbe de Pau* [*sic*]," who gazes into the future through a "philosophic telescope, calculated to diminish all objects, according to the squares of the distances, as has been hinted." Through those "inverted optics," the abbé spies such wonders as "[t]he long-lost pigmies on th' Atlantic shore," but, as the Wits make clear, the real land of degeneracy lies on the opposite strand, where "all fools believe" the lies of charlatans like de Pauw.[11]

In response to their critics, some of the European theorists of degeneracy retracted their attacks on America and its peoples. The most famous such reversal came from Raynal. In the 1780 edition of his *Philosophical and Political History*, the abbé declared that there had been a great mistake: in fact, the English settlers of North America had not degenerated like the inhabitants of other European colonies.[12] But, as it turned out, Raynal's retraction was too little too late. Well into the nineteenth century, the degenerative effects of the American climate would be widely assumed by Europeans, including many, if not most, of the travel writers who published their impressions of this country for audiences on both sides of the Atlantic. Although European travelers saw the American climate as unhealthful for men and women alike, they focused the bulk of their discussion on the latter. By the antebellum period, the slenderness, sickliness, and premature aging of American women had become such a cliché that most writers simply took it for granted. Many also took for granted that the climate and women's health were at their worst in New England, a region notorious for the harsh extremes and instability of its weather and the delicacy of its women.

The portrait of American women's health that emerges from the European travel writers in the antebellum period is consistently dismal. While travelers conceded that American women were beautiful, perhaps the most beautiful in the world, many saw their charm as inseparable from their premature decay.[13] One had to appreciate an American woman's looks today, because tomorrow they might well be gone. The notion that the American climate made people old before their time went back to the followers of Buffon, but, whereas writers like Kalm and de Pauw emphasized the premature aging of Creole males, the antebellum travelers focused on the early decay of American females. Frederick Marryat found the country's climate "not . . . favourable to beauty, which, compared to the English, is very transitory, especially in the eastern states; and when a female arrives at the age of thirty, its reign is, generally speaking, over."[14] Isabella Lucy Bird believed it ended long before that. In *The Englishwoman in America* (1856), she declared that "a girl of twenty is too apt to look faded and haggard; and a woman who with us would be in her bloom at thirty, looks *passée,* wrinkled, and old."[15] Skeptical of such accounts, the German Friedrich Von Raumer resolved "not . . . to repeat what other travellers have said of American women. I will recall to mind the fact, however, that they admire the beauty of the female sex in the United States, and at the same time assert that they soon grow old and lose their teeth. And certainly, for my own part, I have seen in no country in the world, among handsome women, so many pale, sickly faces."[16] Many European travelers believed that in America a female could not expect to retain her looks into adulthood, instead going straight from blooming adolescence into toothless middle age.

Along with her premature aging, European travelers were also struck by the American woman's paleness and thinness. British writers in particular found the American ladies wanting when measured by their own rosier, more buxom feminine ideal.[17] A few complimented American females on their fair complexions, but more found them "pallid" or "faded." Many English travelers also faulted the American ladies for their angularity and spareness.[18] Frances Trollope found them wanting in *tournure* and "the formation of the bust, which is rarely full, or gracefully formed."[19] The Scottish writer Thomas Hamilton described the American female form as "an aggregate of straight lines and corners altogether ungraceful and inharmonious. There is an overweening proportion of bone. . . . a certain tendency to *scragginess.*"[20] According to Isabella Bird, the only American women immune to this tendency were those of "recent English extraction," who "retain their good looks into middle life, and [in their] advancing years produce *embonpoint,* instead of angularity."[21]

European travelers blamed the American woman's delicate health on causes ranging from overheated homes to lack of exercise to poor diet, but the favorite culprit was the climate. Breaking with their Buffonian predecessors, many antebellum European travelers found the American climate too dry, rather than too humid, but they fully agreed about its enormous health risks.[22] From the sultry South to the frigid North, European travelers believed the American climate was undermining health in every region. Harriet Martineau claimed that the only healthy Americans she found were in the upper elevations of the Alleghenies, the state of Michigan, and the port city of Charleston, where the women spent much of the year on their piazzas.[23]

But of all the American climates, New England's was commonly seen as the most unhealthful. European travelers warned about the region's east wind, extreme temperatures, and variable weather.[24] Noting that the women of Boston "appear delicate and not strong," Fredrika Bremer blamed the climate, which is "not considered good on account of the cold sea-winds."[25] Martineau faulted New England's "fierce extremes" of temperature, observing, "The very low average of health there, the prevalence of consumption and of decay of the teeth, are evidences of an unwholesome climate which I believe are universally received as such." Recalling how she suffered one subzero day in Boston, she shuddered, "It is a wretched climate."[26] Charles Wentworth Dilke advised, "If New Englanders would look about them, they would see that their climate has of itself developed brains at the expense of brawn, and that, if national degeneracy is to be long prevented, brawn must in some way be fostered." Warning that the region's colleges needed to do more to promote exercise, Dilke noted, "The women show even greater signs of weakness than the men."[27] Charles Lyell blamed the climate, not overwork, on the "care-worn expression in the countenances of the New Englanders."[28] He admitted that the Anglo-Saxons could acclimate to such weather, but it might take several centuries.

Although some Yankees emphatically rejected the idea that their climate was causing them to degenerate, others conceded it was true. Among the latter were several of New England's leading men of letters, including Emerson, Holmes, and Hawthorne, all of whom blamed their region's climate for making the Yankees more delicate than their English cousins. Yet, whereas Emerson and Holmes were openly envious of the larger, stronger, healthier English body, Hawthorne was more ambivalent. The romancer acknowledged that, in a purely physical sense, the English body was superior, but from a moral and aesthetic point of view, the more delicate American body seemed preferable.

Both Emerson and Holmes endorsed the notion that the American climate had caused the Anglo-Saxon to degenerate on these shores. Traveling in England in 1847, Emerson was struck with admiration and envy by the size, vigor, and ruddiness of the natives. He wrote home to Elizabeth Hoar, "When I see my muscular neighbors day by day I say, Had I been born in England, with but one chip of English oak in my willowy constitution!"[29] He elaborated the point when he wrote up his impressions of that trip in *English Traits* (1856): "The English at the present day have great vigor of body and endurance. Other countrymen look slight and undersized beside them, and invalids. . . . They are round, ruddy, and handsome; at least the whole bust is well formed, and there is a tendency to stout and powerful frames."[30] Crossing the Atlantic in the opposite direction from so many antebellum British travel writers, Emerson reached precisely the same conclusions about the American climate's degenerative effects on the Anglo-Saxon body.

Oliver Wendell Holmes also believed that "climatic influences here are getting up a number of new patterns of humanity, some of which are not an improvement on the old model."[31] In *The Autocrat of the Breakfast-Table* (1858), he made clear his dissatisfaction with the new-model males: "I am satisfied that such a set of black-coated, stiff-jointed, soft-muscled, paste-complexioned youth as we can boast in our Atlantic cities never before sprang from loins of Anglo-Saxon lineage."[32] Holmes believed his Anglo-Saxon countrywomen were faring no better. At one point the Autocrat worriedly considers the consequences of marriage for the "pallid" schoolteacher in his Boston boardinghouse: "Talk about military duty! What is that to the warfare of a married maid-of-all-work, with the title of mistress, and an American female constitution, which collapses just in the middle third of life, and comes out vulcanized India-rubber, if it happen to live through the period when health and strength are most wanted?"[33] Despite these signs of degeneration, the Autocrat declares that the effects of the American climate on humans and other living things are still unknown. He calls for a Buffonian comparison of species of flora and fauna common to the Old and New Worlds, beginning with man. The goal would be to investigate the workings of "the creative force" in the two hemispheres, but, as his remarks on elms suggest, Holmes already suspected what the study would yield: "The American elm is tall, graceful, slender-sprayed, and drooping as if from languor. The English elm is compact, robust, holds its branches up, and carries its leaves for weeks longer than our own native tree."[34] Like the American Anglo-Saxon, the American elm is a slender, drooping, more languid version of its English counterpart. The Autocrat tries to convince himself that the reverse could be true, "that the American is the Englishman reinforced," but everywhere he looks in New England—from the soft-muscled gentlemen to the pallid schoolteachers to the languid elms—the evidence suggests otherwise.[35]

Some Yankees who conceded that the English body was bigger, stronger, and healthier nevertheless refused to see it as better. Nathaniel Hawthorne readily acknowledged that climatic differences had made the English Anglo-Saxons physically superior to their American cousins. On the other hand, Hawthorne maintained that there was a fine line between ruddy health and gross materialism, and the English had crossed that line. This is particularly apparent in the book he based on his years in England, *Our Old Home* (1863), where he offers equally uncomplimentary portraits of English and American middle-aged bodies, painting the former as excessively fleshy and the latter as distressingly lean. But, when he takes up the issue of female beauty, Hawthorne clearly prefers the delicacy of the Americans, which he sees as a sign less of degeneration than of moral refinement. He celebrates his countrywomen for an ethereal charm that far surpasses the Englishwoman's mere physical beauty.

In *Our Old Home,* Hawthorne freely indulges his taste for caricature, offering a series of starkly opposed portraits of English and American bodies. He claims the differences are most striking among both nations' middle-aged citizens. Whereas English people of a certain age are elephantine and sluggish, middle-aged Americans are desiccated and haggard. The contrast is particularly obvious in the women. Hawthorne recalls looking in vain in England for a type of autumnal female who is so familiar in the States: "thin, care-worn, and frail. . . . slender-framed and haggard."[36] What greeted him instead was the imposing form of the English dowager: "She has an awful ponderosity of frame, not pulpy, like the looser development of our few fat women, but massive with solid beef and streaky tallow; so that . . . you inevitably think of her as made up of steaks and sirloins."[37] Hawthorne admits that the dowager looks imposing—she reminds him of "a seventy-four gun ship in time of peace"—but for all her size and strength, she is finally not so formidable. He doubts that she has "greater courage, fortitude, and strength of character, than our women of similar age." Thrust out of her social milieu, the dowager, he suspects, "would be found powerless and timid."[38] If the middle-aged American woman was a physical weakling, the English dowager was a moral one.

Hawthorne presents similarly opposed caricatures of middle-aged English and American males. Invited to a banquet attended by lawyers, he muses on the aging of the Englishman: "[T]he comeliness of the youthful Englishman rapidly diminishes with years, his body appearing to grow longer, his legs to abbreviate themselves, and his stomach to assume the dignified prominence which justly belongs to that metropolis of his system. His face . . . gets red and mottled, and developes [*sic*] at least one additional chin, with a promise of more." Hawthorne claims that the dominance of the "animal part" of the English lawyer can sometimes make the intellect hard to find.[39] In contrast, the Yankee lawyer's mentation is literally inscribed on his features. Hawthorne observes that "the bar of any inland county in New England . . . might show a set of thin-visaged men, looking wretchedly worn, sallow, deeply wrinkled across the forehead and grimly furrowed about the mouth, with whom these heavy-cheeked English lawyers, slow-paced and fat-witted as they must needs be, would stand very little chance."[40] Whereas the English lawyer is all stolid flesh, the Yankee lawyer is all probing intellect. Hawthorne seems uncertain which is worse.

Hawthorne offers a modest proposal to remedy the complementary physical flaws of the English and Americans: the United States should annex England and transfer thirty million of its inhabitants "to some convenient wilderness in the great West." Their places would be taken by

> half or a quarter as many of ourselves. . . . The change would be beneficial to both parties. We, in our dry atmosphere, are getting too nervous, haggard, dyspeptic, extenuated, unsubstantial, theoretic, and need to be made grosser. John Bull, on the other hand, has grown bulbous, long-bodied, short-legged, heavy-witted, material, and, in a word, too intensely English.[41]

At a time when some racial theorists believed the Anglo-Saxon could only survive the degenerative American climate with constant reinforcements from England, Hawthorne argues that the reinforcements need to go both ways.[42] Neither climate can give the Anglo-Saxon body everything it needs.

But, when he turns to the issue of female beauty, Hawthorne abandons his evenhandedness and openly champions the slender American physique. Granted, he admits that after living several years among the buxom English ladies he began to cast a critical eye on his countrywomen,

> I often found, or seemed to find, if I may dare to confess it, in the persons of such of my dear countrywomen as I now occasionally met, a certain meagreness, (Heaven forbid that I should call it scrawniness!)

> a deficiency of physical development, a scantiness, so to speak, in the pattern of their material make, a paleness of complexion, a thinness of voice.

Rather than try to talk himself out of his growing attraction to the buxom English physique, he rejects the very notion of locating beauty on the body. He admits that "from a lower point of view," the English ladies "were perhaps a little finer animals." But Hawthorne advocates a higher point of view that says the true measure of a woman's beauty is the "ethereal charm" of her moral refinement—in other words, her ability to transcend mere animal nature. By this standard the American women are more beautiful; indeed, Hawthorne upholds the "fair creatures as angels." Whereas the Englishwoman is lovely because of her body, the American women is lovelier because of her disembodiment. Granted, we have seen Hawthorne describe the slimness of middle-aged American women as a sign not of moral superiority but of physical degeneration. Yet he abandons that view when it comes to his "angels," replacing the critical terms he usually uses to describe the thin American body with laudatory ones—his countrywomen are "fair" not "pale," "ethereal" not "haggard."[43]

Hawthorne also abandons his idea of putting flesh on the bones of the American female by transporting her to the moister English climate. Indeed, he argues that it would be a fatal mistake to try to turn the American angel into a buxom Englishwoman. Dismissing the superior physical charms of the latter as "a few additional lumps of clay on their shoulders and other parts of their figures," he declares, "It would be a pitiful bargain to give up the ethereal charm of American beauty in exchange for half a hundredweight of human clay!"[44]

To make such an exchange would be to reverse the process Hawthorne describes in *The Scarlet Letter* (1850). There he interrupts his narrative of Hester Prynne's punishment to reflect on the process of moral and physical refinement that has transformed the beefy Puritan matron into the delicate nineteenth-century Yankee lady, "every successive mother has transmitted to her child a fainter bloom, a more delicate and briefer beauty, and a slighter physical frame, if not a character of less force and solidity, than her own." This process has cost Yankee women bulk and strength. They no longer possess the "broad shoulders and well-developed busts, and . . . round and ruddy cheeks," of the Puritan matrons who jeer Hester.[45] But the Yankee female's physical losses are accompanied by moral gains. She would never dream of joining her female ancestors in calling down a harsher punishment on the head of an erring sister. In short Hawthorne leaves no doubt that the exchange of English flesh for American moral refinement is a good bargain.

The Yankee True Woman and Her Irish Other

Hawthorne was far from alone in viewing the Yankee woman's delicacy as a sign not of physical degeneration but of moral refinement. Beginning in the 1820s, conservative cultural authorities enshrined delicacy as a central tenet of the gender ideology that has come to be known as the cult of True Womanhood. As Barbara Welter writes, the cult idealized the middle-class woman for her "piety, purity, submissiveness and domesticity."[46] Many of the cult's adherents believed the True Woman's values were written on her body. They celebrated her physical delicacy—her slender physique, small features, pale complexion, and even invalidism—as proof of her moral virtues.[47] According to Amy Louise Reed, "Delicacy was her chief characteristic. It was sought and attained at a great price, because it was considered as the visible sign of an ethereal, spiritual nature, a moral sensitiveness and purity superior to man's."[48] In the words of that enthusiastic promoter of True Womanhood, *Godey's Lady's Book,* "Woman's spiritual strength seems perfected in her physical weakness."[49]

The theater of the True Woman's spiritual strength was her household. Urged to "make home her whole world," the True Woman wielded significant power in it.[50] She bore primary responsibility for child rearing, a role of paramount importance to the emerging middle class. At a time when experts on parenting increasingly advocated loving moral education over the old-fashioned model of patriarchal discipline, many hailed the True Woman as the ideal parent.[51] The True Woman's champions also celebrated her ameliorating influence over her husband. Convinced that males were by nature more passionate, aggressive, and worldly than females, they hailed the True Woman for gently urging her man into the paths of righteousness. Many saw the True Woman's moral influence over her husband as inseparable from her delicacy. How could any man disappoint a wife who was at once his moral superior and physical dependent? The True Woman's virtues were calculated to stroke, rather than threaten, the male ego.

The True Woman's champions also saw her physical delicacy as the sign of her moral superiority to working-class and/or nonwhite women. Just as the ethereal beauty of the True Woman marked her transcendence of the physical world, the sexuality and physical strength of working-class and nonwhite women marked their grounding in it. That was true in the antebellum South, where proslavery writers painted the mistress as a True Woman, whose angelic purity stood in stark opposition to the "easy chastity" of the slave woman.[52] Apologist for slavery William Harper argued that the slave woman's alleged immorality had a bracing effect on her mistress's chastity, making her purer than northern white women.[53]

A similar dynamic operated in New England, where it was the Irishwoman who served as the Yankee True Woman's hyperembodied, libidinous Other. Many Yankee writers viewed the Irishwoman's defiance of the canons of True Womanhood with a mixture of fascination and dread. In touristic accounts of Hibernian urban neighborhoods and rural settlements, they detailed the various ways Irishwomen flouted the cult's tenets of piety, submissiveness, domesticity, and purity. The Irishwomen in their works are loud, coarse, drunken, and physically violent. They fight with their husbands and neglect their children. They put their bodies and private lives on public display, doing domestic chores in the open air and gossiping from house to house. Often unchaste, they are always robustly sexual, as evidenced by the enormous broods of children who follow in their wake.

Hawthorne was particularly fascinated with the Irishwoman's defiance of the cult of True Womanhood. In his travel writings and notebooks from the 1830s, he consistently portrays the Hibernian female as the antithesis of his ethereal feminine ideal. Although hostile to the Irish as a group (at one point he describes them as "the scum which every wind blows off the Irish shores—the pauper dregs which England flings out upon America"), he cannot hide his admiration for the Irishwoman's sturdy physique and independent, outspoken demeanor.[54] In an 1836 sketch, Hawthorne rails against the Irish who "swarm" at Burlington, Vermont, dismissing the males as well-fed loungers. Yet he obviously finds the females more interesting: "[T]he women strode about, uncovered in the open air, with far plumper waists and brawnier limbs, as well as bolder faces, than our shy and slender females." The fecundity of these Irishwomen is readily apparent in "their progeny, which was [*sic*] innumerable," with "the reddest and the roundest cheeks of any children in America."[55] Aboard a steamboat on the same trip, Hawthorne escapes from the stuffy gentility of the grand cabin to gaze at the Irish immigrants who are bedding down on the forward deck. He takes in sights that include "[s]lender girls . . . preparing to repose their maiden-like forms on the wide, promiscuous couch of the deck." Hawthorne is saddened to think of the corrupting effects of migration on young women who, he speculates, might well have known the protection of "fond fathers" and the counsel of "watchful mothers."[56]

Yet, for the most part, Hawthorne prefers to think of Irish females not as slender, innocent girls but robust, experienced women. That is his perspective in *The American Notebooks,* where he records an 1837 visit to the Augusta, Maine, home of his friend Horatio Bridge. In repeated excursions to a nearby settlement of Irish laborers, Hawthorne takes full advantage of the chance to peek into their violent, impoverished, disorderly lives. He devotes most of his attention to the Irishwomen, including one who is served a warrant "for throwing a brick-bat at a fellow," another who sings sweetly to her children while washing clothes in the river, "though an immoral woman and without the certainty of bread or shelter from day to day," and a third who "is a lady of very indifferent morals, and sells rum and [wears frilled] dresses."[57] But Hawthorne seems most taken by one "old lady of somewhat dissipated habits," whom Bridge vainly tries to evict from her shanty: "He persisting—she took her stand in the doorway of the hut, and stretched out her fist, in a very amazonian attitude—'Nobody' quoth she, 'shall drive me out of this house, till my praties are out of the ground.'" Nor does this woman pay any mind to "her husband—or the man who passes for such," who feebly tries to still her. Hawthorne surmises that after he and Bridge departed the woman probably fought with her man, "it being a custom with the Irish husbands and wives to settle their disputes by blows; and it is said that the woman often proves the better man."[58] Poor, drunken, brawling, and, possibly unchaste, this woman could not be further from Hawthorne's ethereal ideal, yet he is clearly intrigued by the flamboyant stand she takes against male power and class privilege.

William Dean Howells betrays a similar fascination with the Irishwoman's defiance of the canons of True Womanhood in his *Suburban Sketches* (1871). In that bemused insider's account of middle-class life on "Benicia Street" in "Charlesbridge" (based on the Howells' early years on Sacramento Street in Cambridge), the author pays warm tribute to the Yankee True Woman, celebrating her tender maternal affections and sensitivity, while affectionately mocking her overprotectiveness. Those traits are on display in the chapter "A Day's Pleasure," when the arrival of a lost boy on their doorstep prompts contrasting responses from the suburban couple, Frank and Mrs. Sallie. When, after repeated questioning, the boy proves unable to supply his last name and address, Frank grows increasingly exasperated and eventually goes to the police, but, conscientious mother that she is, Mrs. Sallie feeds the boy cookies and starts making plans to adopt him.

Yet, despite his clear respect for the domestic values of the Yankee True Woman, Howells spends much of the book fleeing them. He devotes many pages to his narrator's wanderings through poor Irish neighborhoods, where he catches glimpses of a livelier, more picturesque, and tragic world—one in which the domestic pieties of True Womanhood do not apply. Strolling in an Irish settlement called Dublin, the narrator is charmed to see that "[s]o much of the local life appears upon the street," as the Irishwomen "gossip from house to house, and the talk is always such a resonant clamoring."[59] He is also fascinated by the emotional expressiveness of these women, so unlike the True Woman's modest reserve. In Dublin's cemetery, he is shaken from his aesthetic musings by the lamentations of two Irishwomen, one of whom throws herself upon a grave: "I was now merely touched as a human being, and had little desire to turn the scene to literary account."[60] One might compare the narrator's response to some ornamented vases he later finds in a junk shop, the handiwork, he imagines, of Yankee spinster sisters, "lingering upon the neutral ground between the faded hopes of marriage and the yet unrisen prospects of consumption."[61] Whereas the pathos of these hypothetical Yankee True Women sends the narrator into a sentimental reverie, he finds the Irishwomen's despair much harder to assimilate: "I could not help feeling that it wanted the atmosphere of sentimental association; the whole background was a blank or worse than a blank."[62] He is even more overpowered by the scene he stumbles on in another Irish neighborhood, where a crowd of boys follows a grocer's cart carrying the body of a girl who drowned herself, apparently over an ill-starred love affair: "[T]hey broke out with wild yells, and danced madly about it, while the red shawl hanging from the rigid feet nodded to their frantic mirth."[63] Shaken from his usual pose of ironic detachment, the narrator blankly records the scene without commenting on it. He is clearly a long way from Benicia Street.

Thinking of Hawthorne's Zenobia, Howells's narrator assumes that the drowned girl would be horrified to "have known in what a ghastly comedy the body she put off was to play a part."[64] Yet such bodily display is typical of the book's Irishwomen, most of whom seem the picture of ruddy good health. The narrator spots Irish matrons who stand with "snowy arms, freshly taken from the wash-tub . . . folded across a mighty chest" or pause in the act of spanking a child with "descending palm . . . arrested in mid air."[65] Howells finds the fertility of these women equally impressive, marveling at their ability to raise huge flourishing families amid the worst living conditions in Boston. The Irish mothers practice a rougher, more casual style of parenting than their overprotective Yankee counterparts—the Irish children mostly seem to run wild when they are not being spanked—but despite it, or perhaps because of it, their offspring thrive. Impressed by the "remarkable" crowds of children in Dublin, the narrator observes that the

Irishwoman's fertility may well "make an end of us poor Yankees as a dominant plurality."[66] He strikes a nativist note, warning of the effects of an Irish takeover on the nation's political and institutional life. Yet Howells usually regards the Irishwoman not with hostility but envy. At a time when Yankee society seemed to have become little more than "a hospital for invalid woman [*sic*]," the Irishwoman was the notable exception.[67]

While they enjoyed gazing on the Irishwoman's coarse strength at a distance, the middle-class champions of True Womanhood grew anxious when she came too close. Many feared that the same unladylike traits that made her so formidable among her own people would allow her to bully the Yankee True Woman. They wrote of pushy Irish matrons who ran roughshod over their delicate Yankee neighbors and belligerent Irish servants who tyrannized their Yankee mistresses. Faced with such a daunting antagonist, the Yankee lady had little choice but to give in.

The presumptively middle-class True Woman was likely to come into close contact with Irishwomen only as servants, but there were exceptions, such as those whose decayed fortunes forced them to live among the Irish. That is the fate of Priscilla in Hawthorne's *The Blithedale Romance* (1852), who dwells with her disgraced father in a shabby apartment surrounded by poor Irish. Their building symbolizes the ethnic turnover of New England, as it had formerly belonged to the colonial governor, who "held his levees in a great room where now slept twenty Irish bedfellows."[68] Priscilla is the True Woman taken to her logical extreme. Not only is she intensely affectionate and meek, but her physical insubstantiality renders her almost spectral. This makes her the antithesis of her "gross and simple" neighbors, who enjoy gossiping about Priscilla and teasing her: "The big, red, Irish matrons, whose innumerable progeny swarmed out of the adjacent doors, used to mock at the pale Western child. . . . They called her ghost-child, and said that she . . . could never, in her densest moments, make herself quite visible."[69] Such rough taunts might not amount to much in themselves, but they do foreshadow the abuses, both large and small, that Priscilla receives from the novel's main characters. It is not too much to say that she learns to be a doormat in an Irish tenement.

Much more disturbing is the mistreatment that Sophia Nevins endures from her Irish neighbors in *Ned Nevins, the News Boy; or, Street Life in Boston* (1867), a novel by Boston Methodist minister and moral crusader Henry Morgan. The daughter of a poor New Hampshire clergyman, Sophia is seduced and abandoned by her fiancé, whereupon she moves to Boston and tries to support herself and her son, Ned, by working as a seamstress. But her health soon fails, as "an educated, refined, delicate female, unaccustomed to toil, cannot endure fatigue like a muscular Margaret or a Bridget."[70] When we meet Sophia, she is lying on her deathbed, waiting for her beloved boy's return: "See those Irish women gather around her! One of them watches the trunk, as if to get hold of it, then looks around the room to see if there is nothing else to steal." Another "thievish Irish woman" checks Sophia's pulse, while surreptitiously eying the ring on her finger.[71] Sophia's neighbors—with one notable exception—remain unmoved by her cries for Ned.[72] Like the vast majority of Irishwomen in the novel, who beat, neglect, and exploit their children, these women are too greedy and self-interested to care about anyone else. Clearly, an Irish tenement is no place for the Yankee True Woman.

But, according to some commentators, not even her own middle-class home could protect the Yankee True Woman from the Irishwoman's abuse. In a period when the Irish dominated domestic service in the urban North, critics of the Hibernian servingwoman—commonly called Bridget or Biddy—charged her with dominating her delicate Yankee mistress. The idea that Bridget ruled the American household was a running theme in that vast body of Gilded Age commentary devoted to the "servant problem." For some it was the stuff of humor. A few mistresses were able to chuckle at their own position as "servants of servants," bond slaves of "remorseless tyrants."[73] One quipped about a traveler from a foreign land who is at first puzzled about the nature of the American political system but eventually concludes that it is "made up of families, each of which was controlled by a despotic power, unseen and hidden, called 'Biddies,' or the 'Irish help,' which was more absolute and tyrannical than that of an Eastern autocrat."[74] With more obvious bigotry, cartoonist Frederick Burr Opper drew Bridget as an enormous, simian-faced "Potentate" who shakes a mighty fist at her delicate, pleading mistress or haughtily dismisses her from the kitchen.[75]

Others saw nothing funny about the Irish servingwoman's alleged domination of her mistress. Domesticity expert Virginia F. Townsend declared, "I have seen very good women, and very sensible ones, too, utterly unnerved and prostrated by the impudence and vociferation of an Irish girl."[76] Many believed the key to Bridget's power was her reputation for abruptly quitting her job, leaving her mistress in the lurch. They told of mistresses who lived in constant fear lest their servants suddenly abandon them with a house full of young children or a table full of dinner guests. The fear had a basis in reality. At a time when the demand for competent domestics greatly exceeded the supply, servants often seized the opportunity to change jobs for reasons that included higher wages, a lighter workload, and a better location. As Faye Dudden argues, a high turnover rate was the inevitable result of an anonymous, competitive urban job market for domestic servants, but many mistresses blamed it instead on a clutch of stereotypically Celtic racial traits: fickleness, disloyalty, and defiance.[77] They complained that Irish servants quit work for the pettiest reasons or no reason at all.

Many commentators believed the True Woman's delicacy left her particularly vulnerable to Biddy's tyranny. They pointed out that a mistress who fired a servant faced two unattractive alternatives—both of which compromised her wifely and maternal duties. She could hire a new servant, in which case she would have to devote days—or even weeks—to training her new employee, who was likely to be an unskilled immigrant, or she could do the work herself. In an essay titled "The Persecuted Woman," one mistress described the drawbacks of the first option. Training "Biddy" meant that she had to sacrifice her sacred obligations to her family: "I am to hear the merry voices of my dear ones in the distance, and cannot mingle my own with theirs, because I am banished for Biddy's good."[78] She ultimately decides to abandon the project after a stint in the kitchen brings her to the breakfast table with red-ringed eyes and a scarlet, swollen face. She reminds herself, "I must not forget a lady's duty. Her lord has honored her by his preferment. Her sweet grace and delicacy won him first. . . . [S]he must keep her hands fair for the melody her fingers rain out to him; her cheeks fresh, her curls bright, for the tenderness of his gazing.[79] Dismissing this "Biddy," the frustrated mistress moves on to a succession of others, eventually resigning herself to her fate as a "persecuted woman."

Some mistresses dreamed of ridding themselves of Irish servants altogether and claiming the dubious title of "the lady who does her own work." But the champions of True Womanhood warned that this was physically impossible for most mistresses. Virginia Townsend described mistresses who collapsed in despair after the departure of their Irish servants: "Many of these women were delicately organized, and heavy household burdens had been laid on slender shoulders."[80] Even in New England, where middle-class Yankees continued to pay lip service to the ideal of universal manual labor, writers warned mistresses not to attempt the work of an Irishwoman. Abby Sage Richardson described her sojourn in five New England households that kept no servants. In one well-maintained home, she was initially pleased to discover that the two daughters did all the cooking and housework, "and, what was best of all, they had robust and splendid health."[81] But later one of the young women confided that she was "all overworked, and well-nigh tired to death." The reason the daughters did the housework, it turned out, was because their Irish servants kept leaving them for jobs in the nearby factories. At another home Richardson encountered an even more worrisome case. "Mrs. B—" had spent a "weary month" vainly searching for competent domestics. Shuddering at the thought of bringing "a dirty Irish girl" into her newly furnished home, she moans, "If I were only strong enough, I would rather do all the work myself." But she is clearly not strong enough, as she has recently returned from convalescing at a watering place. Richardson notes how their frustrations with Irish servants had prompted many of her friends to consider the same exotic alternative. "I believe I'd try a Chinaman, if I knew where to get one," Mrs. B— declares.[82] In reality, there were almost no "Chinamen" to be "gotten" in New England in 1871.[83] But caught between her own poor health and Bridget's tyranny, some Yankee True Women were ready to try anything.

The Medical Moralists

The cult of True Womanhood's assumptions about female beauty and morality were by no means universally accepted. Beginning in the antebellum period, commentators from across the ideological spectrum warned that the delicacy of American women—especially those in New England—was a sign not of beauty and moral refinement but of poor health. Those warnings would crescendo in the Gilded Age, as two groups of commentators—both with a large Yankee contingent—debated the causes of and remedies for the American woman's physical delicacy. One group, aptly christened "medical moralists" by Carroll Smith-Rosenberg and Charles E. Rosenberg, was dominated by conservative male physicians.[84] They blamed the delicacy of native-born white women on their indulgence in a variety of self-destructive practices, including excessive education; overreliance on servants; fashionable habits of dressing, eating, and socializing; and, most scandalous of all, abortion and contraception. The medical moralists deplored these practices as a threat not only to individual women but also to their entire race. They warned that each of these sins threatened a woman's ability to bear and raise healthy children. When a native-born woman wore tight corsets or studied too hard, she effectively abandoned the field of motherhood to her immigrant rival, who—the medical moralists insisted—never stooped to those vices. In New England the medical moralists presented the Yankee woman with a clear choice: she could either drive her race to extinction by persisting in her selfish and self-destructive ways or she could return to her grandmother's healthy lifestyle of hard work, moral reproductive practices, and devoted maternity.

That ultimatum, and many of the assumptions that undergirded it, were contested by the other major group of commentators on female delicacy in the Gilded Age, the feminists. While the latter agreed with the medical moralists that fashion was undermining female health, they opposed the conservative physicians on other key issues. Most feminists questioned the idea that women's health in New England had deteriorated since Puritan times; many thought it had actually improved. Most rejected the notion that housework was the key to women's health, and some even saw it as a health risk.[85] Many feminists also thought the medical moralists were wrong about the effects of climate on physiology (which were immediate, not slow and gradual) and wrong about the health of immigrant women (which was poor, not robust). But the primary bone of contention between the two groups was education, which the feminists saw as a major boon to women's health rather than the grave danger the medical moralists described. Citing the benefits of education, the feminists argued that women's health in this country was improving most swiftly in those places, like New England, where females had the best chance to go to school.

Although the medical moralists saw the poor health of native-born women as alarming in itself, they were particularly worried about its implications for the nation's demographic future. By the 1860s it seemed obvious that the future would belong to the immigrants, as census figures consistently revealed that immigrant mothers were giving birth to more babies than were native-born ones. The disparity was particularly acute in New England, where the Yankees—early adopters of family limitation—maintained the lowest birthrate of all US ethnic groups, and the press was filled with stories about the Puritan descendants' imminent disappearance amid a rising tide of immigrants.[86] Among the leading Cassandras were Yankee medical moralists, such as Nathan Allen, John Ellis, and Edward Clarke, who took the population statistics as proof that something was desperately wrong in New England culture, particularly among the women of the middle and upper classes. The conservative physicians believed their people's declining birthrate was partly involuntary, a result of inherited reproductive problems, and they sympathized with Yankee women who wanted to have babies but couldn't. Yet the medical moralists were also convinced that most of the decline in the Yankee birthrate was a deliberate result of narcissistic and risky behaviors by Yankee females who refused to do their maternal duty, thereby hastening the extinction of their people. It was these wayward females who drew the bulk of the medical moralists' wrath. They sought to shame and/or cajole Yankee women back into the paths once trodden by their grandmothers but now mostly traveled by the region's female immigrants.

Some medical moralists thought a key cause of Yankee women's poor health and low birthrates lay in their overreliance on immigrant servants. Countering the advocates of True Womanhood who bemoaned the Irish servant's tyranny over her delicate mistress, the medical moralists insisted that the beleaguered mistress had only herself to blame for her sufferings. They argued that many women undermined their own health and that of their daughters by overrelying on foreign-born domestics.[87] The most tireless advocate of this view was Lowell physician Nathan Allen, who gushed about the physical and moral benefits of domestic labor: "No kind of work or exercise is so well calculated to develop all parts of woman's physical system, as housework. . . . [N]ature expressly designed it for the healthy development of woman's constitution."[88] Although in his role as trustee of Amherst College Allen was "instrumental" in establishing that all-male institution's Department of Physical Culture, he was dismissive of the movement for female exercise and physical education.[89] Allen conceded that a female might get some benefits from outdoor sports or "regular gymnastic exercises," but only housework provided the strenuous, steady activity she needed; moreover, "the knowledge obtained from these exercises is worthless, compared with that acquired in the performance of domestic duties."[90]

Allen believed the widespread employment of immigrant domestics in New England was a primary reason so many Yankee women were sickly and sterile. This was an issue not only for the middle- and upper-class Yankee females who *had* servants but also for working-class Yankee females who refused to *be* servants on the grounds that service was widely considered to be menial "immigrant" work. Allen saw the hiring of immigrant domestics as part of a larger trend whereby Yankees were turning over all their manual labor to the foreign born. He warned that the results already looked ominous for his people: "Judging from a physiological stand-point, the introduction of this foreign element into New England, instead of proving a blessing, may result in one of the greatest misfortunes that ever befell any race or people."[91] Although Allen saw immigrant labor as a threat to the health of all Yankees, he believed the female Puritan descendants were the primary victims: "One obvious effect of employing foreign domestic help has been to impair the constitution and health of New England women. This is a most serious injury in its relations to the family, and especially in its bearings upon the welfare of the race."[92]

Like other medical moralists, Allen believed freedom from domestic labor

Fig. 5. Nathan Allen. Frontispiece from Nathan Allen, *Physical Development; or, The Laws Governing the Human System* (1888).

was especially devastating for middle- and upper-class girls, as it denied them the strength and stamina they would need as housekeepers. Perhaps even more worrisome, it also left their domestic sentiments undeveloped. Allen contended that through a steady regimen of housework "home and the family are pretty sure to secure a strong attachment," but without it a girl was susceptible to the allurements of fashion and inappropriate education.[93] He contrasted the sickly, nervous Yankee girls of his day with their hardworking, rosy-cheeked ancestors, reminiscing about the golden age "fifty or one hundred years ago," when "nearly all New England girls were trained up to domestic labor, commencing early and continuing year after year."[94] Those girls grew up to be "mothers of large families, performing in most cases their own work, seldom feeling an ache or a pain, and living to a good old age, scarcely knowing what weakness or sickness was."[95] Allen maintained that in contemporary New England such shining examples of maternal health were only to be found among the foreign born: "The general health and constitutions of our young women do not compare with the women living fifty years ago, or with the Irish, Scotch, or English women of the present day."[96] The main thing those old-fashioned Yankee women shared with "present day" immigrants was a daily dose of strenuous domestic labor. Like a number of domestic advice writers from the period, Allen believed the immigrant servant was reaping the physical benefits of hard work that in the old days had gone to the native-born female. As his fellow Yankee Harriet Beecher Stowe put it, "The times, in New England, when all women did housework a part of every day, were the times when all women were healthy. At present, the heritage of vigorous muscles, firm nerves, strong backs, and cheerful physical life has gone from American women, and is taken up by Irish women."[97]

In short Allen held contradictory attitudes toward the region's immigrants. In their capacity as domestic servants, he feared them as a threat to the Yankee woman's health—and ultimately the survival of her ethnic group. But as exemplars of healthy, hardworking maternity, he cherished foreign-born females as reminders of what Yankee womanhood had once been and might one day again become. He celebrated the region's immigrant mothers as the metaphoric heirs of "our grandmothers," clearly hoping the literal heirs of those grandmothers would take notice.[98]

Along with the immigrant domestic servant, most medical moralists believed their chief antagonists in the struggle to keep the Yankee female healthy and at home were fashion and education. They thought both pursuits posed grave threats to the minds and bodies of all females, especially pubescent and adolescent ones. They based their understanding of the threat on the era's dominant physiological theory. Like most physicians of the day, the medical moralists assumed that the body was a closed system to which the law of conservation of energy applied: energy expended in one activity had to be drawn away from others. For pubescent and adolescent girls, this meant that the considerable vital force (aka nervous energy) required to develop their complicated reproductive systems had to come from other parts of the body. (Most physicians believed this was less of a concern for boys because their presumptively simpler reproductive systems required less energy to develop.) Unfortunately, by overstimulating a girl's nervous system, education and fashion left her with nothing to grow on.[99] As Carroll Smith-Rosenberg and Charles Rosenberg put it, "The brain and ovary could not develop at the same time."[100] Many physicians believed the failure to protect girls from nervous overstimulation had left them with overdeveloped brains and underdeveloped bodies. They warned that the consequences would be borne not only by the girls themselves—who were said to suffer a shocking array of physical and nervous illnesses—but also by their children, providing they were able to bear any. Offspring of sickly, neurasthenic mothers with deformed uteri and milkless breasts, the next generation of American children was bound to be nervous and delicate itself. Some physicians warned that the nation would have to turn to immigrant mothers to provide the steady-nerved, strong-armed citizens it required.

Of all the unhealthful environments for a growing girl, the medical moralists believed the world of fashion was among the worst. They contended that a steady round of balls, parties, and social calls produced females whose nervous systems were overdeveloped at the expense of the rest of their bodies. According to Nathan Allen, the fashionable female soon came to crave stimulation like a drug: "A cultivation of the brain and nervous system, exclusive of other parts of the body, demands constant excitement and stimulants. In this state of things, children are a trouble and a burden; domestic labor a tax and penance . . . [and] the fashionable call and company, the last novel and romance, have the strongest attractions."[101] In contrast, Allen asserted, New England's immigrants were immune to the attractions of the fashionable life. As a result, "these women have generally a large development of the muscular and vital temperaments, while very few of them have an excess of the nervous temperament. This difference in organization explains why they have so many more children than the American women."[102]

According to Allen, the difference in physical "organization" also explained why immigrant mothers were so much more successful in nursing their babies. In one of his trademark alarmist—and utterly unsupported—claims, Allen observed, "Formerly New England women found little difficulty nursing their offspring; this is true at the present day with the English, the Irish, and the German women living in our country. But not more than one-half of our young New England mothers can now properly nurse their offspring, and this number is every year decreasing." Allen attributed the Yankee woman's breastfeeding problems to her asymmetrical growth: "The nervous system has been developed unduly, while the sympathetic, affectional, and muscular natures have been stinted. The failure to nurse offspring shows something radically wrong."[103] Fashion had literally rewired the Yankee woman's body.

The medical moralists believed that, along with imbalanced growth, fashionable living posed a variety of other health risks to Yankee females, none of which threatened foreign-born females. Echoing the attacks on fashion by innumerable antebellum health reformers, feminists, and regular physicians, the medical moralists inveighed against late hours, rich food, lack of exercise, and, above all, constrictive clothing.[104] They cataloged a variety of ills allegedly caused by corsets and tight dresses, including irregular heartbeat, shortness of breath, dyspepsia, costiveness and other digestive complaints, stooped shoulders, and displaced uteri.[105] The medical moralists predictably warned that the fashionably dressed mother passed her ills down to her children. In 1892 retired physician John Ellis declared, "Fashionable habits of dress—tight lacing, which is worse to-day than ever before—has, to a large extent, destroyed the ability of the New England and other native American women to bear healthy and well-developed children, and to properly nurse them after they are born."[106] He urged readers to consider the small waist as a sign not of beauty but of degeneracy: "The intelligent, conscientious man, as he looks at a deformed or small waist, looks beyond the present time and sees a home often made miserable by the nervousness and sickness of a wife, and the sufferings of puny, imperfectly developed and half-starved and dying children, which results so frequently follow tight dressing." Ellis maintained that any man who complimented a woman on her small waist was either "vain and foolish" or a "flatterer who has some selfish object in view."[107] Noting that women had helped protect men's health by supporting prohibition, he urged men to return the favor by passing laws "to prevent the publication and sale of the fashion plates which contain such miserable caricatures of the female form, and which enter our homes but to pervert and destroy our young girls."[108]

At a time when fashionable dressing seemed pervasive among the native born, the medical moralists contended that one had to look among the immigrants to find a natural female waist. Ellis quoted an unnamed "medical friend" who claimed things had reached such a pass that "it is difficult for us to separate our idea of a natural waist from the quaint dress of an immigrant."[109] Actually, corsets and tight dresses were also quite popular among foreign-born females, whose thirst for American fashions and willingness to spend their hard-earned dollars to get them—even sacrificing their food budget in some cases—has been well documented.[110] But the medical moralists generally overlooked this fact, instead romanticizing immigrant women for their unfashionably loose clothing and healthy physiques. Allen concluded an extended discussion of the dangers of fashionable dressing by observing, "these complaints were entirely unknown to our grandmothers, and are but little known now with the English, German or Irish; they are peculiarly prevalent with the New England women."[111] Ellis concurred, "We have but to compare the female forms we see around us, with the models of feminine beauty which have come down to us in stone or on canvass [*sic*], or with the best developed and most symmetrical forms which we occasionally see, especially among immigrants, at this day, to realize how great [is] the deformity so almost universally prevalent among the native female population of our country."[112] The medical moralists believed foreign-born women still boasted the natural silhouettes so common in the paintings and sculptures of the old masters, and so rare among the fashionable daughters of New England.

The Yankee medical moralists also praised immigrant women for shunning what most saw as the fashionable woman's most immoral and self-destructive practices, contraception and abortion. To judge from their dropping birthrates, family limitation was common among Protestant women of all social classes, but the medical moralists singled out the fashionable woman (and, to a lesser extent, her feminist sister) as the chief perpetrator. They painted her as a selfish hedonist, willing to risk injury or even death to avoid a pregnancy that would force her to give up the frivolous pleasures of high society. The medical moralists found such behavior shocking anywhere, but particularly so in New England, which prided itself on its Puritan history of large families, devoted mothers, and moral reproductive practices. Yet, whereas those traditions seemed all but dead among the Yankees, they lived on among the region's immigrants. The medical moralists watched with a mixture of envy and admiration as Irish and French Canadian Catholic women bore a disproportionate share of the region's babies and won widespread praise for their moral reproductive practices. Joining in that praise, the medical moralists argued that it was the region's foreign-born females, not their fashionable Yankee rivals, who most resembled the Puritan foremothers.

In singling out the fashionable woman as the chief perpetrator of family limitation, the Yankee medical moralists were largely inspired by their colleagues in the physicians' crusade against abortion and contraception. Launched in the 1850s by Boston gynecologist Horatio Robinson Storer, the physicians' crusade successfully lobbied state legislatures over the next three decades for tough new restrictions on abortion and, secondarily, contraception. It sought to overturn a two-hundred-year-old legal tradition that held abortion to be legal up to the point of "quickening" (fetal movement). As Janet Farrell Brodie writes, the physician crusaders saw to it that "[i]n some states it became illegal to obtain an abortion at any stage of pregnancy: abortionists began to face charges of second-degree homicide or manslaughter and women seeking abortions faced criminal prosecution."[113] Many of the physician crusaders also supported the movement to criminalize contraception, which led to the passage of the federal "Comstock Law," as it came to be known, banning the dissemination of information about abortion and contraception, as well as the even more restrictive "little Comstock laws" passed by many states. Under the new legislation, fourteen states outlawed private conversations about abortion or contraception and eleven states made it illegal to possess information about contraception. Connecticut went furthest, banning even the act of contraception itself.[114]

While the physician crusaders blamed abortion and contraception on a variety of causes—from feminism to lax laws—many of them named fashion as the primary culprit.[115] In a typical attack, Storer insisted, "The demands of fashion shorten or prevent nursing, the demands of fashion often forbid a woman from bearing children; but whether this is attained by the prevention of impregnation, or by the induction of miscarriage, it is almost inevitably attended . . . by a grievous shock to the mother's system, that sooner or later undermines her health if even it does not directly induce her death."[116] Storer warned that abortion and contraception both left the fashionable woman with a fearsome catalog of ills. The former caused "uterine displacement," "painfully neuralgic breasts," "disabled limbs," "impatient bladders," "obscure abdominal aches and pains," "severe and intractable headaches," and "general hypochondria and despondency," while the latter caused nervous diseases and uterine problems.[117] According to Storer, the only forms of family limitation that did not endanger the health of a woman, and in some cases her partner, were abstinence and the rhythm method. He even ruled out withdrawal, the most popular form of contraception at the time, declaring: "[T]here can be no doubt that intercourse, unless *complete,* is prejudicial to the health of both parties."[118]

Although they were obviously influenced by Storer and his fellow physician crusaders against abortion and contraception, the Yankee medical moralists lacked their single-minded focus on family limitation, a difference that sometimes led to conflicts between the two groups.[119] But, when it came to the causes and consequences of abortion and contraception, the medical moralists generally echoed the physician crusaders. The two groups agreed that family limitation was particularly rife among the fashionable. In horror the medical moralists described elite social circles where the birth of a child was met with indifference or even dismay and where childlessness actually enhanced one's status. John Ellis quoted a letter from a clergyman who appealed to him, "You, as a physician, cannot help but know how great a misfortune pregnancy is considered by many women, who are so perverted in their ideas as to consider it something to be ashamed of, and that it is positively vulgar to have any sign of child bearing." Such women allegedly wore tight corsets during pregnancy, "knowing that it endangers the life of the child which they would be only glad to lose."[120] Nathan Allen agreed that there was a bias against babies among "what is called cultivated and refined society." He claimed that many Yankee women, having lost their maternal instincts, went into marriage with the intention of remaining childless, "They compliment those who have none or a very small number of children, while comments not pleasant or becoming to hear, are made respecting those who have large families." Allen contended that in fashionable circles it was increasingly considered "vulgar and sensual" to have several children."[121]

According to the medical moralists, the main reason the fashionable woman avoided maternity was not because it enhanced her status but because it interfered with her pleasure. They painted her as a supremely narcissistic creature, who refused to trade the self-indulgence of high society for the self-sacrifice of the nursery. Motherhood meant putting someone else's needs first, and the fashionable woman recoiled from that. The medical moralists tried to show her what she was missing. Ellis quoted a clergyman who argued that abortion would end only when women were taught "the paramount obligations of the family relation, a clear knowledge of the laws of health bearing upon this point, a correct moral sense, an appreciation of the honor and blessing of maternity, and a clear sense of the truth that human life is sacred at all periods."[122] Nathan Allen likewise combined moral attacks on family limitation with praise for the sacred joys of maternity, "woman's brightest crown, her grandest privilege." He urged Yankee females to cultivate maternal love, "the noblest and purest of all the instincts or affections in woman."[123]

The medical moralists complemented their appeals to the fashionable woman's dormant maternal instincts with dire predictions about what would happen if she continued to practice family limitation. Like the physician crusaders against abortion and contraception, they described both practices as grave threats to women's health. Allen maintained that the "evil effects" of contraception "upon physical organization are incalculable," while abortion "has a far more destructive influence upon human welfare and increase than war can possibly have."[124] Ellis was slightly more tolerant of contraception, deeming it permissible in those "rare cases" in which a history of difficult births indicated that a woman's life was likely to be "seriously endangered" by another pregnancy. Abortion, on the other hand, was always a "fearful crime," which "kills the child and always seriously endangers the life of the mother."[125]

The medical moralists believed abortion and contraception were wrong for all women, but doubly so for the descendants of the Puritans. They found it bitterly ironic that Yankee women should become internationally notorious for reproductive practices that defied everything New England womanhood supposedly stood for. Allen charged his fellow Yankees with neglecting the religious beliefs and moral principles of their forebears: "There is . . . too little value set upon the worth of an immortal soul. If parents can bring into existence and rear up for endless bliss a never-dying spirit, how great the privilege! But these considerations, so powerful in the early settlers of New England, have greatly ceased to influence our people."[126] Ellis claimed he had personally witnessed the decline in parental instincts among his people. He reminisced about his boyhood, when early marriages and huge families were far more common among the Yankees than at present. Ruefully noting that the nation was actively enticing "hundreds of thousands of comparatively ignorant foreigners," Ellis insisted that there were better ways to increase the population: "Would it not be as well to cultivate the parental instinct among the descendants of the Puritans? Our fathers and mothers were no ignoble people, and does not humanity and patriotism require that their descendants should shun those false doctrines and evils which are destroying our native race?"[127] It was time for the Yankees to stop disgracing their ancestry.

Yet, as the medical moralists repeatedly pointed out, it was the "ignorant foreigners" rather than "the descendants of the Puritans" who seemed best suited to carry on New England's most cherished parental traditions. In an era when many Yankees charged the immigrant mother—the Irish mother in particular—with reckless breeding and indifferent parenting, the medical moralists strongly disagreed. Ellis and his colleagues consistently attributed to the region's female immigrants the very virtues of fecundity, robust health, intense maternal love, and moral reproductive practices that they so admired in their own grandmothers. Some made the comparison explicit, as when Allen compared the fertility and vigor of "the earlier settlers of New England" with that of his contemporaries, "the better portion of the Irish race, whether living in Ireland or America, together with what may be called a middling class among the English and the Scotch."[128] Allen also made clear that it was the immigrant mother, not her Yankee rival, who most resembled "our grandmothers" in her attitude toward family limitation. Thus, after lashing fashionable Yankees for their hostility to children, Allen mourned, "what a change in this respect between the women of the present day, and those of a hundred years ago." But, as the doctor made clear in the next sentence, not all present-day women had lost their maternal instincts: "The 'arts of destruction and prevention of human life' . . . are comparatively unknown among the Irish, English, and Germans of New England."[129]

Allen was far from alone in invidiously comparing the immigrant female's attitude toward family limitation with that of her fashionable Yankee rival. Such comparisons were a staple of the physician crusaders against abortion and contraception, who routinely warned that the contrast between native-born and immigrant attitudes toward family limitation was rapidly changing the nation's demographics.[130] Although the evidence suggests that some immigrants (German Protestants and Jews in particular) played a significant role in providing and procuring abortions in the Gilded Age, the crusaders, like most Americans, took for granted that family limitation was exclusively a native-born phenomenon.[131] The medical moralists endorsed this view. Ellis quoted a German clergyman who told him, "The German men are afraid to marry American girls, because the latter are not willing to bear children, whereas the Germans love children and desire to have them."[132] Such tributes to the immigrant mother are striking coming from men who generally made little effort to hide their nativism. To the contrary, the medical moralists were openly dismayed at the prospect of an immigrant-dominated New England. Thus, we may assume that their real motive in praising the immigrant mother for her moral reproductive practices was to shame her Yankee rival into reforming. If appealing to the Yankee woman's Puritan heritage failed to stop her family limitation, perhaps flattering the immigrant mother would do the trick.

Along with fashion, the medical moralists saw "improper" education as a chief cause of the Yankee female's supposed delicate health. By improper they meant both coeducation and the "separate identical education" of males and females at both the secondary and postsecondary levels.[133] The medical moralists supported education for females, but they believed it needed to be tailored to accommodate their specific physiological needs, particularly those centered on their developing reproductive systems. Invoking the era's mechanistic theory of human physiology, the medical moralists warned that female students were devoting too much vital force to mental activity and not enough to their growing reproductive systems. The medical moralists believed the health consequences of this asymmetrical growth were devastating for the nation's female students, who were widely reported to be suffering from an epidemic of nervous and gynecological ills. Convinced that education was robbing native-born females of their physical and mental health, as well as their ability to reproduce, the medical moralists warned that the nation would have to look to immigrant mothers to supply the next generation of Americans.

Although conservative physicians and social reformers had been warning of the health risks of female education since midcentury, their voices grew louder in the Gilded Age in response to the rapid expansion of female educational opportunities at both the secondary and college levels.[134] Not surprisingly, many critics of female education identified New England as ground zero for sickly schoolgirls and college women. The region had long stood in the vanguard of female education: the birthplace of pioneering female educators like Mary Lyon and Catharine Beecher, it was also home to the first public high schools for girls. But, according to the medical moralists, Yankee females were paying a steep price for their knowledge. Nathan Allen claimed, "Nowhere in the world is female education carried to such an extent as in New England," and consequently, the "ill health" of the Yankee females "has become proverbial."[135] Philadelphia nervous disorder specialist S. Weir Mitchell concurred. Noting the "hardness of line in form and feature" of the Yankee girls, he partly blamed the climate but insisted that the main cause was excessive education: "In New England . . . the forcing system is at its wicked worst."[136]

New England was also the home of some of the leading critics of this "forcing system," including clergyman, moral crusader, and author John Todd, whose *Woman's Rights* (1867) included a condescending attack on women's higher education:

> Alas! must we crowd education upon our daughters, and for the sake of having them "intellectual," make them puny, nervous, and their whole earthly existence a struggle between life and death? If it ministers to vanity to call a girl's school "a college," it is very harmless, but as for training young ladies through a long intellectual course, as we do young men, it can never be done—they will die in the process.[137]

As he no doubt anticipated, Todd provoked strong rebuttals from feminists.[138] Yet the leading critic of female education in those years was not Todd but Edward Hammond Clarke, a member of Harvard's Board of Overseers and a former Harvard medical faculty member.[139] In his best-selling volume, *Sex in Education; or, A Fair Chance for the Girls* (1873), Clarke painted a deeply disturbing picture of the ill effects of education on the health of the nation's females. Appearing in sixteen editions over the next decade and a half, *Sex in Education* was essential reading for anyone interested in female education.[140] Supporters of higher education for women took particular note. In the months after Clarke's book appeared, alumnae, students, physicians, and instructors from institutions that included Vassar, Oberlin, Antioch, Michigan, and Mount Holyoke published testimonials challenging his claims about the debility of college women.[141] But even Clarke's most determined opponents found it difficult to dismiss his arguments. Writing just a few years after women had begun attending college in significant numbers, the doctor had raised fears about the risks of female education. Bryn Mawr president M. Carey Thomas recalled how Clarke's book had overshadowed her efforts in the 1880s to plan the academic organization of her institution: "We did not know when we began whether women's health could stand the strain of college education. We were haunted in those days by the clanging chains of that gloomy little specter, Dr. Edward H. Clarke's *Sex in Education.*"[142]

Sue Zschoche argues that Clarke's major achievement in *Sex in Education* was to reframe the debate over women's rights—educational and otherwise—in terms of physiology.[143] As the doctor himself put it, "The problem of woman's sphere . . . is not to be solved by applying to it abstract principles of right and wrong. Its solution must be obtained from physiology, not from ethics or metaphysics."[144] Clarke believed that educators needed to take into account the female student's unique bodily needs, particularly those of her reproductive system, the marvelous "engine within an engine" that supposedly took so much vital force to develop and perfect.[145] He insisted that female students needed regular breaks from bodily and mental effort, especially during menstruation. Specifically, Clarke recommended that females between the ages of fourteen and eighteen study one to two hours a day less than males and that they reduce or even stop (depending on their individual needs) their schoolwork each month during menstruation.[146] Clarke contended that females who followed these guidelines could learn as much as males: "Boys must study and work in a boy's way, and girls in a girl's way. They may study the same books, and attain an equal result, but should not follow the same method."[147]

Clarke warned of grave consequences for female students who failed to follow his advice. Declaring that "[t]he system never does two things well at

Fig. 6. Edward H. Clarke. (Courtesy of Harvard University Archives, HUP Clarke, Edward H. [1].)

the same time," he maintained that females who studied intensively while ignoring the demands of their bodies were risking permanent damage to their nervous and/or reproductive systems.[148] He cited examples of ambitious female students whose uninterrupted labors had left them with a range of nervous illnesses, including insomnia, neuralgia, headache, hysteria, and brain degeneration.[149] But Clarke was more concerned about the effects of ignoring "the periodical tides of her organization" on the female student's reproductive system.[150] He cited the cases of his female patients (not all of them students), whose valiant and foolhardy effort to best the males at their own game had brought on an array of gynecological and reproductive ills: "[p]eriodical hemorrhages," "amenorrhœa," "dysmenorrhœa," "menorrhagia," and the "arrest of the development of the reproductive apparatus" (this final condition manifested in small breasts).[151] Clarke left no doubt that these young patients had permanently damaged their reproductive systems. He sarcastically summed up the case of "Miss A—": "She is now what is called getting better, but has the delicacy and weaknesses of American women, and, so far, is without children." Moreover, she would likely remain so, as "the evil of her education will infect her whole life."[152]

Clarke believed the health of educated females was poor across the nation, but nowhere more so than in his native region. He thought it was "the misfortune of this country, and particularly of New England, that education . . . has popularly stood for studying, without regard to the physical training or no training the schools afford."[153] As a result, it was in New England that the schoolgirls and college women were sickest. Clarke recalled what Lady Amberley had said to him after visiting the Boston public schools: "I never saw before so many pretty girls together. . . . They all looked sick."[154] Like other New England medical moralists, Clarke traced a steady deterioration in Yankee women's health over the decades: "Our great-grandmothers are pointed at as types of female physical excellence; their great-grand-daughters as illustrations of female physical degeneracy." He tried to console himself with the thought that, under an appropriate educational regime, "our great-grand-daughters may recapture their ancestors' bloom and force."[155]

But at present the women who most resembled "[o]ur great-grandmothers" were the ones who had escaped the alleged horrors of the American educational system, namely, immigrants. Like other medical moralists, Clarke held up the robust health of the female immigrant as a model for her sickly Yankee rival. He quoted Nathan Allen's pointed questions, "Why should there be such a difference between the women of our times and their mothers or grandmothers? Why should there be such a difference between our American women and those of foreign origin residing in the same locality, and surrounded by the same external influences?"[156] The answer, for Clarke—and to a large extent for Allen as well—was the "identical" education of the sexes. And where that phenomenon was most pervasive—in places like New England—the disparity between the health of native-born and immigrant females was bound to be worst. Citing British essayist W. R. Greg, who claimed that the "cultivated classes" were less fertile than the "uncultivated ones," Clarke theorized that education was the main contributing factor. He warned that if elite girls continued to receive the same schooling as boys, "the race will be propagated from its inferior classes. The stream of life that is to flow into the future will be Celtic rather than American: it will come from the collieries, and not from the peerage."[157]

According to Clarke, Irish immigrants were not alone in surpassing Yankee females in strength and fertility. He argued that as one traveled up the east coast to Nova Scotia and then across the sea to Europe, the females got progressively healthier. The cause, he insisted, was not climate but education. He quoted letters from two German correspondents, one claiming that German girls were required to abstain from school and other activities during their periods and the other insisting that girls in northern Germany left school entirely at fifteen.[158] Clarke urged that similar precautions be adopted in the United States. Otherwise, "it requires no prophet to foretell that the wives who are to be mothers in our republic must be drawn from transatlantic homes. The sons of the New World will have to re-act, on a magnificent scale, the old story of unwived Rome and the Sabines."[159] Clarke was not the first to make such a prediction. Since the antebellum period, writers had warned that the Yankee male would eventually reject the sickly Yankee female as a mate in favor of her robust immigrant rival, but such intermarriages were still relatively uncommon in the Gilded Age.[160] In all likelihood, Clarke was not out to change that. Instead, he was probably resorting to the medical moralists' old ploy of flattering the foreign-born female to provoke changes in her native-born rival: faced with the prospect of losing her man to an Irish "Sabine," perhaps the Yankee college woman would heed Clarke's warnings about the risks she was running.

The Feminists Fight Back

Thanks in large part to their professional stature, apocalyptic rhetoric, and publicity savvy, the New England medical moralists attracted an outsized audience. Commentators in every part of the country and even overseas dutifully repeated their warnings about the poor health, self-destructive lifestyles, and low birthrates of Yankee females.[161] In New England the immigrant press eagerly quoted Nathan Allen's dire predictions that the Yankees would soon disappear in a sea of "foreigners."[162] But not everyone was taken in. Women's rights reformers across the country went to work exposing the dubious premises, poor science, and antifeminist agenda of the conservative physicians. Not surprisingly, the Yankee feminists led this counterattack. They had the most at stake in the debate, inasmuch as Allen and Clarke had named their region the epicenter of women's health and reproductive problems. The New England feminists sharply rebutted the medical moralists' portrait of the Yankee female as a sterile, overeducated invalid. They also exposed as a myth the conservative physicians' declensionist history of women's health in New England. In reality, the Yankee feminists argued, the health of the Puritan descendants had steadily improved since the seventeenth century as a result of better knowledge of physiology and the successful acclimation of the Anglo-Saxon race to the New World. But, according to the Yankee feminists, the female immigrant had missed out on these benefits. They dismissed the medical moralists' portrait of the foreign-born female as an icon of blooming health and fertility, depicting her instead as the victim of unhealthy living and working conditions, as well as a demanding new climate.

To be sure, the Yankee feminists by no means always disagreed with the medical moralists. Particularly when it came to the perils of the fashionable lifestyle—late hours, unwholesome food, tight clothes, abortions, and contraceptive devices—the women's rights reformers were fully in accord with the conservative physicians.[163] The two groups' consensus on that issue is not surprising, as fashion had been the bête noire of commentators on women's health of every ideological stripe since the antebellum period.[164] But there was little common ground between the medical moralists and feminists when it came to female education. Although some New England feminists, including veteran reformer Thomas Wentworth Higginson, agreed that females were physiologically more vulnerable to the strains of education than males, most scoffed at the idea.[165] A number of them pointed out that Clarke had provided no evidence—aside from a few anecdotal examples—to support his claims about the dangers of "identical" female education.[166] This led to a call for scientific research into the health of the nation's educated females, which was answered by several studies, including one by the Association of Collegiate Alumnae.[167] That organization sent a survey to its nearly 1,300 members, asking them detailed questions about their health and that of their parents. The association published the results of the 705 responses it received in the report *Health Statistics of Women College Graduates* (1885), which includes tables quantifying various aspects of the graduates' health, work, and reproductive histories, together with analysis by the chief of the Massachusetts Bureau of Statistics of Labor, Carroll D. Wright.[168] Refuting Clarke's thesis, Wright found that the refusal to rest during menstruation was not a major cause of health problems in college women. Nor did college seem to affect the overall wellness of females; about the same number of respondents reported improvement in their health during their college years as reported deterioration. Wright concluded that it was time to put the whole debate to rest, for "the seeking of a college education on the part of women does not in itself necessarily entail a loss of health or serious impairment of the vital forces. Indeed, the tables show this so conclusively that there is little need, were it within our province, for extended discussion of the subject."[169]

Whereas Wright cautiously concluded merely that education had no negative effects on the female scholar's health, most feminists were convinced that it had a demonstratively positive one. They identified several important health benefits the female scholar could expect from her studies: instruction in physiology taught her about her body and how to maintain its health; rigorous coursework provided a focus for her energies that might otherwise be wasted in fashionable dissipation; interaction with her fellow students provided pleasant stimulation and companionship; physical education gave her a regimen of safe, supervised exercise; and her studies gave her a purpose in life that made her more careful about her health. [170] Countering Clarke's case studies with their own, they told of sickly females whose health had been restored by going to school.[171] Ada Shepard Badger recalled one invalid girl who seemed to be declining into insanity, when, as a last resort, she was placed in school: "She soon began to revive under a regimen of mathematics, languages, and art-culture, and in two years was in a state of perfect health."[172] In short the problem with American females was that they had too little schooling, not too much.

If education improved female health, it stood to reason that females would be sickest where their chances for learning were worst, and that is precisely what the feminists argued. As Badger explained, "Nowhere in our own country does the average woman present so feeble and diseased an aspect as in those parts of the West and South where education is of the smallest moment to her."[173] To see the truth of this assertion, Yankee feminist Caroline Dall argued, one need only "watch the crowd pouring out of a western railroad station."[174] The medical moralists might claim that New England's commitment to female education was making its women the sickest in the nation, but, according to the feminists, the reverse was actually true: it was in the uneducated West and South that women were feeblest.

The Yankee feminists argued that education had contributed to a steady improvement in New England women's health since the settlement era. This obviously put them at odds with the declensionist narrative so energetically and successfully promoted by the medical moralists. Caroline Dall observed, "We are often told that the health of women now is not as good as it was generations ago, and this has been repeated and repeated until everybody believes it."[175] Thomas Wentworth Higginson chalked up that belief to the universal human tendency to idealize the past: "We look around us, and see many invalid or childless women. We say the Pilgrim mothers were not like these. We cheat ourselves by this perpetual worship of the pioneer grandmother. How the young bachelors, who write dashing articles in the newspapers, denounce their 'nervous' sisters, for instance, and belabor them with cruel memories of their ancestors!" Higginson encouraged those sisters to take with a big grain of salt all the stories about their heroic foremothers who "reared a family of twelve or thirteen children; spun, scrubbed, wove, and cooked; lived to eighty-five, with iron muscles, a broad chest and keen, clear eyes." Albeit impressive, this "imaginary Amazon" was a myth, the creation of the medical moralists and their allies, who used it to impose their conservative social vision on young women.[176] In reality, Higginson insisted, Puritan women were far more likely to die at a young age than their present-day descendants. While conceding that it is "desirable, certainly, to venerate our grandmothers," Higginson was "inclined to think, on the whole, that their great-granddaughters will be the best."[177]

Like other Yankee feminists, Higginson largely credited the improving health of the great-granddaughters to their superior knowledge of physiology. He observed, "There are undoubtedly many moral and physiological sins committed, tending to shorten and weaken life; but the progress of knowledge more than counterbalances them."[178] Annie Howes believed the progress of knowledge was essential, given that the physiological sins of the ancestors were still taking a toll on the present generation: "It is difficult to estimate what proportion of our bodily weakness must be traced to former ignorance of the laws of hygiene, but from what record [*sic*] tells us of the lives of the olden New England dames, they frequently sinned against Nature and we suffer the penalties of their transgressions." Howes maintained that it was their "very limited knowledge of the many laws of sanitary science" that led the foremothers to commit these physiological sins in the first place.[179] Thus, to ensure further improvements in women's health, it was imperative to increase public knowledge of physiology by creating more educational opportunities for females.

The Yankee feminists also attributed the improvement in women's health to the successful acclimation of their race in the New World. Convinced that the medical moralists had badly underestimated the physical rigors of transplantation, they argued that the New England climate had taken a severe toll on each wave of immigrants, beginning with the Puritans. Caroline Dall complained that Clarke "alludes to 'the pallor of our women' as if it were a new thing, whereas the second generation born upon these shores bore witness to it. It was observed by travellers one hundred and fifty years ago. As to the endurance of the duties of motherhood, and the proportion of surviving children born to them, our women are far in advance of the first generation, born and reared across the water." Noting that it was not uncommon for Puritan men to bury up to four wives, Dall contended, "The change of climate was at the bottom of this early fatality." She argued that the health of the Puritan descendants had "steadily improved" over subsequent generations as they acclimated (though she admitted that progress had stalled in recent decades due to the spread of "French fashions, vices, and habits").[180]

Higginson likewise believed the Yankee female had benefited from the acclimation of her race in the New World. While acknowledging that "the process of acclimating the English stock in America has been a severe one," he concluded that "there is much more reason to hope than to fear for the result." Higginson reasoned that even the low birthrate of Yankee women might proceed "in part from physical advancement rather from than physical decay," since in modern New England many people who never would have survived childhood in Puritan times now grew up to have one or two children of their own. Moreover, while it was true that the Yankee woman had fewer babies than her Puritan foremothers, far more of her offspring survived. Higginson took these as encouraging signs that his race had finally gotten its footing in the New World.[181]

Yet, if the Yankee female was winding up her long struggle with the New England climate, the region's immigrants were still in the early stages of theirs. For the Yankee feminists, this largely explained why the region's immigrant females were so unhealthy. They ridiculed Clarke's claim that it would take more than a century for the New World climate "to transform the sturdy German fraulein and robust English damsel into the fragile American miss."[182] In fact, wrote Caroline Dall, "The influence of climate does this in one generation for our Irish and German population. Standing in the mills at Lawrence, the pale faces and constant cough of the operatives will attest these words to any competent observer."[183] Higginson also claimed to have witnessed the deleterious effects of climate on the region's immigrants. At the height of the controversy over *Sex in Education,* he declared, "I have seen this change very nearly effected, in a single generation, among the children of English, Irish, French Canadians, and even the Nova Scotians whom [Clarke] so praises; and this actually without the influence of schooling, or almost without it." Higginson blamed the "delicacy" of the second generation on "the effect of climate, change of diet, [and] change of living." He thought the decay was nearly as visible among boys as girls (he quoted a physician in a manufacturing town who claimed that second-generation Irish American males were "the unhealthiest class of the community").[184]

Over the following decade, however, Higginson and other Yankee commentators would increasingly single out the Irish American *female* as the chief sufferer from the New World climate. He advanced this position by way of refuting Nathan Allen's invidious comparison between Yankee and immigrant women, based on their health and maternal instincts. In defense of the former, Higginson quoted an unnamed authority (identified only as "one of the most eminent physicians in this region") who maintained: "(1) that there is now visible a decided increase, not diminution, in the instinct of parentage and the desire of offspring, among American-born women of [the] English race; (2) that there is a gain now going on, not a loss, in the facility of child-bearing; (3) that there is a gain, not a loss, in the function of lactation or nursing."[185] According to Higginson, Allen was even farther from the truth when it came to the Irishwoman. Whereas Allen hailed her as an icon of maternal love and moral reproductive practices, Higginson attacked her as a reckless breeder who lost more children to careless parenting than she raised to maturity.[186] He cited Yankee physician Edward Jarvis, who maintained that the high infant mortality rate of the Irish nullified their high birthrate.[187] Higginson offered the hypothetical example of two neighboring families, one native born with three children, the other Irish with six: "If the American family, through care and providence, rear all their three children, and the Irish family, through recklessness and improvidence [*sic*] rear only two of their six, where is the gain?"[188] If the medical moralists were right about the superior maternal instincts of the Irishwoman, then why did she lose so many more babies than her Yankee rival?

Yet Higginson believed it was acclimation, rather than poor parenting, that posed the main threat to the Irish in America. He quoted his eminent New England physician friend as stating that "the thing really to be anxious about just now is not the physiological condition of the English but the Irish stock in America, from the rapidity with which pulmonary weakness is developing itself among the Americanized Irish."[189] Higginson believed the chief victims of that disease were young, second-generation Irish American women: "Within sight of my window is a small house, very healthfully located, where a fine family of young women of Irish parentage, are dying off with a regularity that seems like a doom."[190] These warnings prompted an Irish American woman from Bangor, Maine, to write Higginson to ask why her people were so susceptible to pulmonary diseases and what could be done about it. Higginson replied that the problem was acclimation: "The Irish immigrant arrives here poor, hardy, athletic, accustomed to the open air and to simple food. His son shuts himself up in a shoe-shop, his daughter in a factory; they eat unwholesome food, forego fresh air, and in one generation we see the change." He noted that the Anglo-Saxon settlers in New England had been forced to adapt to an outdoor life, while the Irish were adjusting to an indoor one. As for the question of how to meet those challenges, Higginson offered only condescending platitudes: "Time brings increased knowledge; the sense of danger; better sanitary regulations; more self-control. The Anglo-American race has been driven back, by experience, to take up again some of the simple habits of its ancestry: open fire-places, hard beds, oatmeal porridge. It will be the same in time with all other immigrant races; they must all adapt themselves to the new world and the new life, or die."[191] Such social Darwinist sentiments may seem surprising in a man who was rightly recognized by the Irish as one of their staunchest Brahmin friends. Appearing in the *Woman's Journal,* they may partly be explained by the Irish Catholics' well-known opposition to feminism.[192] But Higginson may also be venting some frustration against Yankee medical moralists like Nathan Allen. Exasperated with their attacks on Yankee women, he likely took some pleasure in smashing their Irish maternal icon.

On the other hand, influential Yankees with no obvious stake in the debates between the medical moralists and feminists also believed the second-generation Irish were having major problems acclimating in New England. Higginson cited a Boston medical commission whose report, *The Sanitary Condition of Boston* (1875), painted a dire picture of the prevalence of disease and death among the city's Irish. While the commissioners conceded that some of the problem lay in unhealthful living conditions, they also maintained that the Irish were particularly susceptible to the two allegedly heritable diseases that were among the city's most fatal: consumption and cancer.[193] This meant that "many of the most potent causes of disease and of death continue in operation through several generations among that part of our native population which is of comparatively recent foreign origin. Especially must this be the case among the Irish stock, which still so largely predominates among us."[194] Having inherited the diseases of their parents, the second-generation Irish were now passing them on to their children.

To prevent the recurrence of this tragic situation, the commissioners called for a study of all America's peoples to "determine for each race its amount of innate healthfulness, its power of resistance to disease, and its degree of adaptability to our climate and institutions." This eugenicist analysis would enable the nation to "favor the immigration of the more robust races, and discourage those who are found to be less capable of adapting themselves to our climate from attempting a fruitless struggle for life on this continent." The Irish would obviously fall in the latter category.[195]

Sociologist Frederick Bushee was equally pessimistic about the prospects of the second-generation Irish in a 1903 study of Boston's ethnic groups. Noting the "low rate of increase of the native born of Irish parentage," Bushee insisted that "the cause is not in the low birth rate . . . but in the exceedingly high death rate."[196] In fact, as scholars have shown, the cause *was* a low birth rate: the fertility of second-generation Irish females was dramatically lowered by their tendency to marry late or not at all.[197] Yet Bushee believed the second generation's slow growth was the result not of conscious decisions about marriage but of the impersonal forces of racial adaptation: "the Irish seem to be subjected to a strong process of natural selection, which is weeding out a large number who are physically unable to survive in their environments."[198] Like the authors of *The Sanitary Condition of Boston*, Bushee seemed doubtful that the second-generation Irish had what it took to survive, much less raise children, in America.

The same skepticism about the prospects of second-generation Irish American females was also voiced in the period's fiction.[199] In William Dean Howells's novella *An Imperative Duty* (1892), the Brahmin protagonist, a physician named Olney, contrasts the first- and second-generation Irishwomen he sees on the Boston Common:

> The old women were strong, sturdy, old-world peasants, but the young girls were thin and crooked, with pale, pasty complexions, and an effect of physical delicacy from their hard work and hard conditions, which might later be physical refinement. . . . Looking at them scientifically, Olney thought that if they survived to be mothers they might give us, with better conditions, a race as hale and handsome as the elder American race; but the transition from the Old World to the New, as represented in them, was painful.[200]

Two decades after *Suburban Sketches,* Howells no longer views Boston's women through the cult of True Womanhood's opposed stereotypes of Irish coarseness and Yankee delicacy. The Irish Amazon is back in full force, but her Yankee foil has lost her delicacy and now appears "hale and handsome." An equally striking change has occurred in the second-generation Irish American female, whom we encountered in *Suburban Sketches* among the "admirably small children" running errands in the streets.[201] Now grown up, she looks anything but admirable, a result—Olney surmises—of her harsh living and working conditions, as well as the "transition from the Old World to the New." In short, she is taking the first steps in the long march of acclimation that the "elder American race" began two centuries before. Olney seems hopeful that the Irish American female will eventually reach her destination, but he also leaves no doubt it will be a painful and arduous journey. Always a close observer of New England culture, Howells seems to be marking a milestone in the relations between the region's two dominant ethnic groups. From now on it is the second-generation Irish American female, rather than her Yankee rival, who will personify female delicacy in New England.

Like Howells's fictional physician, most of the participants in the debate over New England women's health focused their attention on the urban population. It was in the city, after all, that such notorious threats to women's health as ballrooms, abortionists, factories, and slums were most likely to be found. Yet, as many commentators pointed out, the region's countryside was no land of milk and honey for New England women. Farmwives in particular were widely reported to be struggling in an era of chronic shortages of domestic labor and increasing domestic responsibilities. But there was no consensus about what should be done to help them, or their husbands and children for that matter. While almost everyone agreed that rural New England faced severe challenges—by most accounts the gravest it had ever confronted—they were deeply divided over how best to respond to them.

FOUR

"Rural New England Is in a State of Transition"

Immigrants and Yankees on the Land

In the period after the Civil War, rural New England was notorious as a place that had seen better days. While some diehards strenuously denied that there was anything wrong with the region's countryside, most commentators, both inside and outside New England, believed otherwise. The author of a controversial attack on the villages of the region's hill country—the area widely seen as the epicenter of rural decay—assembled an ominous catalog of epithets about the place from his supporters: "'a catastrophe,' 'a decline in civilization,' 'a sickly condition,' 'degeneration,' 'demoralization,' 'decay.'"[1] The doomsayers pointed to various signs of rural decline, including dying villages, crumbling farmhouses, impassable roads, and dropping birthrates. Many believed that the region's agriculturalists were abandoning their farms in droves, unable to compete with the vast, fertile fields of the West. Some observers claimed that rural New England's morals were also decaying. They wrote lurid articles in the national press about hill towns where couples cohabited without marriage, babies were born with birth defects caused by inbreeding, and young people lacked ambition and hope.[2] A few commentators even warned that the physical and moral degeneracy of the rural Yankees was beginning to approach that of the poor whites of the South.[3] It was a terrible comedown for a countryside that had long thought of itself as the nation's standard-bearer for republican values and moral probity.

In recent decades scholars have refuted the idea that rural New England suffered a catastrophic decline in the Gilded Age. Some even maintain that the region's farm economy was quite healthy. Michael Bell contends that

New England farms were more productive and profitable than those in other regions, and Paul Munyon argues that, for the farmers of New Hampshire, the late nineteenth century was a time of "growing prosperity."[4] Others characterize the era as one of stagnancy, or at best slow growth, for the region's farmers. John Black shows that, despite the widespread talk of abandoned farms, the period saw no significant change in the region's aggregate farmland and only a slight decline in its total number of farms.[5] In his study of Chelsea, Vermont, Hal Barron finds the local economy "slowed down and stabilized," with the number of farms and their average size holding steady throughout the period.[6] Barron argues that a similar stability characterized Chelsea society, which "was much more stable, much less subject to the constant turnover and flux that characterized nineteenth-century society."[7] Chelsea's population had grown older and more homogeneous as younger people moved away, antebellum conflicts over politics and religion faded into the distance, and a consensus of "settled rural respectability" took hold.[8]

Yet, for all of its apparent stability, the New England countryside in the late nineteenth century was also undergoing a series of wrenching changes. As one observer put it, "Rural New England is in a state of transition."[9] The primary engine of change was the growth of urban America, which exerted an escalating influence over the nation's countryside. This trend was particularly pronounced in New England, where rampant suburbanization and a modernizing transportation network literally brought the city to the farmer's doorstep, dictating the crops he grew, the clothes he wore, and the ambitions of his children. Along with urbanization, the New England farmer also had to adjust to an agricultural economy strained by chronic labor shortages, dwindling production of cereals, declining wool prices, and high taxes. True, the years also brought new economic opportunities for the farmer, particularly in the form of urban consumers' seemingly insatiable demand for milk, butter, eggs, poultry, fruits, and vegetables, but to supply any of those products the agriculturalist had to solve his labor problem. Finally there was the challenge of depopulation. Since the antebellum years, many communities in rural New England had been losing population, as Yankees, mostly the young and unpropertied, left for the city or the West, to be replaced by far smaller numbers of immigrants. While the region's farm economy adjusted remarkably well to depopulation, cultural and political institutions suffered. Schools lost students, church attendance dwindled, and public spirit declined. Local farmers' clubs and Granges provided much needed sociability, cultural enrichment, and activism, but, by the end of the nineteenth century, the slow and difficult process of reconstructing the institutions of the countryside—exemplified by the Country Life Movement and the campaign to close and consolidate small rural schools—had only begun.

The challenges facing rural New England after the Civil War were widely recognized. Indeed, there was a vibrant cottage industry devoted to discussing them. That was particularly true within the region, where two groups that I will call "traditionalists" and "progressive farmers" took the lead in debating what had gone wrong in New England's countryside and what should be done to fix it. Although both groups included members from a variety of backgrounds and occupations, the traditionalists were particularly diverse. They included the most conservative farmers—oftentimes, although by no means always, the smaller ones—as well as urban journalists, politicians, and reformers who had never plowed a field.[10] What held this motley group together was a vision of the New England countryside as a stronghold of the rural republican values of universal manual labor, egalitarianism, thrift, and a deep and abiding attachment to the land.[11] The traditionalists believed those values had been established in the region by the Puritan settlers and handed down to their descendants, the rural Yankee folk. Yet, according to the traditionalists, the moral fiber of the rural Yankees was now being eroded by the city, particularly when it came to their attitudes toward labor, consumption, and mobility. The traditionalists hoped to save the countryside by staving off the influence of the city and reviving the republican lifestyles and values of their ancestors.

The traditionalists' diagnosis of the crisis in rural New England was rejected by the region's progressive farmers, a group that included agricultural professors at the region's colleges and the wealthiest, most entrepreneurial farmers. Although they, too, were convinced that the revival of rural New England called for a return to core values, they defined those values diametrically opposite from the traditionalists. The progressive farmers embraced agrarian capitalism and the higher living standards, greater risks, and larger profits that went with it.[12] Urging agriculturalists to think of themselves as "business farmers" and "agricultural entrepreneurs," they advocated a variety of reforms to make agriculture more lucrative, including expanded operations, more hired labor, scientific methods, the latest implements, and the strategic abandonment of marginal farmland. They also rejected the traditionalists' hostility to the city, calling for more, not less, integration between the markets and cultures of rural and urban New England. The progressive farmers even crafted an image of the Puritans as risk-taking "men of progress" to serve as suitable forebears.[13]

Despite their many ideological and social differences, there was one way in which the traditionalists and progressive farmers strongly resembled each other. Both groups relied heavily on the figure of the immigrant to define what it meant—and did not mean—to be a rural New Englander. Yet neither the traditionalists nor the progressive farmers could agree among themselves about the proper relation of the foreign born to their regional ideals. Some members of both groups viewed immigrants in straightforward nativist fashion, constructing them as derided Others to their notion of a rural New Englander. But, in a surprising number of cases, both traditionalists and progressive farmers hailed the foreign born as better embodiments of rural New England values than the Yankees themselves. Their motives for doing this are often hard to fathom. Some seemed to be trying to shame Yankee backsliders back into the path of virtue. Others appeared genuinely convinced that the foreign born were better prospects for reviving rural New England than the Yankees. Yet, whatever their motivations, the traditionalists and progressive farmers who hailed Irish, French Canadian, Swedish, and Polish immigrants as saviors of the countryside helped contribute to the new pluralist ideas about regional identity that were emerging in New England at the end of the century. Those ideas had potential implications far beyond the region. After all, if rural New England—that legendary stronghold of Puritan values and Anglo-Saxon bloodlines—could keep its distinctive character while welcoming immigrants, then what place couldn't?

"Work, Work, Work"

Most traditionalists and progressive farmers agreed that farm labor lay at the center of many of rural New England's difficulties. Both groups recognized that the nature of farm labor and the class and ethnic backgrounds of those who did it had undergone seismic changes since the early nineteenth century. Those transformations have been widely discussed by historians, who demonstrate that the social status of farm laborers dropped throughout the rural North in the middle decades of the century. This was largely a function of changes in the farm labor work force and the capital requirements of farming. In the early nineteenth century, farm laborers (males were called "hired hands" or "help"; females were "hired girls," "helpers," or "help") were usually young, single, native-born males and females who worked for wages to support their parents' farms or to provide for their own future in the form of a dowry or a payment on farmland. They were often employed on seasonal or temporary terms, as farmers hired additional hands to help with haying or harvest, and farmwives employed more help when there was a birth, illness, or death in the family, as well as during the summer busy season when those extra hired men had to be fed. These young workers were generally treated as social equals by their employers, especially when, as was often the case, they were relatives or neighbors. Hired hands and helpers generally worked at the same tasks, ate at the same table, slept under the same roof, and sat in the same pew as the families of their employers. In most cases shared bonds of class, ethnicity, community, and religion led farm families to view their hands and helpers as members of the family. One sure sign of those bonds are the many reports of hired men who married the farmer's daughter.[14]

Yet, by the middle of the nineteenth century, farmers could no longer rely on their own children and those of their neighbors to fill their labor needs. As rural New England youth increasingly migrated to cities, factory towns, and the West, their places were taken by a new breed of farm laborers, who differed from their predecessors in several key ways. First, these latter-day farm laborers were poorer, often drawn from a class of landless workers that would expand as property distribution patterns in older settlements became increasingly unequal. Second, they were older. Unlike early nineteenth-century hands and helpers, for whom wage labor was often a step toward becoming a farmer or farmwife, their successors often spent decades or even their entire lives working for others. The agricultural ladder proved a fairy tale for most of these new laborers, who found it increasingly difficult to accumulate enough savings to buy a farm. In contrast to their young, unmarried predecessors, the midcentury farm laborers were often married with children. They comprised what one historian has called a "more permanent agricultural proletariat" than their predecessors.[15] Third, farm laborers were increasingly likely to be immigrants. The unprecedented waves of newcomers arriving from Europe and Canada permanently changed the face of farm labor.[16] That was particularly true in New England, where the foreign born would come to dominate the farm labor work force in some districts. After the Civil War, as before it, the largest group of non-Yankee farm laborers was Irish, but, as the decades passed, the Irish were increasingly joined by workers from other ethnic groups. By 1900 the Irish, English Canadians, and French Canadians were the largest contingents of agricultural laborers in the region, but the Poles, Scandinavians, British, and Germans were also heavily represented.[17]

In sum Gilded Age agricultural laborers were far more vulnerable to exploitation than their predecessors had been, and farmers made them feel their inferiority in ways both large and small. Some farmers and their wives now forced domestic employees to submit to the title of "servant" and treated them as menials (though many rural domestic laborers—both native born and immigrant—managed to retain the title and status of "helper"), and they increasingly referred to their male employees as "labor" rather than the more egalitarian "help."[18] One Massachusetts commentator observed that many farmers preferred to hire immigrants because they could be paid less and were "satisfied to be regarded as servants," whereas "the natives are likely to be exacting and very independent."[19] Perhaps most tellingly, both farmers and their employees complained that the latter were no longer treated with the respect they once enjoyed. One Connecticut agriculturalist mused, "Why then the laborer himself should receive so little true consideration from those who employ him upon the farm, I am at a loss to explain. It would seem, in numerous instances, as though he was from the beginning to the end of his service nothing more than a free slave, a drudge, to be fed and lodged, and worked to the limit of his ability."[20] The question was not whether farm laborers were disrespected—almost everyone agreed they were—but whether they deserved it or not. One's answer to this question depended on one's opinion both of the native-born youth who were abandoning farm labor and of the older immigrants who, in many cases, were replacing them.

The sharpening class divisions between farmers and their employees were controversial throughout the rural North, but nowhere more so than in New England. There the traditionalists and progressive farmers debated the significance of the changing status of farm labor for the region and the nation as a whole. For their part, traditionalists viewed the growing class divide as a threat to New England's rural republican values. Convinced that universal manual labor lay at the center of those values, they worried that many Yankees, particularly those of the younger generation, now saw farm work as beneath them. In contrast, the progressive farmers were much more sanguine about the widening class divide. Rejecting the traditionalists' moralizing view of farm work, the progressive farmers urged the agriculturalist to think of manual labor as just another expense in his ledger, rather than a source of values for his family. Some progressive farmers even constructed the agriculturalist's identity over against the farm laborer. They believed rural New England needed a class of subordinate workers to boost the profits and social status of its farmers.

Most traditionalists saw the worsening class divide on New England's farms as a function not of structural changes in the region's labor force and land distribution patterns but of the moral failings of its inhabitants.

If farm labor no longer got the respect it deserved, the fault lay with the people rather than the social and economic systems in which they lived and worked. Yet the traditionalists disagreed about which people were primarily to blame. One camp blamed the Yankees—particularly those of the younger generation—accusing them of abandoning farm work out of an aristocratic contempt for manual labor. Another camp faulted immigrant farm workers, charging them with giving manual labor a bad name through their ignorance, laziness, and incompetence. But no matter whom they blamed for the decaying status of farm labor, all traditionalists believed the primary victims were the rural Yankees, who seemed to be paying a moral and physical price for breaking with their ancestors' tradition of honest labor.

The traditionalists who accused rural Yankees of aristocratic attitudes toward manual labor were themselves divided over the source of those attitudes. Some fulminated against farmers who refused to "work, work, work" as long and hard as their ancestors or who hired laborers when they were perfectly capable of doing the work themselves.[21] While most traditionalists favored the new labor-saving machines—including mowers, horse rakes, and sulky plows—that had revolutionized farming since midcentury, some worried that they were encouraging a spirit of idleness in the region's agriculturalists. They thought a farmer with too much time on his hands was likely to fall into bad habits and neglect his farm.[22] Others believed the problem lay with dissatisfied farmwives who refused to support their husbands' efforts.[23]

But most traditionalists presented the Yankee farmer and his wife as victims rather than villains in the story of manual labor's declining status. They warned of aging farmers who had to give up their farms and farmwives who were worn out or even worked to death, all for want of good help. The culprits in these sad tales were often the Yankee farmer's children, who refused to soil their hands with honest labor. Connecticut agriculturalist L. F. Scott told of an old farmer in Litchfield who had been devastated by the departure of his three sons: "The old man sits in his arm-chair, with the tears running down his furrowed cheeks in torrents, as he exclaims: 'Joseph is not, and Simeon is not, and will ye take Benjamin away also?'"[24] Newport, Vermont, editor D. M. Camp warned that the idea "that manual labor is degrading" was bringing forth "a noble fruitage of dudes and dudees in the region."[25] The traditionalists disagreed about where the younger generation had acquired its alleged contempt for manual labor, variously blaming the schools, the influence of the upper class, and overindulgent parents, but they all agreed that such sentiments were one of the primary threats to the region's survival.[26]

Traditionalists believed young Yankees sacrificed both virtue and health when they abandoned farm work for nonmanual pursuits. Convinced that manual labor was an ideal school of character, the traditionalists drew a moral distinction between members of the rising generation of Yankees and their predecessors, who allegedly owed their success in life to the values they acquired on the farm.[27] Like the Puritans before them, the traditionalists held that it was the very difficulty of manual labor that made it so morally beneficial. They invoked the example of the region's settlers, whose back-breaking toil supposedly had turned them into exemplary men and women. D. M. Camp acknowledged that the settlers of his state had suffered much, "And yet out of that very discipline came the strongest, noblest men and women the state has ever seen—not educated, not cultivated, not refined as to day [*sic*], but healthy, happy, and noble in character and life."[28] He warned farmers not to shield their children from manual labor in an effort to make their lives easier. The best parents were those who submitted their children to the same discipline of toil that had ennobled and strengthened their ancestors.

The traditionalists insisted that the abandonment of manual labor was also taking a physical toll on the Yankee farmers' children. They believed the primary victim was the farmer's daughter. Echoing the medical moralists discussed in chapter 3, the traditionalists warned that young Yankee females endangered their health when they abandoned domestic labor. Addressing a Connecticut agricultural meeting, L. F. Scott thundered, "*Satan. . . .* is telling our daughters that it is degrading to go into the kitchen and help their mothers do the necessary work of the household, a work which God evidently designed woman to perform, by adapting woman to the work, and adapting the work for the woman."[29] He contrasted these idle daughters with their ancestors, who pulled flax, spun tow, and enjoyed "contentment and rosy cheeks, such are seldom seen at the present day."[30] Some traditionalists recommended that the farmer's daughter restore her health through exercise, but far more recommended housework.[31] The latter remedy had the additional benefit of lifting the burden from the overworked farmwife.

While many traditionalists believed the Yankee farmers' children could be persuaded to return to the field and kitchen, others were more pessimistic. The latter sometimes predicted that the younger generation's contempt for manual labor would lead to an immigrant takeover of rural New England. After scolding the rising generation of Yankees for its refusal to do manual labor, L. F. Scott claimed that "about one-half our farmers would sell their farms to-day if they could, but there are few buyers except the foreign element, and that is destined to own and control this country—not a very bright picture." He maintained that the only way to keep the farms of New England out of immigrant hands was "*retrenchment;* go back as far as practicable to the well-trodden paths of our worthy ancestors."[32]

But other traditionalists countered that the best way to return to "the well-trodden paths of our worthy ancestors" was to hand rural New England over to the immigrants. They contended that, when it came to their attitudes toward manual labor, it was the foreign born who best resembled the Puritans. In 1884 literary lion James Russell Lowell observed, "Irish peasants are buying up the worn-out farms of Massachusetts, and making them productive again by the same virtues of industry and thrift that once made them profitable to the English ancestors of the men who are deserting them."[33] Massachusetts politician John D. Long also believed immigrants were taking up the Puritans' work ethic along with their farms. Contributing to an 1891 *New England Magazine* symposium titled "The Future of the New England Country," the ex-governor predicted that the region's countryside would soon experience a revival, thanks in large measure to the immigrant farmers who were taking the place of the departing Yankees: "[O]ur citizens of foreign birth are seeking and have sought the New England farms, and are there going through the experiences which made our own ancestors self-supporting farmers," such as "raising large families of boys and girls, and keeping them at work indoors and out of doors, at home." For Long it was the experience of building a family farm in New England—not the ethnic background of the farmer—that brought out the traditional virtues of the rural New Englander. The Yankees might be turning their backs on farm work, but as long as immigrant families were willing to submit to the rigors of rural life, the republican values of the countryside seemed safe. Long conceded that the immigrants were bringing changes to the region, particularly in its ethnic and religious complexion: "It will be a different life from that of a generation or two ago. It will be, not a unique, but a conglomerate population. It will not be of one faith, but of many faiths." Yet balancing these changes was the comforting resemblance the immigrants bore to Long's hardworking rural Yankee ancestors. It was that promise of continuity amid all the changes that allowed him to conclude, "There is no fear for the future of New England rural life."[34]

Another camp of traditionalists scoffed at the idea that immigrants were reviving respect for manual labor in rural New England. These nativist traditionalists blamed immigrant farm laborers for degrading the very idea of farm work through their ignorance, shiftlessness, and incompetence. They argued that the region had betrayed its egalitarian ideals—and sacrificed the republican influence it had formerly exerted over the rest of the nation—by importing a mudsill class. The nativist traditionalists also worried about the effects of a degraded immigrant laboring class on the children of the Yankee farmers. They maintained that young Yankees were learning to think of manual labor as beneath them and thereby losing out on the moral and physical benefits of honest work. Yet the nativist traditionalists generally did not blame the young Yankees for eschewing manual labor. At a time when it was increasingly coming to be seen as "immigrant work," they sympathized with those who avoided it.

In 1888 Geoffrey Champlin warned of the eroding status of farm labor in an essay published in the *North American Review* titled "The Decline of New England." He believed one of the chief causes of the region's decay was the class divide that had emerged between farmers and their hired help: "The equality which once existed between man and man—between employer and employé—has been changed: there are fewer 'help' and more 'servants.'" Champlin reminisced about the "good old days" forty years earlier when everyone did manual labor and class differences were minimal: "[W]e can recall how men and women labored without their labor lowering them in the social scale or preventing the development of their mental powers, how the squire left the scythe in the field while he leaned on the fence and talked about crops, or investments, or the latest political news, to the farmer or the farmer's hired man." Champlin partly blamed the new stratification on "rich and idle" summer visitors who undermined the republican values of the countryside, but he also fingered immigrant farm laborers. He argued that the foreign-born workers brought their Old World degradation with them: "[H]owever worthy the foreign laborer may be, something of his former state of servitude still lingers about him and humiliates him into a lower caste than the descendants of the former tillers of the soil."[35]

For most nativist traditionalists, however, it was not the foreign-born laborers' past degradation but their present inadequacies that marked them as socially inferior. The nativist traditionalists justified their retreat from egalitarianism by detailing the various ways immigrant farm laborers failed to measure up to their Yankee predecessors. They reminisced about the skill, independence, intelligence, and self-respect of the old-time Yankee hired men and female helpers, and they shuddered at the clumsiness, ignorance, and servility of their foreign-born replacements. Many nativist traditionalists frankly announced that immigrant laborers did not deserve the respect accorded their predecessors. In an era of immigrants, it no longer made sense to treat farm laborers as equals.[36]

Yet, while they agreed that immigrant laborers deserved to be treated as second-class citizens, most nativist traditionalists felt uneasy about doing so. Like Geoffrey Champlin, many saw the introduction of a foreign-born mudsill class as a repudiation of rural New England's republican values. They reminisced about the "good old days" when the region still stood for universal manual labor. Some nativist traditionalists also worried about the effects of an immigrant laboring class on the values and health of the rising generation of rural Yankees. In 1857 a writer in the *New England Farmer* warned that the widespread employment of "ignorant foreign help" on the region's farms was turning young Yankees away from manual labor: "The younger members of the family, especially, are growing up with the idea that the . . . harder and more unpleasant part of the labor, which is done by Irish help, is unsuitable for them, is a degradation; and they learn to despise it."[37] The author claimed that the employment of immigrant farm laborers was also taking a physical toll on Yankee females: "The health of our females has deteriorated since spinning and weaving have been given up, and the labors of the kitchen and dairy have been transferred to foreign females."[38] Such warnings would multiply over the following decades, as nativist traditionalists painted the region's growing cohort of immigrant farm laborers as a major threat to the health and/or values of young Yankees. In 1874 New Hampshire politician Warren Brown wistfully recalled the days when hiring out was a rite of passage for rural Yankee youth:

> Many a young man who started in life as a farm laborer has arrived at wealth, and filled important and responsible positions of trust in the state and nation. The habits of industry, economy, and sobriety, learned and practised [*sic*] on the farms, were the groundwork of their success in life. If the young men of the present day began life with the correct habits, industry, and patience of those who have preceded them. . . . [w]e should not find in every paper cases of fraud and embezzlement, and the long list of crimes which result from an attempt to live without honest labor.[39]

Rather than blame his young Yankee contemporaries for straying off the farm into a life of crime, Brown reserved his ire for their immigrant replacements, whom he found "ignorant, unskilled," "incompetent," "idle," "dishonest," and sometimes "immoral."[40] Brown clearly believed foreign-born farm workers had degraded agricultural labor as an occupation. Thus, he didn't blame Yankee youth for rejecting it. Brown held out hope that, with better pay and working conditions, farmers might attract a better class of laborers, but he seemed reconciled to the fact that they would not be Yankees. Despite his best effort to keep a stiff upper lip about the changing work force, he could not resist reminiscing about the days when Yankee youth built strong muscles and strong characters on the region's farms: "To us of the present day those times seem a paradise."[41]

"*Study* More and *Toil* Less"

Another group of commentators on rural New England remained unruffled by the widening social and economic divisions between farmers and their laborers. Indeed, the region's progressive farmers advocated practices that were calculated to increase that stratification. Refusing to see universal manual labor as a regional ideal, the progressive farmers believed rural New England stood for agrarian capitalism. They called on farmers to unlock the full economic potential of their farms by thinking of themselves not as manual workers but as capitalists who purchased and managed the labor of others. Denying the moral and physical benefits of manual labor, the progressive farmers encouraged agriculturalists to view it in strictly economic terms. While few of the region's husbandmen were willing or able free themselves from all physical toil, many did take steps to separate themselves from farm laborers. This was particularly true in their treatment of their employees, whom they increasingly fed and housed apart from their own families. While such segregation obviously violated rural New England's strong egalitarian traditions, it became easier to justify in an era of immigrant farm labor. Many progressive farmers insisted that the new class of farm laborers did not deserve the respect accorded to its predecessor.

Like the traditionalists, the progressive farmers called on New England agriculturalists to respect regional values regarding manual labor, but the progressive farmers had a different conception of those values. The rural New England they valorized was a land not of universal manual labor but of "business farmers" and their hired employees. The progressive farmers urged agriculturalists to live up to this regional ideal by hiring more labor and expanding their operations. In 1856 Professor J. A. Nash demanded, "Will New England farmers be true to themselves, and to the old cradle of American liberty? Never has the encouragement for farmers to hire labor, put their land to producing, and go ahead, been as good as now."[42] The call for larger farms and more hired labor would be regularly sounded by progressive farmers in the decades after the Civil War, many of whom believed the Yankee agriculturalist had grown too risk averse.[43] Progressive farmers disagreed about whether that conservatism stemmed from out-migration (which supposedly winnowed away the most ambitious and aggressive farmers), the force of habit, or the Yankee farmer's diet of pork and corn, but they all hoped he would overcome it.[44] Professor J. W. Sanborn complained that the region's farmers had "narrowed and narrowed the farm operations, until relatively less capital and less labor were employed upon them than in old times." He saw such retrenchment as a betrayal of "our stalwart ancestry, who bravely cleared our fields, erected our homes . . . and transmitted to the sons capital to continue them."[45] By hiring more labor, New England's farmers would recover the capitalist spirit of the Puritans.

In calling for agriculturalists to use more hired labor, the progressive farmers primarily were trying to make New England farming more profitable. They argued that many of the region's farms were simply too small to generate sufficient revenue: farmers needed to expand their operations by buying land, investing in machinery, and hiring more labor. The progressive farmers sneered at the modest ambitions captured in a popular song celebrating the farmer's happiness as "A little farm well tilled / A little wife well willed."[46] In fact, proclaimed farmer and businessman Joseph B. Walker, "an enterprising New England husbandman, worthy of his blood and of generous soul, wants a good-sized wife and a good-sized farm; with fruitfulness within doors and fruitfulness without."[47]

Even with the new labor-saving implements, a big farm still required lots of labor, and the progressive farmers urged husbandmen to hire it. True, some spoke of using the new machines to free the farmer from dependence on "the caprices and exactions of those whose aid he would otherwise be obliged to secure at any price, and upon almost any conditions."[48] But most progressive farmers understood that even the best-equipped agriculturalist would still need employees, and the bigger the farm, the greater the need. In an era of high labor costs, this would require significant capital, a fact that some progressive farmers frankly acknowledged. They urged farmers to be bold and creative in finding new sources of financing, for example, by taking on partners or seeking investors. They assured farmers that the economies of scale they would achieve by expanding their operations would more than cover their increased costs of financing, machinery, and labor.[49]

The progressive farmers also advocated hiring additional labor in order to free the farmer for more productive nonmanual work such as bookkeeping, keeping up with the agricultural press, and managing the labor of others. Underscoring their own commitment to what some derided as "book farming," progressive farmers urged farmers to "*study* more and *toil* less."[50] They promised that farmers would increase their profits if they spent less time in "wasteful" manual labor and more time keeping up with the stream of publications emanating from agricultural experiment stations, state agricultural boards, and the agricultural press. Observing, "It pays to 'hire hands' and save a head, on a farm," a speaker at a Connecticut agriculture board meeting presented hired labor as the key to gaining time for the farmer to educate himself.[51]

In urging the agriculturalist to avoid manual labor, the progressive farmers also hoped to elevate his social status. Convinced that farmers no longer received the respect they deserved from mainstream society, the progressive farmers believed much of the problem lay in the popular association of farming with mindless drudgery.[52] Their solution was to limit the farmer's association with manual labor and those who did it. This partly explains the progressive farmers' enormous enthusiasm for farm machinery. J. W. Sanborn underscored the enhanced esteem that came with the new technology, "Our genteel driver in fresh spirits, as he rides his fertilizer distributer, doing better work than by hand . . . revolves in his mind with pride the increasing ease and dignity of farming."[53] Fertilizer distributors and other modern implements would become status symbols as a gap opened between farmers who could afford the new equipment and those who couldn't.[54] Machinery manufacturers encouraged implement envy among farmers with ads featuring prosperous-looking agriculturalists perched masterfully on the latest equipment (figure 7).

Progressive farmers also sought to boost the agriculturalist's social status by elevating him above his employees. They celebrated the growing class divide between farmers and their hired help. J. W. Sanborn argued that simply by hiring more labor the farmer automatically enhanced his status: "[I]n working capitalized lands, the farmer is made more of a capitalist and less of a laborer; employing more labor makes the farmer more of an executive or business man."[55] In 1899 a progressive farmer writing in the *Nation* argued that the widening class gulf in rural New England confronted the agriculturalist with a choice: "He may accept the new conditions and become himself a landed proprietor and agricultural *entrepreneur* on the new scale, or he may resign his independence and become a hired man."[56] A few progressive farmers believed the gap between farm owners and laborers would continue to expand until much of New England's farmland had passed into the hands of absentee urban owners. These proprietors would leave the day-to-day operation of their farms to a class of college-educated managers, "men who themselves never swung a scythe or held a plough."[57]

Granted, most progressive farmers did not want to see agrarian capital-

Fig. 7. Bullard Improved Hay Tedder advertising card. (Courtesy of the Special Collections Department, Iowa State University Library.)

ism taken this far, but they did believe that agriculturalists should treat their employees just as manufacturers and merchants treated theirs. Above all this meant maintaining a clear separation between employer and employee. At an 1887 Connecticut Board of Agriculture meeting, a "Mr. Cables" insisted that drawing the class line was the key to a smooth-running farm.[58] Like many farmers in the region, he employed immigrants hired through employment agencies in New York City. (By the end of the century, farmers could "order" the number of foreign-born workers they desired—and even request a specific nationality—by filling out a form and sending it to one of the many employment agencies in the city.)[59] Cables declared that he had discovered the secret to managing his immigrant workers, "if you hire this class of men, there is one thing you must not do. Don't go out into the field with them to work. If I put myself on a level with this foreign class of men I don't get any work done when I am not in the field, but if you put one of their own class ahead you will have no trouble."[60] Cables urged farmers to preserve their authority by relying on an immigrant foreman to supervise the laborers in the fields.

Many progressive farmers also urged agriculturalists to maintain a distance from their employees in their homes. Most obviously, this meant that laborers were no longer viewed as "one of the family." Progressive farmers increasingly called for laborers to be housed in tenements or boardinghouses away from the farmer's household.[61] As Sally McMurry has shown, progressive farmers justified this segregation as a means both of easing the burden on the farmwife and of protecting the privacy of the farmer's family.[62] McMurry argues that progressive farmers designed their homes with an eye toward isolating their families from their employees. Unlike their antebellum predecessors, Gilded Age progressive farmers who published plans for farmhouses took pains to protect the family's private living spaces from the public rooms that received outsiders.[63]

Given that many progressive farmers and their wives had once hired out themselves, the hardening class divisions on New England's farms made them feel defensive, but they insisted that the present generation of immigrant workers did not deserve the same respect as their Yankee predecessors.[64] In a speech at an 1883 Connecticut agricultural board meeting, educator and former hired man L. P. Chamberlain critiqued farmers for their lack of sympathy toward their employees.[65] In response two farmers in the audience spoke in favor of keeping one's distance from the help. A "Mr. Hyde" explained that things had changed since the days when Chamberlain had hired out:

> Whom does the farmer employ for his help to-day? Is it the class of men whom he would employ twenty years ago—men whom he wants to take into his family? Why, it has been said, and I think very justly, the farm laborer is often a foreigner, perfectly ignorant of the business which we entrust to him, and probably of the domestic relations. It is a very grave question whether a man wants to hug one of them to his bosom as a companion.[66]

A "Mr. Sedgwick" agreed that laborers belonged in boardinghouses or tenements, rather than the farmer's house:

> What do you want to board your men in your family for? A hired man can board himself cheaper than you can do it, and you have all the trouble and annoyance of having a sweaty, perspiring man at your table, when you don't want him. If you have company, you can't have such a man as that at the table with them, and you feel sort of disagreeable about it.[67]

Such open expressions of contempt for farm laborers suggest how much things had changed on many New England farms since the day when the hired man was often a neighbor or relative. Sounding like the nativist traditionalists, many progressive farmers attacked immigrant laborers as ignorant incompetents who bore little resemblance to the Yankee hired help of old.[68]

Yet, unlike the nativist traditionalists, the progressive farmers did not worry about the moral effects of immigrant farm labor on their children. Rejecting the view of manual labor as school of character, some progressive farmers celebrated young Yankees who abandoned it for nonmanual occupations. In response to the eternal question—"How shall we keep our boys on the farm?"—one writer defiantly proclaimed, "We ought to be profoundly thankful, considering what the farm now is as a business, that we can not keep them there."[69] To be sure, most progressive farmers were deeply disturbed by the hemorrhaging of young people from rural New England, but they believed the lion's share of the blame lay with the farmer rather than his children. The progressive farmers charged Yankee agriculturalists with driving off their offspring by working them too hard, paying them too little, and denying them the comforts of a middle-class home.[70]

The progressive farmers had even more sympathy for farmwives, whom they saw as the primary victims of severe farm labor. As Sally McMurry has pointed out, the burdens on farmwives probably grew after the Civil War due to rising standards of housekeeping and the increased use of male farm labor.[71] Many farmwives were still tasked with housing and feeding the help, as well taking care of their own families. Progressive farmers sought to relieve overworked farmwives by urging farmers to hire more domestic help and stop boarding their hands. They appealed to the farmers' sympathies with stories of old-fashioned agriculturalists who worked their wives to the point of death or insanity—New England insane asylums were rumored to be filled with farmwives—by overrelying on family labor.[72]

Yet, for most progressive farmers, the chief embodiment of backward attitudes about farm labor was not the old-fashioned Yankee farmer but the stereotypical European peasant. Whereas the progressive farmer replaced human labor with modern machines, the peasant still used hand tools. Whereas the progressive farmer sought to free his family from severe toil, the peasant worked his wife and small children in the fields. And whereas the progressive farmer used as much hired labor as possible, the peasant avoided it at all costs. In short the peasant was the embodiment of the grinding, mind-numbing, exploitative toil that the progressive farmers were trying to rise above. In the course of urging New England farmers to use more machinery, J. W. Sanborn declared, "I do not call any farming successful that puts wooden shoes on to the manager like a French peasant with his 10 acres and hand tools."[73] Other progressive farmers insisted that the European peasant continued to display the same backward attitudes toward manual labor after he immigrated to the United States. They warned that a huge class of ignorant, foreign-born drudges were settling on the farmlands of the United States and working them with the most primitive, labor-intensive methods.[74] Some progressive farmers found amusing the immigrants' alleged overreliance on muscle. More than one speaker at an agricultural meeting likened such hard-toiling farmers to the Irish fiddler whom celebrity violinist Ole Bull supposedly encountered at a fair. When Bull asked the Hibernian musician whether he played by note or ear, he replied, "Be main strength, be jabbers."[75] But other progressive farmers saw nothing humorous about the immigrant farmer's dependence on main strength. They feared that his cost advantages would soon make farming unfeasible for anyone who was not a peasant or a native-born farmer willing to work like one.

Recent studies have shown that the stereotype of the immigrant farmer as a peasant drudge had little basis in fact. As Kathleen Neils Conzen points out, since the nineteenth century, most immigrant groups have "quickly accepted the logic of American settlement systems, crops, and farming methods. . . . [I]mmigrants who migrated to achieve economic security for their families found little reason to challenge the imperatives of environment and market."[76] While it is true that in other areas of their lives (e.g., religious beliefs, inheritance practices, social customs) rural immigrants often resisted local norms, when it came to their farming methods, they were only too eager to adopt them.[77] Indeed, by the turn of the century, some native-born observers in the Middle West considered immigrant agriculturalists to be more progressive and more willing to spend their money on expensive implements than were their "American" rivals.[78]

Back in New England, most Yankees were not ready to admit that an immigrant could be a progressive farmer, though a few were willing to consider the idea. That was the case in the Connecticut River valley, where the Poles were establishing a reputation as up-and-coming agriculturalists. After arriving in the valley in the 1880s as farm laborers, within two decades the Poles were successfully raising onions and tobacco on land they had purchased from departing Yankees.[79] Nativist commentators attacked the Polish farmer as a peasant invader who was driving out the Yankees by working his wife and small children in the fields, but more sympathetic Yankees demurred.[80] Writing in the *Smith College Monthly,* senior Elizabeth Stearns

Tyler argued that the typical Polish farmer of western Massachusetts "uses as up-to-date methods and implements as the American does."[81] While she conceded that Polish women still did field labor, she confidently predicted, "This drawback which . . . is shared by all European farming classes, will be done away with by education."[82] A reporter for the *Greenfield (MA) Gazette and Courier* agreed that the Polish farmers of his district were lifting themselves out of mindless drudgery. Although he expressed some anxiety that the Poles might become a "peasant class," he seemed fairly confident that they would not, declaring, "The Poles are progressive farmers and not afraid to spend money for machinery and improvements." He saw signs of their "enterprise and progressiveness" in their interest in the extension programming of the Massachusetts Agricultural College (which had recently held its second "Polish farmers' day") and in their judicious use of financing, writing, "As business men the Polish farmers have shown themselves superior to many native born tillers of the soil."[83]

Some writers seemed genuinely confused about whether the immigrant farmer was rising above manual labor or not. That appeared to be the case for Connecticut journalist Clarence Deming, whose 1903 article "Broken Shadows on the New England Farm" hopefully described "certain gleams that already have begun to break into the encircling gloom." Asserting that "the new elements passing to the farm are foreign," Deming cited two examples of those "elements" in an unnamed town in Connecticut.[84] The first was a Swede who had prospered on a tobacco and dairy farm, working it "by modern scientific methods" and employing two hired hands. The second was another Swede who had successfully reclaimed an "abandoned" farm nearby, "working sometimes continental fashion with his wife in the field." Having portrayed the immigrant agriculturalist as both progressive farmer and peasant drudge, Deming cast him in a third role: modern-day Puritan. He argued that the secret to success in New England agriculture was "old-fashioned industry, thrift and self-denial—the substitution of the old economy and hard work for a rule under which the ancestral farm luxuries have come to be classed as the necessities of to-day. The incoming foreigner who takes up the farm is simply going back to its ancestral conditions."[85] The immigrant, it should be noted, was "going back" to the farm's ancestral conditions, not his own. Echoing the traditionalists who hailed the industrious foreign-born farmer as the true heir of the Puritans, Deming suggested that the core values of rural New England—"industry, thrift, and self-denial"—would survive, even as its ethnic cast changed, for "the old blood flows out and the new blood flows in."[86] It is hard to know what to make of such traditionalist sentiments in an essay that pays homage to progressive farming. Deming may be genuinely uncertain, both about the kind of farming practices necessary to revive rural New England and about the immigrants' relation to those practices. In an era when both issues were hotly debated, it was easy to get confused.

"*Wife, Silk* and *Satin; Boy, Greek* and *Latin.*"

One aspect of rural New England about which there was no uncertainty was the rise in living standards. Both traditionalists and progressive farmers would have accepted Deming's claim that the luxuries of an earlier era "have come to be classed as the necessities of to-day." A series of Gilded Age marketing innovations—including nationally advertised brands, mail-order houses like Montgomery Ward and Sears, Roebuck, and large manufacturers employing armies of traveling salesmen—were rapidly filling the imaginations and homes of rural Americans with a host of new commodities. By the 1870s farmwives could use their sewing machines, store-bought fabrics, and Butterick patterns to imitate the latest styles of their city sisters.[87] The age of homespun seemed centuries, not decades, in the past. The rise of rural consumerism was particularly pronounced in rural areas with easy access to the city. That was the case in rural New England, where the spread of trolleys and improved roads hastened the integration of much of the countryside into the urban marketplace.

Yet, while everyone agreed that the consumerism was on the rise in rural New England, they sharply disputed its consequences for the region's farm families. On one side, the traditionalists condemned what they saw as an epidemic of extravagance among the rural Yankees. Convinced that the farmer's goal was a "competency" (aka "competence")—the golden mean between too much wealth and too little—they feared both the moral and economic effects of closer ties to the urban marketplace, and they called for a return to the spartan lifestyles that they associated with their Puritan ancestors. In contrast, the progressive farmers celebrated rural consumerism precisely because it promised to knit the region's farm families more tightly into the urban marketplace. They believed a rising rural living standard would spur agricultural reform and stanch the flow of young people to the city.

As in the case of their debate over farm labor, the traditionalists and progressive farmers were internally divided over the relation of immigrants to the countryside's rising living standards. Whereas some traditionalists believed the thrift and self-sacrifice of the region's foreign-born farm families made them the true heirs of the Puritans, others attacked the newcomers as sordid materialists who had all of the Puritans' austerity but none of the religious and cultural ideals that redeemed it. The progressive farmers were also split on the question of the immigrants' living standards. While many progressive farmers saw competition from hardscrabble foreign-born farm families as *the* major threat to the domestic comfort of rural Yankees, others argued that rural immigrants were rapidly improving their standard of living. Yet, wherever they came down on these questions, both traditionalists and progressive farmers agreed that immigrants had a crucial light to shed on the meaning of consumerism in rural New England.

Most traditionalists viewed the rising rural living standard as contrary to their normative attitudes toward wealth and consumption. Those attitudes were encapsulated in the concept of the competency, the ideal of economic moderation that dated back to the Puritans. A family with a competency had enough wealth to be financially independent, but not enough to be at risk of turning corrupt or autocratic. In an era of unprecedented inequalities of wealth—symbolized in those two new American social types, the robber baron and the tramp—competency harked to the nation's mythical past as a republic of independent freeholders. That was precisely the type of society that the traditionalists hoped to revive in rural New England.

Many traditionalists believed farming was the perfect occupation for a family seeking a competency. They liked the fact that if he worked hard, the farmer would probably never fall into the ranks of the dependent poor, but they were equally pleased that he would likely never become rich either. This led the traditionalists to protest the efforts of the progressive farmers to expand the region's farms. Some couched their protests as warnings against the corrupting influence of wealth.[88] After hearing progressive farmer Stephen L. Goodale call for larger farms at a Maine agricultural meeting, a member of his audience—who described himself as the owner of "a considerably large farm"—strongly objected, "I do not believe it to be true that a great property is desirable. A farmer who is worth five to ten thousand dollars is as well off as anybody in the world; he is well enough off, and if he aspires for more, he sometimes does that which is not right."[89] He warned farmers not to let their minds "run after fine carriages, and stylish horses and horse racing."[90] Other traditionalists believed farmers faced a comparable moral threat in the temptation to turn speculator, which seemed to carry a particular allure for the Yankees.[91] Whereas the speculator amassed vast sums overnight through luck, daring, and in many cases "questionable methods," the farmer slowly and steadily built his competency through honest labor and thrifty living.[92] And whereas the speculator often became "bankrupt in fortune and character," the farmer worked in a "safe and honorable business."[93] Indeed, the traditionalists believed that farming, if faithfully pursued, insulated one from the moral hazards surrounding more speculative and lucrative occupations: "Its moderate profits and hard labor do not allure speculators who overrun a good business."[94] Yet, as the traditionalists sadly conceded, even farmers who resisted the urge to get rich quickly still faced the temptation of living beyond their means. Many believed that the extravagance of the rural Yankees was making a mockery of their reputation for republican austerity. Some warned that consumerism was putting the financial well-being of the region's farms at risk. One cited an "honest, industrious farmer" who was "asked why he did not succeed better in his business relations. . . . His reply was, '*Wife, silk* and *satin; boy, Greek* and *Latin.*'"[95] Traditionalists frequently blamed the farmer's financial troubles on his free-spending children—sons who demanded not only expensive educations but also costly guns and watches, as well as daughters who insisted on the latest fashions.[96] Yet, in an era that saw an increasing "defeminization" of agriculture—with farmers taking over most production, including such traditional women's tasks as dairying and poultry keeping, and farmwives increasingly focused on housekeeping and consumption—most of the blame for extravagance inevitably fell on females.[97] What if, contrary to the song lyrics, the "little wife" was *not* "well willed"? Traditionalists warned of an escalating struggle between free-spending wives and hard-pressed farmers: "Soon the milk from the dairy has to be sold, then the cows, and finally the farm sold, and with it all their earthly happiness."[98] Traditionalists advised aspiring farmers to marry sensible young women who were prepared to work hard and live simply, not the spoiled daughters of fashion: "[T]he ball room is a poor place to choose a wife."[99]

The traditionalists saw extravagance as a danger not only to the farmer's pocketbook but also to the broader community in which he lived. They argued that high living infected rural communities with a spirit of rivalry, envy, and social pretension that was contrary to the region's republican ideals, and they reminisced about the simple days of yore, when a social gathering might take the form of an apple, spinning, or cornhusking bee: "The young people went to those bees many times in their home-spun—they saw each other as they *were.*"[100] The traditionalists viewed extravagance as particularly worrisome because of its contagiousness. Once one farm family took up fashionable ways, its neighbors were sure to follow. The *New*

England Farmer illustrated this emulative process in a parable titled "Labor and Luxury." It told of ten families that decide to form a farming community. All goes well for the first few years, as the farms thrive and the families use their growing wealth to educate their children and improve their standard of living. But things quickly deteriorate when some of the families visit "foreign cities, and imbibe a taste for display and luxury, and undertake to copy, at home, the style of living they have seen abroad." The families abandon farming for the fashionable pursuits of opera, elegant living, carriage riding, and fancy dressing. The effects are soon felt by their neighbors, who come to disdain farming and long for the high life. Eventually, the little "society" cannot feed itself and must pay high prices for food while its fields lie fallow. In an era when Americans faced rising food prices, the moral of the story was clear: "*An extravagant style of living*" left one vulnerable to the vagaries of the market.[101] To regain their independence, farmers needed to go back to producing more and consuming less.

While the *New England Farmer* blamed rural extravagance on the influence of "foreign cities," many traditionalists believed it was just as rampant in domestic ones. They warned that the runaway consumerism of the city had penetrated the countryside through a variety of means, including drummers who hawked shoddy luxury goods, magazines with fashion plates that made farmwives and daughters lust after expensive, impractical clothing, and—in an era when urbanites increasingly vacationed in the countryside—city tourists, whose luxury and idleness inspired envy in the natives: "The show, the glitter, the greater wealth of the new comers, create a disparity which humiliates or offends the old settlers, and they move away; while those who stay cannot escape the pernicious influence of a large and wealthy idle class."[102] In a controversial essay in the *Atlantic Monthly,* Boston journalist and reformer Alvan Sanborn spelled out the dangers of urban consumerism for the rural Yankees. Sanborn contended that "an exaggerated notion of the luxury and gentility of city life" was causing rural New Englanders to ape urban styles of clothing, home furnishings, house design, and housekeeping:

> If these attempts to put away old country fashions were genuine reachings out towards a higher life, there would be no good reason for deploring them; but they are so plainly mere affectations that they are thoroughly pernicious. The standards they are based upon are ready-made importations, not the natural and healthy outgrowth of rustic conditions.[103]

Sanborn's portrait of the rural Yankees as "hopelessly under the spell" of urban salesmen did not win him any friends in the New England countryside.[104] One respondent sarcastically described him as "a bright young man, who . . . writes for the Atlantic Monthly all sorts of things that aren't so, about New England rural life."[105] Yet many rural Yankees shared Sanborn's fear of the growing influence of urban consumerism over the countryside. Warning that "[f]armers and farmers' families are imitating more and more the habits and fashions and extravagances of city life," agriculturalist John F. French quoted a reporter who estimated that Maine farmers annually wasted fifty thousand dollars on shoddy "patent" appliances like churns and washing machines.[106] Another traditionalist condemned the free-spending ways farm boys learned from their city cousins, "I have heard farmers say that they about as lief bury a boy as to let him go to the city."[107]

Short of keeping their children away from the city, few traditionalists had any ideas about stemming rural extravagance. Many seemed resigned to the disappearance of the "plain living and high thinking" rural New Englander. Yet some traditionalists insisted that the old ways *were* being carried on, not by the Yankees but by the immigrants who were replacing them. They celebrated the region's foreign-born farm families for taking up the traditions of thrift and self-sacrifice that had been abandoned by the free-spending Yankees. Praising rural New England's immigrants, Alvan Sanborn declared, "They alone are willing and able to lead simple farm lives, such as the pioneers of the West or the original New England settlers lived. The native Americans are now too impatient, too extravagant, too proud, under the changed conditions, to be successful farmers."[108] Other observers agreed that it was the region's immigrants, rather than its Yankees, who were carrying on the Puritans' legacy of frugality and self-denial. New Hampshire governor Frank Rollins praised the "new stock" pouring into his state: "It has perhaps more of the spirit of our forefathers than the natives. I am sorry to say it, but I fear it is so. They are willing to make more sacrifices, work longer hours, live less expensively, and have more ambition, and they will succeed. . . . The new stock understands the principles of the fathers, the principle of sacrifice."[109] Echoing those who celebrated the immigrant farmers for their "Puritan" work ethic, these traditionalists declared the region's foreign-born farm families—not its Yankees—the true heirs of its seventeenth-century settlers.

Another camp of traditionalists strongly disagreed, finding nothing Puritan-like in New England's immigrant agriculturalists. They judged the region's French Canadians "easy-going" and "thriftless," a poor substitute for the "thrifty, public-spirited farmers who preceded them."[110] In contrast, they found the Poles thrifty, but for all the wrong reasons. The nativist traditionalists argued that the austerity of the Puritans had been motivated by their faith, whereas the Poles made thrift an end in itself. In a 1903 essay titled "The Pole in the Land of the Puritan," Edward Kirk Titus invoked that opposition to attack the Polish farmers of western Massachusetts. Titus admitted that the Pole did resemble his Puritan predecessor in some ways, for "the former possess[es] in marked degree physical endurance, industry, frugality—qualities very largely contributory to the material success of the latter in his original role as pioneer."[111] But, whereas the Puritan had been frugal, the Pole was downright miserly. Titus luridly wrote of elegant colonial homes now converted into cheap Polish boardinghouses and butcher shops where Polish men "hang about . . . like hungry dogs, and eagerly snap at some dusty or tainted neck or flank offered for two or three cents a pound."[112] Titus acknowledged that the Poles had contributed tremendously to the region's farm economy, but he was more struck by the damage they had done to its ideals: "In spite of many faults, the Puritan hitched his wagon to a star, but the Pole sees more pulling power in a bankbook, and his mind is fixed on things of the earth, earthy."[113] A Northampton journalist reached similar conclusions in a story on the Polish farmers in the neighboring towns. He agreed with Titus that the Poles had some qualities that strongly recalled the region's Puritan settlers, "Their indomitable courage and industry is comparable only to the pioneer spirit of the early settlers." But there was nothing Puritan-like in the Pole's scrimping domestic habits, for his "unsanitary and nomadic housekeeping is a world removed from the radiant old New England housewifery." After describing the lengths to which the Pole would go to fatten his bank account—sleeping eight to a bed, eating spoiled food—the reporter concluded that "his search for the dollar, which excludes almost every other interest, has little relation to Puritan ideals."[114] The Poles were giving plain living a bad name.

"The Rightful Demands of a Massachusetts Home"

On the other hand, not all rural New Englanders embraced austerity as an ideal for themselves or the region's agriculturalists. To the contrary, the progressive farmers saw the spread of rural consumerism as something to be applauded rather than attacked. They believed a higher standard of living had several key benefits. First, it forced the farmer to modernize his agricultural practices and become more attuned to the market to cover his rising domestic expenses. Second, it helped rural New England maintain the high standard of civilization that distinguished it from rival farming areas in other parts of the country. Third, it closed the gap between rural and urban lifestyles, thereby stemming the out-migration of young people.

But, while the progressive farmers saw a rising living standard as a feasible goal for Yankee agriculturalists, they were divided over whether it was attainable for immigrants. Many attacked foreign-born farmers as degraded peasants who lacked the desire and ability to live better. Those progressive farmers feared that competition from cheap-living peasants would force the Yankee farmers to descend to their level or get out of the business. But another camp of progressive farmers defended the immigrant agriculturalist as an ambitious striver who would soon equal or even surpass the living conditions of the Yankee. These writers believed the superior market orientation of the immigrant farmer made him the best hope for keeping the living standard high in rural New England.

Unlike the traditionalists, the progressive farmers saw rural New England's rising living standard as a benefit, rather than a burden, for the Yankee husbandman. They readily acknowledged that higher domestic expenses put pressure on the farmer to be more profitable, but most believed this was precisely what New England's agriculturalists needed. Observing that "there has never been a time in the history of New England farming when the standard of life on the farm was as high as it is to-day," returned native son Albert Gardner Robinson showed how this trend had impacted one progressive farmer in western Massachusetts.[115] He asked the man to compare his own machine-aided labors with the manual toil of his father. The farmer replied, "I work just as much and, in a way, just as hard. But it is an easier kind of work, and I get more out of it. I have to." Robinson explained that "the demands made upon him by the life of his generation made this increase imperative."[116] Another progressive farmer argued that the presence of one or two "well-ordered farms" could spur a similar rise in productivity in a whole community: "It costs more to live because one needs more in order to be satisfied. It seems clear that this upward pull . . . must in the near future cause a sharp rise of wages, and at the same time drive to the wall the small farmer whose ability or resources will not allow him to keep up."[117]

Faced with a higher cost of living, the farmer had two choices: make more money or quit. When the traditionalists proposed a third option—curtail consumption—the progressive farmers scornfully replied:

> It is often asserted that, if our farmers would live as frugally as our forefathers did, they might accumulate money. They have no right to be content with any such mode of living. This is an age of progress in the things that contribute to man's well-being; the farmer not only has a right to a place in the procession, but should demand it.[118]

Equally defiant, another progressive declared, "I have no patience with the advice to farmers to be economical. We want to see no economy for farmers that others do not practice."[119] Whereas traditionalists valued farming in part because it enforced thrift on rural households, progressive farmers wanted farm families to consume just as much as their prosperous urban cousins.

The heat with which the progressive farmers rejected the call to economize suggests how much was at stake in the issue. The progressive farmers believed the farmer had a moral obligation to his calling, his region, and his family to keep up with the general rise in living standards. Worried that the social status of their vocation was eroding, they warned farmers not to fall behind other occupations: "The car of progress is on the track and going at a rate of speed never before realized. We have our choice to keep pace with it or be crushed by it."[120] Also at issue was the reputation of New England. The progressive farmers prided themselves on the high level of civilization in their region's countryside. They often cited the cultural and material amenities of rural New England—its comfortable homes, good schools, and proximity to the city—as its chief advantage over other regions with longer growing seasons and better soils.[121] But penny-pinching farmers negated these advantages when they cut their living expenses to the bone. Finally, the progressive farmers believed that the agriculturalist had a moral obligation to his family to provide a comfortable lifestyle. Reversing the traditionalists' preachments, the progressive farmers argued that the real danger in rural New England was not extravagance but miserliness, and they condemned farmers who fattened their bank accounts and farms by pinching their families. Such farmers were rightly served when their children departed for the city.[122] The progressive farmers argued that any farmer worth his salt cheerfully provided his family with the domestic comforts it demanded, while viewing the rising costs as an incentive to greater innovation and effort. The idea was to make *and spend* more money.

As supporters of rural consumerism, the progressive farmers looked fondly on the city, which provided the countryside with both a dazzling array of new consumer goods and a culture increasingly oriented around buying them. Many took heart in the belief that living standards in rural New England were rapidly approaching urban levels.[123] The progressive farmers rejected the traditionalists' fears of what urban consumerism was doing to rural youth. Whereas the traditionalists sought to lessen the contact between rural youth and the city, the progressive farmers strived to increase it.[124] Agricultural science professor Charles S. Phelps explained:

> The contact of the younger generation with the life of the city is making new and more progressive methods of living almost a necessity. To-day, on many farms, the "best room" is none too good for the family. Musical instruments are found in a large proportion of the country homes; a daily paper, some of the best magazines, and often the leading novel of the day are not uncommon.[125]

Rather than attacking the younger generation for its self-indulgence and extravagance, the progressive farmers praised it for elevating the culture and comfort of the region's farmhouses. They believed domestic life in rural New England would continue to improve as the farmers' children learned more about the consumer styles and cultural opportunities of the city.

But many progressive farmers worried that the standard of living on New England farms was more likely to fall than to rise. While they blamed a number of culprits—declining grain prices, rising taxes, out-migration—their favorite scapegoat was the immigrant farmer, whose bare-bones lifestyle made him a formidable competitor to those who aspired to more comfort and culture. Some progressive farmers feared that the Yankee agriculturalist would soon be faced with the agonizing choice of descending to the immigrant farmer's level or giving up farming altogether. But others insisted that, despite his modest beginnings, the immigrant farmer was already doing his part to lift the standard of living in rural New England.

Among progressive farmers who considered the cheap-living "foreign" farmer a threat, there was a debate about whether he was even present in New England. Some saw him as an external menace who endangered the Yankee farmer from overseas or the West. Physician and progressive farmer George Austin Bowen warned that the Yankee farmer was engaged in a global competition against "degraded and low-priced labor" from South America, Australia, and Russia. He predicted that if American agriculture were not protected from these external threats, "we shall see it passing into such hands as are carrying it on in other parts of the world, a debased, spiritless peasantry."[126] Other progressive farmers believed the peasants were already menacing the Yankees from within the United States. They described a regional struggle between old-stock New Englanders and foreign-born westerners. Convinced that the latter had several unfair advantages in their favor—free land, cut-rate rail freights, virgin soils—these progressive farmers were particularly incensed by the newcomers' scrimping lifestyle. Charles A. Mills described it as an unfair fight, "matching the expenses of the rudest and simplest mode of living against the rightful demands of a Massachusetts home."[127] Yale agriculture professor William H. Brewer saw the conflict in even starker terms, pitting the "comfortable, and even luxurious" homes of rural New England against the sordid hovels of the West.[128] Insisting that "[a]griculture in New England is the most strictly American vocation left here," Brewer believed the Yankee farmers were endangered by the cheap-living immigrants of the West: "These foreign peasants, like a cloud of locusts, have settled on American land . . . in many ways lowering the average level of farm life."[129] He warned that if something were not done soon, all American farmers—including those in New England—would be depressed into a peasant class.[130] Claiming (inaccurately) that the US government maintained the standard of living of nonfarm laborers by excluding immigrant competitors, Brewer asked for the same protection for farmers.[131] In the meantime, he took some comfort in the thought that, as the last of the free lands were being taken up, the western "peasant" was losing one of his unfair advantages.[132] While Brewer believed the cheap-living immigrant farmers were largely confined to the West, other commentators warned that they were also making inroads in New England. In 1878 minister J. W. Lees reported, "New England statesmen are telling us . . . that the business of New England farming is falling into the hands of an ignorant foreign element, whose low ideas of life will sink the business into the squalor of European peasantry."[133] A decade later, a writer in *Popular Science* maintained that the takeover was well under way: "Very rapidly, in New England, the farms are passing into the hands of the foreigner, or distinctly peasant element, a class which reduces the necessities of life to the simplest scale."[134] Progressive farmers proposed a variety of remedies to even the Yankee farmer's odds against the immigrants—from improving rural education to changing tax and tariff policies—but cutting his living standards was not one of them.[135] A writer in the *Nation* proudly noted the Yankee farmer's reply to those who suggested that he "live on as little as the Irish or the French": "He thanks them for their good advice, but answers that he can do better. And so he can."[136] It was better to get out of the business than live like an immigrant.

Yet some progressive farmers refused to see the immigrant farmer as a degraded, scrimping peasant. In an 1878 address, J. G. Crawford argued that, thanks to their superior market savvy, the region's immigrant agriculturalists were actually living better than many Yankees—better in particular than that lamentable species of Yankee husbandman who was too cheap to invest in his farmstead: "Should you visit his farm, and you need not travel a great distance to find it, you will see a house without paint, the brick falling from the chimney; carts, wagons, drags, harrows, and old logs filling his dooryard." Eventually, "Mr. Shiftless" heads to town or the poorhouse and is replaced by an immigrant, who builds "a comfortable home, upon the ruins of the unprofitable farmer." The key to the foreign-born farmer's success is his single-minded focus on the market: "The American farmer will sell nothing he can eat, and the Irishman will eat nothing he can sell."[137] By giving the market what it wanted, the Irish farmer was able to meet his family's own expanding consumer desires. Crawford believed it was a lesson many Yankees needed to learn.

By the turn of the century, some observers claimed that—contrary to their reputation for stinginess—the region's Poles were also doing their part to raise rural living standards. A *Boston Globe* reporter quoted a South Deerfield businessman's impressions of the neighboring Polish farm families: "When they come to this country they want to purchase coarse, rough articles, such as they have been accustomed to. In a little while they want a higher grade. You see, they are just like all the rest of us." Even more striking as proof of the Poles' rising living standards were the success stories cited by that same reporter. There was "Hen House Joe" Burnosky, who once lived in an old henhouse, but now owned the two-hundred-acre "Deacon Cleary" farm, complete with a farmhouse that was "modern throughout." Equally impressive was Roman Skibisky, a young farmer who had made a killing speculating in onions and now "lives in what was formerly one of the fine old mansions on the broad main street of Sunderland." Declaring that "[h]istory is repeating itself," the *Globe* reporter celebrated the Polish farmers as "ancestors" who were "planting an old race in a new country," just as the Puritans did before them. Granted, traditionalists would have been have been appalled at the idea of an onion speculator, much less a Polish one, being promoted as the heir of the Puritans. But from the perspective of the progressive farmers, it was precisely that market orientation that made the Poles resemble New England's settlers. As the *Globe* reporter put it, "That they are the founders of strong families of the future for New England none who study them can doubt."[138]

Whom the Land Loves

While issues like farm labor and living standards sharply divided the traditionalists and progressive farmers, their most fundamental difference concerned the farmer's proper relation to the land. Rural New Englanders had long been known for their ambiguous relation to their native soil. On the one hand, they were famous for loving it—stones and all—above every other place on earth. On the other hand, they were also notorious for leaving it, particularly for lands farther west. Both impulses are evident in a popular subgenre of sentimental poetry, featuring relocated Yankees who, despite having found prosperity on the fertile fields of the West, still long for "[t]he hills of old New England around my childhood's home."[139] In a century in which much of rural America would suffer from depopulation, the flight of Yankees from the New England countryside received the lion's share of attention in the national press. For many writers, the abandoned New England farmhouse stood as the most poignant symbol of a phenomenon affecting communities from eastern Nebraska to the Down East. Partly this was a function of timing. Rural depopulation was widespread in New England in the antebellum period, decades before it arrived in the West (with the exception of parts of Ohio). Partly it was a matter of reputation. Depopulation seemed particularly poignant in a New England countryside that had long presented itself as the nation's republican heartland—the home of the town meeting, the "plain living, high thinking" Yankee farmer, and the shot heard 'round the world. Partly it was a matter of visibility. The empty farmhouses and shrub-grown fields of New England were familiar sights to the eastern publishing classes, for whom the troubles of the rural West were but a distant rumor.

For these and other reasons, writers found it hard to resist the idea that rural New England's population troubles were somehow unique. Exceptionalist thinking could overtake even the most tough-minded observers. The chief of the Massachusetts Bureau of Statistics of Labor, Horace G. Wadlin, closed an 1891 pamphlet on abandoned farms in his state by describing them as part of a global phenomenon, "not confined to Massachusetts, to New England, to the West . . . nor to the United States. It is one of the features of modern civilization."[140] Noting that many of New England's farmers—namely, those with easy access to urban markets—were doing quite well, he urged readers to resist the temptation to sentimentalize: "The partial desertion of the once thriving villages, that were the centres of the idyllic New England life of the past, touches our sentiments and arouses our emotions. But the matter must be viewed from quite another stand-point than that of sentiment."[141] Yet his own emotions became aroused as he considered what the countryside had traditionally meant to the region:

> The farms of New England have in the past nurtured strong and brave men, but it was not because of any specially favorable economic conditions. It was the New England character, the New England home life, the New England respect for the church and school, which, frequently in the face of adverse circumstances, developed the New England citizen.[142]

In short the abandonment of New England's farms *was* exceptionally tragic, because it also signified the loss of the type of citizen that had been nurtured on them. Wadlin doubted that those farms could make citizens of the same caliber out of the immigrants who were taking them over: "It is, of course, doubtful if immigrants who are led to take up this land can withstand the inducements constantly tending to draw them away to the larger towns." The Yankees of old were ready to commit the "hard labor and . . . self-denial" it took to make a farm; the immigrants were not.[143] Thus, the departure of the Yankee farmer marked the end of rural New England's unique contribution to the region and the nation.

The vast majority of traditionalists and progressive farmers agreed with Wadlin that depopulation posed a unique challenge in rural New England, but they had very different responses to it. While most traditionalists assumed that the phenomenon was partly the result of larger structural forces—including urbanization, western competition, falling commodity prices, and the decline of rural industry—they focused more on the alleged moral causes. The problem, they argued, was that the Yankee farmer lacked sufficient attachment to his native soil to withstand the temptation to rove. Invoking the familiar stereotype of the rootless, mercenary Yankee, many traditionalists saw the descendants of the Puritans as simply too deracinated and greedy to settle down and live contentedly as farmers. Some believed the remedy for this situation was to nurture ties to the soil among the rural Yankees, especially farm children. Others despaired at the thought of reforming the Yankees and began looking elsewhere for a new generation of New England farmers. Some saw hope in the region's immigrants, who seemed to possess the love for the land that the Yankee so notoriously lacked. Celebrating the foreign-born agriculturalist's attachment to the Yankee's abandoned ancestral acres, these traditionalists believed they had found the solution to depopulation in rural New England.

In contrast, the progressive farmers had little patience with a naive attachment to place, even if that place was a New England farm. While they encouraged the Yankee farmers to love their homes and teach their children to do likewise, they believed such sentimental concerns had to be subordinated to the larger goal of making New England agriculture more productive and profitable. To that end they promoted ideas for financing, managing, and cultivating farms that were often calculated to weaken, rather than strengthen, the farmer's ties to the soil. Convinced that much of the region's marginal farmland actually needed to be abandoned, the progressive farmers regularly defended the farmer's right to move, and they warned Yankee agriculturalists not to stay put merely because their ancestors had. Some progressive farmers argued that it was precisely that habit of irrationally clinging to the soil that doomed the immigrant farmer to a life of unnecessary privation. But others strongly disagreed, contending that the real stick-in-the-mud was the Yankee agriculturalist, who could take a lesson from the highly mobile native-born and immigrant farmers of the West.

The Gilded Age traditionalists who portrayed the Yankee as a restless wanderer were only the latest in a long line to do so. Since the late eighteenth century, that stereotype was familiar not just in New England but everywhere the Yankee had set foot; indeed, the figure of the peripatetic Yankee was inescapable in American folklore and popular culture. But, while everyone agreed about the Yankee's remarkable mobility, they fiercely disagreed about whether it was a good thing. The Yankee's champions celebrated his ceaseless movement as proof of his energy, buoyancy, and enterprise. Many of them frankly acknowledged that it was money that kept him in motion. After paying tribute to the globe-hopping enterprise of his fellow Yankees, the Reverend John Todd declared that the "one trait in the character of New England people peculiar to them. . . . is the ardent, unquenchable love of money."[144] Some spun tall tales about the lengths—literally—the Yankee would go for a "spec": "Away up in Greenland he has administered the cold-water pledge; sold matches in Norway; peddled Yankee notions as far off as he could get . . . made an independent fortune by selling eggs; taught a whistling school in Constantinople; exhibited the striped pig to the world, not excluding *the elephant.*"[145] In contrast, other writers maintained that the Yankee roved for less mercenary motives—a thirst for novelty, a zeal for reform, or a sheer love of movement for its own sake. In "Self-Reliance," Emerson romanticized the "sturdy lad from New Hampshire or Vermont, who in turn tries all the professions, who *teams it, farms it, peddles,* keeps a school, preaches, edits a newspaper, goes to Congress, buys a township, and so forth, in successive years, and always, like a cat, falls on his feet."[146]

Whether they saw their hero as a money-hungry speculator or a peripatetic man of parts, the Yankee's champions hailed him as the fitting representative of an American population that seemed always to be in motion. In honor of their hero, they collectively referred to all American expatriates—whether they hailed from Maine or Missouri—as the Universal Yankee Nation. These partisans saw their hyperactive idol as the representative American: "The live Yankee is but the eccentricity of a truly wonderful people; the moral and physical impress of New England is stamped upon the universe; we owe her our nationality, and the world owes her admiration and respect."[147]

Yet, for many writers, the Yankee's restlessness was anything but a virtue. They saw it instead as a sign of deep moral flaws: greed, deracination, and a shocking coldness toward the mother region. The Yankee's critics attacked him as a rootless mercenary who lacked the patience and love for the land ever to amount to anything as a farmer. Some of the sharpest criticisms came from the Yankee's rivals in other regions: the New Yorkers who resented the New England migrants of the late eighteenth century, the southerners who bristled at Yankee carpetbaggers during Reconstruction, and the folks in every region who came out on the short end of a trade with the ubiquitous Yankee peddler.

Yankee mobility was also the subject of harsh criticism inside New England, particularly from traditionalist agricultural writers, who believed the key to the countryside's survival lay in fostering a class of resident proprietors with a deep and abiding attachment to the soil, who could then pass on that attachment to their children. Many traditionalists painted the Yankee migrants as gullible victims of the siren song of the city or the new lands of the West. They warned that while a few migrants met with financial success, most did not, and many lost everything. They assured the prospective migrant that he was better off staying in New England, "where, with proper application to business, he may secure a competency and a happy home."[148] According to the traditionalists, migration also carried enormous moral risks for the rural New Englander. The dangers were greatest in the city, where sturdy farm-bred youths quickly declined into sycophantic clerks or moneygrubbing speculators, but the West also had its moral pitfalls. Charles McDaniel—a farmer and large landowner in Sullivan County, New Hampshire—described his encounter with a "far Western farmer or ranchman," who recalled how he had gone west about thirty-five years earlier with fifteen or twenty other young men, all of whom "had been unsuccessful, or 'gone to the bad.'"[149] The moral of the story, McDaniel concluded, was that the living was so easy in the land of olive trees and oranges that a man soon grew "too lazy to be anything but a tramp, and a consumer of wine if he can manage to get it." That wasn't a problem back east, "where nature has done less by way of this spontaneous production," and as a result, "man has acquired habits of skill, industry, and perseverance, which have given character and stability to our Eastern agricultural community."[150] If New England was less than ideal for growing crops, so much the better for its ability to grow upright, hardworking men and women.[151]

Nativist traditionalists worried that the restlessness of their fellow Yankees was leaving rural New England vulnerable to an immigrant takeover. In an essay narrating his enraptured return to his ancestral Massachusetts farm after a long sojourn in Minnesota, Herbert Wendell Gleason critiqued his fellow Yankees for their lack of home feeling: "[W]e have especially erred, it seems to me, in neglecting adequately to preserve and perpetuate the old New England idea of *home.*"[152] At a time when traditionalists offered various strategies for nurturing home ties in rural Yankees (e.g., socializing more with neighbors, beautifying the farmhouse, and encouraging sons to make improvements), Gleason hoped the newly invented tradition of Old Home Week might do the trick.[153] Nevertheless, he remained concerned that the Yankees' lack of a "'fatherland' instinct" was leaving the countryside undefended against the foreign hordes: "The spirit of commercial greed has wrought sad havoc with the ideals of our fathers. We have allowed aliens to come in and steal our birthright."[154] Gleason underscored the immigrant threat with a quote from British historian James Bryce, who blamed the Irish and French Canadian newcomers for destroying the "homely simplicity and keen intelligence" of the traditional Yankee farm community.[155]

Other nativist traditionalists agreed that there was little "homely simplicity" among the region's immigrant farmers; if anything, they seemed less attached to their new homes than the Yankees they were replacing. Professor Amos Currier—himself a Yankee migrant to Iowa—blamed the loss of home feeling in New England on the rise of a renter class in place of the "hardy yeomanry, with whom the love of natal soil and home and simple life has been almost a religion." Although Currier condemned *all* renters, not just immigrants, he seemed especially dismissive of French Canadians, doubting that this "floating population," with its strong ties to Canada, could ever put down roots in rural New England.[156]

But other traditionalists strongly dissented, insisting that foreign-born farmers had much to teach their Yankee rivals when it came to home ties and attachment to the soil. They found it deeply ironic that the newcomers could care more for the Yankee's ancestral acres than he himself did, but that seemed to be the situation in rural New England, where the immigrant farmers' land hunger was apparently matched only by the Yankee's eagerness to sell out. While some traditionalists held out hope that the Yankee would start acting like his immigrant counterparts, others believed it was up to the foreign born to restore home feeling in rural New England.

The notion that immigrant and Yankee farmers had categorically different relationships with the land was not unique to New England's agricultural writers. To the contrary, it can be found across a wide range of popular and scholarly writings on rural America. One encounters it in commentary not only on New England but also on places like the Old Northwest, where Yankee migrants settled alongside immigrants. In almost every case, writers drew the same basic contrast between Yankee and immigrant attitudes toward the soil. They claimed the Yankee was primarily not a farmer but a speculator, who "skinned" his farm by cultivating it in the most exploitative manner, before selling out—often to an immigrant—and moving on. Speaking of the Yankee, Wisconsin historian Joseph Schafer observed, "To him land was a desirable commodity, but by no means a sacred trust."[157] In contrast, the land *was* a sacred trust to the immigrant farmer, who, Shafer wrote, "tended to hold on, through good years and bad years, as if his farm were the one piece of land in the world for him and his."[158] Some writers believed the Yankee speculator and the foreign-born farmer had played complementary roles in the settlement of the West. Whereas the Yankee was first on the scene, boldly going into the wilderness to buy up promising sites for farms, mills, and towns, the immigrant was more cautious, preferring lands closer to market and often willing to pay a premium for land his predecessor had partly improved.[159]

Recent studies have challenged the assumption that Yankees and immigrants had fundamentally different attitudes toward the soil. It is true that in some locales (often those with highly concentrated ethnic settlements) foreign-born farmers were more likely to persist on their farms than their Yankee neighbors, but in other places the Yankees were more persistent than some immigrant groups.[160] Moreover, when immigrant farmers did stay put, they were generally motivated not by a sentimental attachment to the soil but by ties to friends and family. As Kathleen Neils Conzen and Robert Ostergren have argued, stable immigrant farming communities brought with them from the old country customs that were calculated to keep farms within families, such as intervivos farm transfers between immigrant fathers and their sons.[161] Along with such inheritance strategies, communal bonds also encouraged farmers to persist on their land. Jon Gjerde argues that links of "kinship and regional background" encouraged stability in some Norwegian farmers in the Upper Midwest (though the same ties prompted others to join group migrations to Norwegian settlements farther west).[162] Gjerde contends that when Norwegian farmers stayed put, it was "due not so much to an emotional attachment to the soil as to benefits derived by the immigrants from compact settlement."[163]

Despite such evidence to the contrary, the hypothesis that Yankees and immigrants held antithetical attitudes toward the soil would dominate both popular and scholarly discourses on rural America well into the twentieth century. Some scholars narrowed the theory to argue that only continental immigrants, not those from the British Isles, displayed an unusual attachment to the land.[164] Others expanded it to contend that all native-born Americans, not just Yankees, were more mobile than all immigrants.[165] Yet even those who argued for an expanded class of mobile Americans often found it difficult to shake the figure of the restless Yankee, who continues to haunt their work as the personification of ceaseless mobility.

Most writers offered historical explanations to support their claims about restless Yankees and rooted immigrants. They argued that the age-old scarcity of farmland in Europe led immigrants to treasure the farms they were finally able to purchase in America, whereas the historical abundance of cheap, plentiful land in America taught the Yankees to take it for granted. Others thought the Yankees had inherited their attitudes toward the soil from their Puritan ancestors. In a 1922 *Atlantic Monthly* essay Mary Alden Hopkins argued that the Puritans were a bookish people who "were never reconciled to being farmers" and as a result, "lived in perpetual conflict with Nature." She blamed them for passing down those attitudes to their descendants: "The New England farmers took and took and took from the land, and they hated the land they looted. The land held back more each year." The conflict escalated until the Yankees finally fled and the "soil had—nervous prostration!" Hopkins believed the story took a fortunate turn with the arrival of "slow-moving, hard-working" Slavs and Italians, whom she credited with reviving the farms in her neighborhood: "They do not fight the land; they live with it and tend it. Under their patient nursing, the soil is gradually recovering its health." The same soil that had resentfully withheld its bounty from the Yankees was rewarding the immigrants with green pastures and high corn stacks. As Hopkins's title suggests, it was easy to tell "Whom the Land Loves."[166]

Anticipating (and perhaps inspiring) Hopkins, many Gilded Age traditionalists held up the "patient," "contented" immigrant farmer as a role model for the perpetually restless and dissatisfied Yankee. Several juxtaposed the hyperactive Yankee with his ethnic foil, the stereotypically phlegmatic German. Conceding that the German farmers of Pennsylvania were "often declared stolid by the fast men of New England," a Keystone state newspaper argued that the Germans were getting the last laugh. The paper contended that, thanks to both multigenerational German Americans and recent German immigrants, agriculture and rural communities were thriving in Pennsylvania, in striking contrast to New England, where progressive Yankee farmers wasted their time growing exotics like opium and rare fruits, while farmland grew up in trees. The paper blamed much of the trouble on the Yankees' weak home ties: "Notwithstanding all that is said about the attachment of the people of New England to their homes, the home feeling is manifestly far less there than in the middle and southern states." The remedy for the problem lay outside New England, specifically in "a large infusion of emigrant farmers from England and Germany, who would reestablish the home feeling and build up permanent agricultural interests." With no hope of galvanizing home feeling in the Yankees, the paper believed New England's salvation lay in importing German farmers and their Anglo-Saxon kinsmen from Britain.[167]

Prompted, perhaps, by the relative dearth of Germans in New England, other traditionalists looked also to French Canadian or Irish farmers to supply the attachment to the soil that seemed so lacking in the Yankees. A writer in a New Hampshire newspaper described how Germans, Irish, and French Canadians were replacing the Yankees in that state's farming towns. While the writer was obviously unhappy with the change, there was no choice: "[W]e have got to have foreign brawn, foreign patience, frugality, and industry, or we shall have nothing." The problem was that the Yankees were simply too "brainy, nervous, [and] restless" to stay.[168] According to a Massachusetts correspondent in the *New York Sun,* it was not too much brain but too little "veneration and ambition" that caused the Yankees to "desert the home of their fathers."[169] But, whatever had killed their home feeling, the immigrants seemed to be making up for it. Even the Irish, famous for congregating in cities and factory towns, were making their way to the land. Some joined Archbishop John Ireland's Catholic colonization movement on the prairies of Minnesota, but others listened to the *Boston Pilot*'s repeated pleas for the advantages of rural New England: "Go not West, young man, until you know the East."[170] Watching the Irish revive the neglected Yankee farms, the *New York Sun* writer concluded, "They love to become landholders. The unsightly, neglected and barren places they have rendered fertile and fruitful in this State by their patient labor is [*sic*] simply incredible."[171] With little hope of instilling such love for the soil in the Yankees, many traditionalists were looking to the immigrants to supply it.

Moving On

Many progressive farmers accepted the traditionalists' dichotomous view of Yankee and immigrant mobility patterns, but not their valuation of them. These progressive farmers saw the Yankee farmer's restlessness as a virtue rather than a vice, since it spoke to his ambition, enterprise, and innovativeness. Convinced that much of New England's marginal farmland needed to be left uncultivated or even abandoned, they celebrated the Yankee who overcame his own sentimental ties to his land and moved on. Some argued that it was his ability to put profits above sentiment that separated the enlightened Yankee agriculturalist from the backward immigrant, who irrationally clung to his tiny plot, entailing misery on his children. But other progressive farmers challenged the dichotomous stereotypes of Yankee restlessness and immigrant roots. Critiquing the Yankee farmers of New England for their inertia and conservatism, these writers held up the farmers of the West—native born and immigrant alike—as the real movers.

In an era when the Yankee farmer was relentlessly attacked for abandoning his native soil, the progressive farmers defended his right to move. Granted, the progressive farmers were careful to speak up for the virtues of a New England home and the importance of cultivating an attachment to the land and a love of farming in the younger generation. Yet, unlike the traditionalists, they argued that the farmer needed to weigh the emotional and cultural benefits of persisting against the opportunity costs of owning a successful farm elsewhere. Some progressive farmers even warned that home attachments could become a trap if they enticed the farmer to remain on unproductive land. As a progressive farmer at a New Hampshire meeting advised:

> I know it is very pretty, almost romantic, to talk of our beautiful hills and valleys, but stern investigation reveals the fact, that a certain portion of our soil never repays the cost of working it, and that the old adage in regard to a home is as true now as ever, still the occupants of such homes simply *stay* there, and live from year to year, denying themselves what their creator intended as the heritage of all.[172]

The speaker argued that such persisters would be much better off moving to richer land (hopefully within the state). Most progressive farmers would have heartily agreed. They understood how hard it could be for a farmer to leave his ancestral acres in an era when so many were speaking against it. Writing in the *Nation,* Charles C. Nott argued that walking away from his land was often the Yankee hill farmer's last great triumph: "[T]here is something grand in the farmer of these mountain towns, who, rising to the heroic treatment of his case, turns away from the fields and fences upon which he has toiled through the better part of his life, and . . . writes upon the closed door, ABANDONED." Nott judged this last act "not unworthy" of the Yankee's "sturdy and upright lineage": ironically, by walking away from his ancestral lands, the farmer proved himself a worthy son of the Puritans.[173]

As supporters of New England agriculture, the progressive farmers naturally wanted to see their colleagues remain in the region, but they were often quite supportive of those who left it. Unlike the traditionalists, who typically attacked the Yankee migrants to the West as dupes and traitors, the progressive farmers commonly celebrated them for their ambition and enterprise. A Vermont writer lauded his departed brethren: "They are helping to spread the leaven of New England throughout the whole Union, and are doing their part to make our country the greatest among the nations."[174] The progressive farmers never lost sight of the fact that the West was New England's daunting rival in the markets for cereals and wool, but they took solace in the belief that the most successful farmers of the West were Yankee migrants. Hartford mayor William Hyde remembered traveling as a boy with his father through a desolate stretch of Wisconsin, where they encountered "foreigners of every degree of poverty." Suddenly, they came upon a neat, thriving farm: "[W]e could have told, gentlemen, before we asked a question, that the man who owned that house and had done that work came from New England." Hyde argued that the relocated Yankee was "only a sample of the kind of men to whom all that great country owes its prosperity, so far as it has any prosperity."[175] Progressive Yankee farmers were making the West bloom.

Progressive farmers who stopped short of encouraging the agriculturalist to uproot himself did not hesitate to suggest other courses of action that would have increased his profits at the cost of weakening his home ties. Many recommended that marginal croplands be allowed to grow up in trees, advice that large numbers of New England farmers seem to have heeded.[176] Some urged farmers to achieve economies of scale by tearing down their fences and forming partnerships with their neighbors.[177] Some called for farmers to preserve their capital by becoming tenants, rather than resident proprietors.[178] And some called for urban investors to purchase New England's farms, hire managers to run them, and use the farmhouses as vacation homes.[179] Granted, most progressive farmers continued to assume that the typical New England agriculturalist would be a resident proprietor, but they were also quite willing to consider alternatives for capitalizing and managing the region's farms, even at the risk of undermining the farmer's "home feeling."

Some progressive farmers believed foreign-born agriculturalists were particularly prone to the mistake of irrationally clinging to the soil. Invoking the familiar dichotomy of immigrant roots and Yankee restlessness, those writers celebrated the Yankee for breaking the home ties that supposedly limited the horizons, and bank account, of his foreign-born rival. At the beginning of a speech titled "The Business Side of Agriculture," J. H. Hale recalled a "good German friend" who once told him, "I think you have a good farm, but . . . I think you would do better if you stayed at home a little more." Hale disagreed: "I have made more on the farm in ten years than he has in twenty, and have had a heap more of fun."[180] As if to prove his point, he casually dropped references to his "fruit-packing house in Georgia" and "a couple of farms" he had recently "picked up" in Connecticut.[181] Clearly, it paid *not* to stay home. In a similar vein, Charles Nott contrasted his farm-abandoning Yankee hero with "the peasants and crofters of other races," who "obstinately hold fast to their small holdings, and divide and subdivide their insufficient farms only to entail intenser misery on their descendants."[182] Deriding the foreign born for their excessive attachment to the soil, these progressive farmers praised the Yankee for knowing when it was time to leave.

Other progressive farmers challenged the stereotype of the rooted immigrant, arguing instead that the best foreign-born agriculturalists, like the best of the Yankees, were open to opportunity wherever it took them. J. W. Sanborn (whose own academic career had taken him from New Hampshire to Missouri to Utah) maintained that the West had attracted the most energetic members of both groups: "The west is peopled by the stirring, ambitious sons and daughters of New England and the better sections of Europe."[183] Sanborn praised the boldness and enterprise of both the Yankee and foreign-born westerners, their large farms, modern implements, and scientific methods. Granted, mobility had its risks, and Sanborn saw a particular danger in the growing number of farm renters in states like Indiana and Illinois. But he seemed even more worried about the inertia of his fellow Yankees back east, castigating them for their "timidity of operation," overreliance on manual labor, and "paralyzed . . . energies."[184] Sanborn's concerns were shared by George Austin Bowen, who warned, "Caution is perhaps a little too fully developed" in the Yankee farmer, "for it is apt to make him conservative, and compels him to keep in the old tracks, rather than to push out in new directions, and tends to take away his dash and enterprise." Like Sanborn, Bowen took heart in the West, where the Yankee had recovered his mobility and enterprise. The key to the Yankee migrant's revival, Bowen argued, was his status as a newcomer in the West, "where he comes in competition with those of almost every nation of Europe, [and] where, like them, he becomes an immigrant, having but one advantage, that of knowing the language."[185] Although no friend of the foreign born, Bowen seemed to envy their freedom from the "old tracks" that bound the New England Yankees.[186] As an immigrant among immigrants, the western Yankee had finally recovered his dash.

The internal debates of the progressive farmers and traditionalists over the immigrant farmer's attachment to the soil, like their intramural disputes over his labor practices and standard of living, can partly be attributed to their ignorance. Most Yankees knew very little about some of the groups—Poles and Swedes in particular—who were taking up the region's farms. But at least some of the confusion was due to self-doubts within the Yankee community. At a time when it was not at all clear that their own ethnic group had what it took to revive rural New England, Yankee traditionalists and progressive farmers were torn over whether to embrace the immigrants as saviors or to attack them as dangerous interlopers. As we have seen, that debate encompassed not only New England proper but also the many other places where Yankee migrants brushed elbows with immigrants. Of all those sites of encounter, many believed it was the Old Northwest that held the key to the Yankees' future in a nation of immigrants.

FIVE

The *New* New England

Yankees and Immigrants in the Old Northwest

For many inhabitants of the Old Northwest, the Gilded Age was a time to reflect on their region's history. They founded state and local pioneer and historical societies to collect the memories of settlers. They subscribed to the *Magazine of Western History,* the Cleveland-based monthly that focused on northwestern history in its early years.[1] They participated in the centennial celebrations of the Northwest Ordinance of 1787 and of cities like Marietta and Cleveland, Ohio. Northwesterners had much to crow about. In a hundred short years their region had emerged as a rising economic and political power, with booming cities, rich farmlands, and a growing pantheon of statesmen. But mingled with northwesterners' intense pride in their region were feelings of loyalty to older places. As a region that had drawn its settlers not only from across the United States but also from much of Europe and Canada, the Old Northwest was a land of many ethnic groups, each with strong memories of, and ties to, its homeland. That was particularly true in the subregion that has been variously dubbed Greater New England, New England Expanded, Yankeeland, the Yankee Runway, and the Yankee West. Beginning in New York, this zone of settlement sliced across the Old Northwest—from northern Ohio to southern Wisconsin—before reaching its western terminus (scholars differ here) somewhere in the Mississippi Valley or the Great Plains.[2] This Yankee-tinged subregion was settled in stages by New England migrants and their children. For example, many of the pioneers who arrived in southern Michigan and Wisconsin in the antebellum years were native New Yorkers whose parents had migrated from New England in the early national period. The centennial celebrations of the Gilded Age prompted many of those northwestern descendants of the

Puritans (with debts to Susan Gray, I shall call them Yankee Westerners) to meditate on the relationship between the Old Northwest and New England. That relationship was also the subject of much discussion among the Yankees back east, some of whom boarded trains to take part in the festivities in the Old Northwest. No centennial celebration along the Yankee Runway was complete without a speech from New England luminaries like senators George Frisbie Hoar and Joseph Roswell Hawley, who knew how to balance praise for their western cousins with tributes to the mother region.

Yet, while everyone agreed that the destinies of New England and the Old Northwest were intimately connected, there was considerable debate over the nature of the bond.[3] Were the two regions metropole and colony? Creditor and debtor? Aging parent and upstart offspring? Although commentators in both regions offered a range of responses to these questions, I will focus on three perspectives that were especially prominent. One group of writers, dominated by Yankee Westerners, fully embraced the era's fashionable Anglo-Saxonist racial theories. They celebrated the Yankee colonization of the Old Northwest as proof of their race's unique gifts for conquering lands, engulfing alien peoples, and founding governments. These writers, whom I have dubbed Greater New Englanders, shared the muscular racialism of their Brahmin Anglo-Saxonist colleagues back east, but not their besieged regionalism. By broadening their definition of New England to include the Old Northwest, the Greater New Englanders constructed a regional identity that could support, rather than undermine, their rampant Anglo-Saxonism. One finds a far more modest view of New England's role in the Old Northwest and the rest of the globe among a second group of commentators whom I call preservationists. They saw New England not as an expanding Anglo-Saxon empire, but as a dwindling cultural and political tradition, one that was rapidly being consumed by the fires of urbanization, industrialization, and immigration. With little hope of saving old New England in the East, the preservationists turned their hopes to the Old Northwest, particularly Ohio's Western Reserve. There they hailed the villages founded in the early nineteenth century by Yankee migrants as living embodiments of old New England, places where one could still encounter homogeneous communities of thrifty, hardworking "Puritans." This nostalgic view of the Western Reserve was more fantasy than fact, but it served the preservationists as a standard for measuring how badly contemporary New England had betrayed its ancestral ideals. In contrast, a third group of commentators, whom I label nationalists, saw little to lament in the demise of traditional New England culture, which they blamed for making the Yankees conservative, narrow-minded, and provincial. The nationalists believed the best cure for these defects lay in the Old Northwest, which allegedly had fostered a more liberal, broad-minded, and all-American breed of Yankees. The nationalists credited the Yankee Westerners with wielding a progressive influence not only on the Old Northwest but also on New England. They reasoned that if anybody could open the minds of those staid eastern Yankees, it was their liberal western cousins.

Aside from their shared interest in the relationship between New England and the Old Northwest, there was little common ground among the Greater New Englanders, preservationists, and nationalists. One thing they did agree on, though, was the importance of immigrants to the relationship between the two regions. Yet even here they had strong differences. Whereas the Greater New Englanders valued immigrants as candidates for absorption into their expanding Anglo-Saxon empire, the preservationists feared the foreign born as one of the chief threats to old New England. For their part the nationalists credited the immigrants of the Old Northwest with exerting a powerful ameliorating influence on the Puritan descendants. They believed that the necessity of negotiating with the foreign born over issues like temperance and education had made the Yankee Westerners far more liberal, tolerant, and national in outlook than their eastern cousins. Ironically, they thought it was "give-and-take" with people from other lands that transformed the Yankee into an American.

The Greater New Englanders

The Greater New Englanders were only the latest in a long line of commentators who saw the Yankee settlement of the Old Northwest as an exercise in cultural imperialism. Since the antebellum period, that perspective had dominated much of the discourse about the Yankee Westerners. Critics frequently attacked the westering Yankees as self-righteous busybodies, bent on subjugating all other groups to their institutions, political reforms, and cultural norms. That charge was perhaps most often heard from Upland Southern migrants to the Old Northwest (whose origins, Nicole Etcheson explains, lay in "the interior border region of the Old South which includes piedmont Virginia, Maryland, North Carolina, Kentucky, and Tennessee").[4] Some Yankee migrants fiercely denied the Upland Southerners' charge of cultural imperialism. The classic example was Vermont-born Stephen Douglas, who sought to reassure Upland Southern voters in Illinois that all Yankee migrants were not abolitionists and all abolitionists in the state were not Yankees.[5] But another group of Yankee migrants eagerly took up the mantle of cultural imperialism. Its members included the ministers who worked for New England–based home missionary societies and the schoolteachers and farmers who wrote home boasting of their success at convincing non-Yankee migrants to adopt New England ways.[6] In the guidebook *Illinois and the West* (1838), A. D. Jones advised his fellow Yankees on the best way to go about influencing their Upland Southern neighbors. Jones warned the prospective migrant not to adopt a superior air around the less educated Upland Southerners: "[L]et him mingle freely and unsuspiciously with his neighbors, and while he sinks his manners to their level, strive to bring up their habits, by a successful example, to the New England standard."[7] At a time of widespread fear of Yankee domination, it paid to be stealthy.

Among the most enthusiastic Yankee cultural imperialists in the Old Northwest were the advocates of Anglo-Saxonism. That racial ideology had fueled Yankee ambitions in the younger region since the antebellum period, when New England home missionaries and reformers invoked Anglo-Saxonist rhetoric to promote their projects and boost their self-confidence.[8] They painted the Yankee migrants in the Old Northwest as the true heirs of their Anglo-Saxon forebears, restless adventurers who boldly marched west, founding states, making laws, and absorbing other peoples. In an 1861 speech supporting home missions, Detroit minister H. D. Kitchel celebrated the racial ties that bound the Yankees of New England to their migrant brethren in the "New England Zone" of the West. Both groups, he insisted, were worthy scions of an Anglo-Saxon people that had always been on the move: "It is in our blood to press Westward. It is the Saxon drift."[9] He traced the historical progress of the race across the Roman Empire into Britain, then across the ocean to New England, and finally across the Alleghenies into the American West. Along the way, the race was "Christianized, then Protestantized, and finally Puritanized," while retaining its capacity to dominate and assimilate other groups. Kitchel believed those racial gifts were superlatively exemplified by the Yankee migrants, whose "plastic and organizing force" enabled them to shape the institutions and ideas of their neighbors:

> A New England family, even if it be not distinctively Christian, is still a vitalizing and organic power—has law in it, and system—knows what a *School* is, and a *Church,* and a *Town-meeting;* and the subtle presence has mastery, and so the neighborhood, the district, town, county, State, is leavened and swayed. It works dimly for a time, amid

> the colonial chaos; but presently, as the social web turns right side up, the figure appears—it's the New England pattern.[10]

Contending that it was "not number, but weight" that gave a group influence over its neighbors, Kitchel believed nothing was weightier than the culture of the Yankees. Indeed, he saw their influence as nearly pervasive: "Not a State, nor a town, scarcely a neighborhood, of the West, but owes thus its shaping and attitude in all essentials, to the early income of a New England germ."[11] As the planters of the seed, Kitchel contended, the Yankees would continue to shape the culture and institutions of the Old Northwest even as their share in its population slipped. The "New England Zone" extended not just along the Yankee Runway but throughout the entire Old Northwest.

Speaking in the early 1860s, Kitchel still took for granted that the Yankee migrants lacked the colonizing force of their cousins back east. He deferred to the superior might of the latter, pleading

> that the old New England will cherish still a lively and effective interest in all this outgrowth of herself. There is danger that you may come to feel an abatement of care in this direction, as if this West . . . now taking on the proportions of manhood, no longer needed the fostering hand or the special sympathy of the East.[12]

Despite his manly appearance, the Yankee Westerner was still a dependent son, reliant on the mother region for strength and nurturing. Specifically, Kitchel called on his Boston listeners to support the American Home Missionary Society in its work of establishing Congregational churches in the younger region: "Impress yourselves purposely on this vast field which you are filling. Pour out through all this New England Zone the full heart of your love."[13] In metaphors that utterly negated the agency of the Yankee Westerners, Kitchel painted them as the passive recipients of the love and energy of their eastern parents. It was up to the latter to ensure the continued domination of the Yankees in the West.

A couple of decades later Kitchel's depiction of the relationship between the Yankees of New England and the West already seemed hopelessly out of date. By that point only die-hard believers still talked of the Yankees of New England as a colonizing force. More objective observers warned that the group would do well to defend its homeland from the vigorous and prolific newcomers pouring in on it. In contrast, the Yankee migrants and their descendants in the Old Northwest increasingly looked like a power to be reckoned with. As each year produced a new crop of influential Yankee Westerners—reformers, educators, business leaders, even US presidents—it seemed clear that the colonizing energies of the Yankees had migrated westward. No longer an awkward adolescent looking to his eastern mother for support, the Yankee Westerner was now a full-grown man ready to take up the standard of Anglo-Saxonism.

The changed relationship between the two regions is especially obvious when one compares the Greater New Englanders of the Old Northwest with their fellow Anglo-Saxonists, the Brahmin scholars of New England. Like the latter, the Greater New Englanders were convinced that they belonged to the world's dominant race, one destined to conquer and populate much of the globe. But the Greater New Englanders parted ways with the Brahmin Anglo-Saxonists when it came to their regional identity. By expanding their notion of New England to include most, and in some cases all, of the Old Northwest, the Greater New Englanders were able to avoid the fears of regional decay that haunted the Brahmins. The Greater New Englanders saw New England not as a dying older region but as a vital and expanding younger one—in short, a New England that towered above the nation's regions just as the Anglo-Saxon ruled its races.

The Greater New Englanders' dispute with the Brahmin Anglo-Saxonists centered on New England's present, not its past. On the latter subject, the two groups were fully in accord. Both understood the region's colonial and revolutionary eras as one long story of Anglo-Saxon triumph. Both depicted the Pilgrims and Puritans as exemplary members of their race, the products of a long history of self-government that began on the coastal plains of ancient Germany, continued in the Anglo-Saxon villages of medieval Britain, and culminated in the town meetings of New England. Both believed New England's settlers had demonstrated their political genius through such achievements as the Mayflower Compact and Connecticut's Fundamental Orders. Finally, both believed the Anglo-Saxon virtues of the Pilgrims and Puritans had been further enhanced by the political and environmental challenges they endured settling New England and fighting for their independence from Britain.

Yet the consensus between the Greater New Englanders and Brahmin Anglo-Saxonists broke down when they turned from New England's past to its present. As I argued in chapter 1, the Brahmins believed their race had seen better days in New England. While in most parts of the world the Anglo-Saxons seemed destined for supremacy, in New England they were rapidly being supplanted by more vigorous and prolific peoples. The

Brahmins saw the decay of their race in its traditional stronghold as a matter of grave concern. If the Anglo-Saxons were defeated in New England, they wondered, what was to prevent the same thing from happening worldwide? The Greater New Englanders took a much more sanguine view of the situation, however. While conceding that their race had declined in New England, they believed it had more than made up for those losses in the Old Northwest. There the Yankee had returned to true Anglo-Saxon form, conquering lands, founding states, and absorbing new peoples—all in the name of New England. The Greater New Englanders pointed to the Yankee Westerners' achievements as proof that they were still the standard-bearers of their race. Far from dying out, the New England Anglo-Saxons had simply shifted the center of their empire westward.

The contrasting perspectives of the Brahmin Anglo-Saxonists and Greater New Englanders are amply displayed by their differing responses to the demographic changes under way in New England. Both groups agreed that the region's weakened Yankee population was no match for the waves of immigrants pouring in on it. But, whereas the Brahmins responded to this situation with anguish, the Greater New Englanders viewed it with remarkable equanimity. Addressing his fellow Puritan descendants at an Independence Day celebration in Connecticut, Senator Thomas W. Palmer of Michigan coolly observed, "It has often occurred to me that [New England's] mission with the Saxon is ended, and that now her work lies with the Celt, the Scandinavian and other strains of blood."[14] Another enthusiastic Greater New Englander, Edward Payson Powell, regarded the immigrant takeover of the mother region with equal complacency.[15] Powell cited financier Hugh McCulloch's prediction that "The change in the character of the population of New England" meant that "the control of the cities and towns will soon be in the hands of men who have not a drop of original New England blood in their veins."[16] Likewise, a writer in the *New York Evangelist*—unnamed, but apparently a Greater New Englander—viewed "with perfect composure" the immigrant takeover of the region's farms: "The land is wide enough to receive them all, and to furnish a home and a support for every honest, hard-working laborer of other countries, whether Irish, or German, or Scandinavian."[17]

It was easy for the Greater New Englanders to concede the mother region to the immigrants when so much of the rest of the country, indeed the world, seemed destined for the Yankees. Powell contended, "New England conquered and carried the sentiments, customs, tastes, township organizations and constitutional forms of Massachusetts and Connecticut to the very Pacific." What is more, "New England ideas are well on the way to girdle the globe with steel and machinery."[18] Palmer concluded that the spread of New England ideas and institutions meant that "[t]he continent is hers"—except, of course, for New England itself, which he had already conceded to the immigrants.[19] The unnamed *New York Evangelist* author insisted, "New England, if it has changed its abode, has not changed its race, nor its force of character. It has only broadened its foundations, and carried its energy and enterprise to new scenes of activity." The writer believed the same relationship between metropole and colonies obtained among the Anglo-Saxons of New England and "Old England." In both cases worrisome signs that the race was decaying at home (e.g., deserted rural villages and abandoned farms) were utterly belied by the energy and enterprise it displayed in its colonies. The real New England, like the real Britain, was at the empire's expanding edges.[20]

The Greater New Englanders' equanimity toward the population turnover in the mother region should not be taken as a sign of pluralism. To the contrary, they were every bit as racialist as the Brahmin Anglo-Saxonists. The Greater New Englanders took immense pride in belonging to the world's most restless, adventurous, and aggressive race. As the *New York Evangelist* writer put it, "The New England race is a conquering race, and is always seeking new worlds to conquer."[21] Another Greater New Englander, Wisconsin journalist and historian Ellis Usher, argued that colonizing the Northwest Territories was no job for the "roving, easy-going" Frenchman; instead, it called for "the hard, compelling hand of the Anglo-Saxon," with his "strange fusion of the overwhelming, compelling, courage of the spirit and the irresistible force of physical endurance."[22] Some Greater New Englanders seemed almost defensive about the century or more their ancestors had tarried in the mother region before heading west, arguing that they had been held there by a love of home, primitive transportation, and the opposition of France and Britain.[23] But once those barriers were down, the Yankees marched toward the setting sun like the Teutonic tribes of old. Palmer insisted, "[T]he instinct of their race was strong within them, and it again took them just two hundred years to wrench a continent from its possessors." Like most Greater New Englanders, Palmer took pains to present the Yankee migrants' aggression as tempered by their faith and respect for the law. The senator placed the westering Yankees at the apex of an evolutionary process, which began with their ruthless ancestors, the Baltic "pirates," who "sailed forth to take by the strong hand." Next came the Puritans, who "did not rely on the arm of flesh but upon that faith which altho [*sic*] at times it carried them to conclusions indefensible . . . still made them God-fearing and humanity-lifting in their efforts and in their results." Last in the procession were the Yankee migrants, who shared all of their ancestors' will to conquer but none of their piratical violence and "indefensible" intolerance.[24] Other Greater New Englanders agreed that the Yankee migrants' aggression was matched by their humanitarianism.[25] Ignoring, among other things, the Yankee Westerners' prominent role in the Black Hawk War, the Greater New Englanders insisted that the Yankees dominated not by the sword but by the power of their ideas and institutions.

According to the Greater New Englanders, those ideas and institutions were pure products of the mother region. They argued that the Yankee took New England with him on his journey west. Dismissing the effect of the new environment on their hero, they maintained that the Yankee remade the Old Northwest in his image, not vice versa. They rejected the widespread belief that migrants "barbarized" on the frontier—losing their religion and respect for the law. Instead, the Greater New Englanders painted the Yankee migrant as unwaveringly faithful to the values and institutions of his native region. Powell cited the popular notion that "a single family alone would not break the laws it had left behind in Connecticut."[26] Many Greater New Englanders denied that the Yankee left behind his laws—or anything else. They described how the institutions of New England sprang up as if by magic everywhere the Yankee set foot: "The New Englander may almost be said to have carried his church and state with him, so soon did they reappear in the wilderness."[27] Many Greater New Englanders thought the Yankee had brought along his domestic life and civil institutions as well. They insisted that you could find authentic New England communities all along the Yankee's path west, each of them complete with churches, common schools, and town meetings. The minister and horticulturalist Powell contended that the Yankees carried with them their familiar Spitzenburg apples, St. Michaels pears, and currant bushes to plant in their new home, as well as a "Connecticut bookcase" packed with volumes by Josephus, Fox, Jonathan Edwards, and Joshua Moody.[28] Palmer maintained that the Yankee Westerners sang the same hymns and told the same legends about New England heroes as their cousins back home: "Forefathers' Day and Thanksgiving were festivals, and the story of the Tea in Boston harbor, Paul Revere's ride, Putnam and the Wolf's Den were as familiar to the boys and girls in the wilds of Michigan and on the prairies of Illinois as in the localities where they had been enacted."[29] The Yankee migrants had transplanted New England to the Old Northwest down to the smallest detail.

The Greater New Englanders were right to believe that the mother region exerted a powerful influence over the Old Northwest, particularly along the Yankee Runway. There, as scholars have shown, the Yankees left a strong imprint on many areas of political, cultural, and social life. To cite some familiar examples, the Yankee Westerners led the movements for common schools, temperance, and antislavery. They accounted for the Republican Party's dominance along the Runway, and they established many of that subregion's cultural and religious institutions, including lyceums, colleges, and Congregational and Presbyterian churches.[30] They also helped shape the subregion's built environment and geography, constructing houses and barns after the New England style and christening towns with New England place-names.[31] Finally, the Yankees played a distinctive role in the subregion's agriculture, raising more wheat and less corn, cattle, and hogs than the Upland Southern and Mid-Atlantic migrants who settled to the south of them. When wheat became unprofitable, the Yankee farmers switched to dairying, producing more milk than their counterparts to the south.[32] The Yankee farmers were known for milking their own cows, earning the derision of Upland Southern and immigrant farmers, who saw that as woman's work.[33]

Yet, despite the Yankees' deep and lasting influence on the Old Northwest, the Greater New Englanders were wrong to view it as an extension of New England. Even along the Runway, Yankee hegemony was strongly resisted by native-born migrants from other regions, as well as immigrants from Europe and Canada. In many instances, this resistance forced the Yankee Westerners to alter or even abandon their attempts to install New England–style institutions and cultural practices. As a result the Old Northwest took shape as the nation's most culturally hybridized and politically contested region, with other groups regularly challenging what they saw as the paternalism, moral superciliousness, and cultural imperialism of the Yankees.

New Englanders in the Old Northwest met some of their stiffest resistance from the Upland Southerners. During the antebellum period, the two groups squared off over issues like common school reform, temperance, and the civil rights of African Americans. To be sure, there were exceptions, but the vast majority of Yankees favored these causes, just as the vast majority of southern migrants opposed them. This was particularly evident in Ohio, Indiana, and Illinois, where support for all three causes came chiefly from the Yankee-dominated northern counties and opposition centered in the Upland Southern–dominated downstate ones.[34]

The battle lines were drawn from 1820 to 1860, when reformers in all three states fought to establish tax-based, free school systems. As Carl Kaestle has shown, it is important not to overstate New England's influence over the common school movement of the Old Northwest. For example, it is wrong to claim—as many have—that Yankee migrants simply transplanted the New England common school to their new western homes. In fact, common school reform occurred simultaneously in the two regions, with eastern and western reformers exchanging ideas, copying each others' laws, and quoting each others' writings. Nor is the traditional account correct in blaming the lion's share of the opposition to common schools in the Old Northwest on Upland Southerners. In fact common school reform was opposed by a variety of groups—including localists who feared losing control over community schools, farmers who opposed taxes, and pluralists who liked diverse schools—some of whom were themselves Yankee migrants. Yet the fact remains that Yankees and Upland Southerners tended to take opposite sides on the issue. This was evident in Ohio, Indiana, and Illinois, where the stiffest resistance to common school reform consistently came from the downstate Upland Southerners and the greatest support came from the upstate Yankees.[35]

Upland Southerners in the Old Northwest also opposed the Yankee-led temperance and antislavery movements. As scholars have argued, the conflict over temperance derived at least in part from the two groups' contrasting social backgrounds. Coming from industrializing New England, Yankee migrants in the antebellum period were far more likely to have been exposed to temperance teachings—generally grounded in middle-class ideologies of self-discipline, self-improvement, and social mobility—than were their counterparts from the agrarian, slaveholding South.[36] Once again there were exceptions—southern migrants who supported temperance and Yankees who opposed it—but the overall pattern held. For example, in the 1855 referendum on the Maine Law in Illinois, most of the northern counties voted in favor, but the measure was defeated by the opposition of downstate southerners.[37]

Not surprisingly, it was the issue of black civil rights that sparked the most heated conflicts in the antebellum years between Yankees and Upland Southerners in the Old Northwest. As Nicole Etcheson has pointed out, the latter were ambivalent about slavery—many had crossed the Ohio River to escape the political domination of the planters—but they were almost universally opposed to African Americans, whom they saw as an inferior race that degraded the status of white labor. Southern migrants in Ohio, Indiana, and Illinois also worried that planters would "dump" their aged and infirm slaves across the Ohio, creating a burden for the southern counties of the three states. They responded by supporting amendments to the three states' constitutions banning (or, in the case of Ohio, discouraging) the immigration of African Americans. After debates in constitutional conventions that saw southern delegates accuse their Yankee opponents of being willing to harm them out of a misplaced sympathy for blacks, the voting followed the familiar pattern: delegates from upstate, Yankee-dominated counties strongly opposed the amendments; and delegates from downstate, southern-dominated counties supported them. In Indiana and Illinois, the amendments passed over the strenuous opposition of the Yankee delegates, although the Ohio measure was defeated when the southerners split their votes.[38]

Along with Upland Southerners, immigrants also offered stiff, sometimes insurmountable, resistance to Yankee reformers in the Old Northwest. The immigrant opposition was particularly strong on the issues of public education and prohibition. As in the case of the Upland Southerners, by no means all immigrants opposed the Yankee reformers on these issues. To the contrary, the immigrant groups that Richard Jensen and Paul Kleppner classify as pietists (i.e., those more concerned with right behavior than right belief) were often as fervent as the Yankees in their support for prohibition and common schools.[39] Many Scandinavian groups rivaled anyone in their enthusiastic prohibitionism, particularly the Swedish and Norwegian Lutherans, who often "out-Puritaned the Puritanism of the New Englanders."[40] Irish Catholics of the Old Northwest were equally fervent in their embrace of common schools, this at a time when conservative priests regularly denied the sacrament to parents who sent their children to public rather than parochial schools.

Yet it is also true that large numbers of immigrants in the Old Northwest opposed the Yankee reformers. This was especially the case for the groups Jensen and Kleppner call liturgicals and ritualists, respectively (i.e., those more concerned with right belief than right behavior). In the antebellum period, the foreign born rightly saw the Yankee-led movement for common schools as a threat to the pluralist, laissez-faire educational arrangements that had dominated the Old Northwest in the early national period. As Kaestle has described, those arrangements included mixed public/private schools, charity schools, and Catholic and foreign-language schools that received some public funding. When Yankee reformers sought to replace this institutional grab bag with state-regulated, tax-supported common schools, some immigrants—Catholics in particular—fought back. They resisted in the 1850s in Ohio, where the state constitution banned public aid to religious schools and the legislature taxed everyone to support the common schools. Archbishop John Purcell of Cincinnati argued that, given the fact that the common schools were sectarian (students were subjected to readings from the King James Bible), Catholic parents should be exempt from taxes. Purcell failed to overturn the law, but he helped launch a long tradition of immigrant and Catholic resistance to Yankee-led school reform in the Old Northwest.[41]

The most famous such battle was the one in Wisconsin over the Bennett law, a measure passed in 1889 by the Republican-controlled legislature at the request of the Republican governor, William D. Hoard, himself a Yankee Westerner.[42] Modeled on the controversial Edwards law of Illinois, the Bennett law required all students in the state's schools to be instructed in English, thus overturning Wisconsin's long tradition of tolerance for foreign-language parochial schools, which chiefly served the state's German Catholic and German and Norwegian Lutheran communities. The passage of the law prompted a fierce struggle between Yankee Republican supporters and Democratic opponents, the latter drawing crucial aid from the Lutheran synods and Catholic bishops. As Richard Jensen points out, the anti-Bennett campaign also collaborated with the parallel movement against the Edwards law (and its author, school superintendent Richard Edwards) in Illinois.[43] The struggle in both states centered on what many saw as the competing rights of immigrant parents and their children. Hoard warned about the "unprogressive elements" that were victimizing the "poor German boys" of Wisconsin. What those boys needed, the governor insisted, was "that unrivalled, that invaluable political and moral institution—our own blessing and the glory of our fathers—the New England system of free schools."[44] But many of the state's German and Norwegian voters disagreed, shifting their support to the Democrats; even the reliably Republican non-Christian Germans broke ranks to help overturn the Bennett law and oust its supporters. In 1890 Hoard lost his reelection bid and the state legislature was turned over to the Democrats for only second time in thirty-five years. The Democrats also swung to power throughout the Old Northwest (including Illinois, where Richard Edwards was defeated) and across the nation. Historians have placed much of the blame for this debacle on the Republican pietists' embrace of divisive cultural issues that drove away immigrant voters. Although the party would begin another long period of dominance in the Old Northwest with the 1896 election, it was only after reframing itself in terms that were more secular, pluralist, and libertarian—in other words, more the party of professionals like William McKinley and less the party of Yankee pietists like William Hoard.[45]

Another sign of the dwindling influence of the Yankee reformers inside the Republican Party was its increasing wariness of prohibition. Since the party's origins, Yankees had been primarily responsible for its consistent—though at times strategically muted—support for temperance in the Old Northwest. Temperance activism in the Old Northwest peaked in the 1880s, as movements arose in all the region's states to submit prohibition amendments to their constitutions. That decade also saw Yankee Republican drys and their pietist allies use local option laws to banish saloons in many counties, townships, and cities.[46] But the Republican drys met resistance not only from their Democratic opponents but also from within their own party. Among the latter, German immigrants were surely the most formidable. Throughout the decades, Germans in the Old Northwest regularly abandoned the Republican Party when it took strong temperance positions, as it did in Indiana in 1856, Wisconsin in 1873, and across the region in 1890.[47] By the late 1880s, the professionals who ran the party understood the price it was paying for militant prohibitionist positions and increasingly steered clear of them. In Ohio William McKinley, Mark Hanna, and John Sherman kept the party out of a campaign to enforce the Sunday closing laws; in Illinois drys limited their efforts to get the World's Fair to close on Sunday; and in cities across the region, a pragmatic new generation of Republican leaders reached out to wet immigrant voters.[48] Detroit Republican Hazen Pingree was especially adept at cultivating the foreign born. A Yankee migrant from Maine, Pingree famously launched his 1889 campaign for mayor of Detroit in a saloon. As Melvin Holli observes, "He drank 'red-eye' whisky with the Irish voters, spoke to German societies, [and] flattered the Poles."[49] While temperance would remain a popular cause among northwestern politicians with rural constituencies, it had become a liability for anyone—even a Yankee Republican—who needed the votes of urban immigrants.

This long history of contestation and compromise between the Yankees and other groups in the Old Northwest was barely acknowledged by the Greater New Englanders. Painting the Yankees as thoroughly dominant in the region, they generally ignored the challenges of outsiders. When resistance does occur in their accounts, it is easily quashed. Ellis Baker Usher recounted the defeat of proslavery southern migrants in the Wisconsin territory: "New England ideas and southern ideas of government . . . met and clashed sharply in the constitutional conventions, and the New Englander won."[50] But for the most part the Greater New Englanders presented other groups as passively following the Yankees' lead. They argued that the New England migrants had established the institutions of the Old Northwest on such a thoroughgoing Yankee basis that other groups had no choice but to respect them. After celebrating the Yankee pioneers of Wisconsin politics, law, education, and business, Usher concluded, "Though few in numbers, the New England men have been potent, and, however the foreign blood has or may predominate, theirs is the pattern that has been set and must be followed."[51] Yet, as Usher well knew, the state's immigrants had often refused to follow the lead of the New England pietists, particularly when it came to temperance and school reform. He had personally helped the foreign born overturn the Yankee pietists' Bennett law while serving as chairman of the Wisconsin Democratic Party's Central Committee in 1887–90.[52] Usher was not alone among the Greater New Englanders in downplaying the immigrants' resistance to Yankee hegemony. Senator Palmer declared, "The Celt, the Teuton, the Scandinavian, the Latin, the Slav, yield obedience to laws copied in a great measure from New England, and gather at town-meetings which impress them for the first time with the responsibilities of freemen. Their children attend schools modeled after New England; [and] read histories of their country in which New England illuminates almost every page of heroic achievement."[53] Ignoring a half century of immigrant opposition to Yankee temperance laws and school reforms, Palmer painted the foreign born as docile followers of the New Englanders.

Perhaps the surest sign of the Greater New Englanders' proprietary attitude toward the Old Northwest was their lack of concern over their dwindling share of the region's population. The mass migration of Yankees to the Old Northwest in the 1820s and 1830s made them the majority in some districts, but that would change after 1840, when the migration into the region became dominated by the foreign born. By midcentury Yankee migrants comprised only 3.8 percent of the population of the Old Northwest as a whole, and the percentage was significantly smaller in southern-dominated Indiana.[54] In short the Greater New Englanders faced a demographic situation in the West that closely resembled the one plaguing the Brahmin Anglo-Saxonists back east. But unlike the Brahmins, the Greater New Englanders generally regarded the rise in their region's foreign-born population with complacency rather than fear. Ellis Baker Usher, for example, insisted that it was not the Yankees of Wisconsin who had joined the state's American Protective Association (the leading anti-Catholic, nativist organization of the 1890s).[55] Confident in the assimilative power of Yankee ideas and institutions, the Greater New Englanders saw the arrival of immigrants in the Old Northwest as an excellent opportunity to extend New England's sway. Indeed, they sometimes took pride in the smallness of their numbers as compelling proof of their ability to dominate larger groups. Usher marveled at the tiny percentage of his state's population (he estimated only 15,000 out of 1.6 million total) that could claim native-born ancestry going back to Revolutionary times: "This is the fact that is most astonishing. . . . and it is quite remarkable, in this aspect of the growth of the state, to find the great influence this little leaven of New England blood has exerted, from the very beginning."[56] Even as the children of the immigrants took power in municipal governments across the Old Northwest, most Greater New Englanders kept their faith in the leavening power of Yankee institutions.

The one partial exception was Thomas Witherell Palmer, who joined his Brahmin Anglo-Saxonist colleagues in calling for the restriction of immigration. In 1887 the senator introduced a bill that would have required of every immigrant a certificate from a US consul attesting to his or her good character and fitness for citizenship. No certificate would be granted to any Mormon, convict (except for political prisoners), "lunatic, idiot," "anarchist, nihilist," enemy of the Constitution, or person likely to become a public charge.[57] In introducing the bill (which was ultimately tabled), Palmer called on some of the favorite arguments of the Brahmin restrictionists: unskilled immigrants undercut the wages and living standards of native-born workers, radical immigrants were a threat to the lives and property of Americans, and southern and eastern European immigrants were racially inferior.[58] But, when he lectured on "New England at the West" the following Independence Day, Palmer presented the foreign born as a benefit to his country, rather than a threat. The reasons for this about-face are unclear, but they may have to do with context. Speaking from the heights of Greater New England, Palmer apparently saw advantages to immigration that were not visible from the Senate chamber. This was evident at the end of the Independence Day speech when he contemplated the future relations of Greater New England and the mother region. While acknowledging that the latter already belonged to the foreign born, he insisted that the former would always be Yankee territory. He even dreamed of the day when the Yankee Westerners, reinforced through crossings with other groups, would recolonize New England: "It may be that the teeming West may at some future day repay the debt incurred by reflecting back a civilization which, flowing from the parent states, has become enriched and multiplied in a wider arena, [and] which has been invigorated and stimulated by a fusion with many races, but of which the base has been furnished by New England."[59] Reversing, for once, the Anglo-Saxon's relentless march to the West, the Yankee Westerner would return for one final conquest in his ancestral home in the East.

The Preservationists

Palmer's dream of reconquering New England in the name of the Anglo-Saxons would have earned guffaws from a second group of commentators on the Yankees of the Old Northwest, the preservationists. These writers believed traditional Yankee ideas and institutions were no match for the corrosive forces of modernity—industrialism, urbanization, materialism, and above all immigration—that had overtaken much of New England, particularly in its southern states. Far from recolonizing New England or expanding it to the west, the preservationists merely wanted to save what remained of it. They believed the best place to do that was not in New England proper, which was already too far gone to preserve, but in the villages it had planted in the early nineteenth century, particularly in that legendary outpost of Yankeedom, the Western Reserve of Ohio. There, they argued, one could still find the republican simplicity, strict morality, deep piety, and racial purity of old New England. At a time when many people saw the Old Northwest as the symbol of the nation's future, the preservationists cherished it as a throwback to New England's past.

The primary embodiment of the preservationists' nostalgia was the New England village. They drew on long-standing myths about the region's so-called center villages to paint them as pastoral islands removed from the main currents of history. As historians have shown, the New England center village was actually a product of the ambition, market orientation, and social pretension sparked in rural New England by the commercial revolution. During the late eighteenth and early nineteenth centuries, town centers across rural New England expanded to meet the commercial and professional needs of outlying rural settlements. The wealthy and ambitious inhabitants of such villages embarked on building and landscaping projects—turning meetinghouse lots into town commons, building imposing federal and Greek revival homes and shops, and renovating churches—to transform the modest town center of the eighteenth century into that icon of New England regionalism, the "white village."[60] But the preservationists chose to ignore this history, instead portraying the center village as a relic of Puritan times that was now threatened by sprawling immigrant cities and factory towns.

In protesting what modernity had done to the New England village, the preservationists resembled their contemporaries, both inside and outside the region, who argued that the "real" New England had moved north to the region's underdeveloped hill country. Since most of the cities, factories, and immigrants were located in the region's south, Dona Brown explains, "Northern New England was increasingly considered the true home of New England's heritage, both moral and racial."[61] But many preservationists believed that *all* of New England, including the hill country, had fallen under the sway of the city. Journalist and author George Perry Morris underscored this point in a discussion of the region's college towns, which, he claimed, best embodied the classic charm of the New England village. Unfortunately, that charm had been obliterated in New Haven, Cambridge, and Providence by "a heterogeneous population and large manufacturing interests."[62] Nor was it to be found in the collegiate "hill-towns" like Amherst, Williamstown, and Hanover, for

> even there, standards of living and conduct among students and instructors have been changed and influenced by the habits and ideals of the universities and the cities. Hence, to see the American college town in all its pristine simplicity and beauty, one now has to go to the new New England, and visit such institutions as Oberlin, Beloit, Knox, Iowa, and Colorado colleges.[63]

In other words, one had to seek out the college towns of the West that had been founded by Yankee migrants and their children.

Many preservationists believed the villages that best captured the spirit of old New England were in Ohio's Western Reserve. There, they insisted, one could still find examples of the traditional Yankee village community that had once been a distinguishing feature of New England life. The preservationists argued that the geographic isolation and ethnic homogeneity of the Western Reserve had protected its Yankee villages from the influence of urban industrial America. But in reality the Western Reserve had always been more ethnically and culturally diverse than the preservationists let on. Their timeless, pastoral portrait of the Western Reserve is thus best understood as a response to the rapid changes taking place back in New England.

It was no accident that the preservationists seized on the Western Reserve as the locus of their nostalgia for Yankee village life, since that is precisely how "New Connecticut" (as it was then called) was marketed by the New Englanders who surveyed, developed, and missionized it beginning in the 1790s. The Western Reserve was originally part of the vast colonial territories of Connecticut, most of which were ceded to the federal government in 1786. But Connecticut reserved (hence Western Reserve) a tract between the forty-first parallel and Lake Erie, stretching from the western border of

Pennsylvania to a point 120 miles to the west. In 1895 most of that territory was sold to a group of investors, the Connecticut Land Company, which surveyed the land, sold lots to settlers and speculators, and promoted settlement. The land company worked closely with the Connecticut Missionary Society, which had been founded by Congregationalists in 1798 to minister to the new settlements in Vermont, New York, Pennsylvania, and the Old Northwest. (After 1801 the missionary society had the support of Presbyterians who joined forces with the Congregationalists under the so-called Plan of Union.)[64] As Amy DeRogatis has shown, both the Connecticut Land Company and the Connecticut Missionary Society promoted the Western Reserve by appealing to their New England audiences' Puritan nostalgia. Thus, land company proprietors laid out villages in what was commonly (but erroneously) understood to be traditional New England fashion, with lots divided into grids around a green bordered by a church and houses. Likewise, the missionary society appealed to potential donors by portraying the settlers of New Connecticut as homogeneous communities of latter-day Pilgrims and Puritans who had given up the comforts of civilization for a new errand into the wilderness.[65] As James Rohrer argues, such Puritan nostalgia was driven in part by the erosion of traditional communal values in Revolutionary era New England. Anxious that economic and demographic growth was fueling individualism and materialism, traditionalists called for a return to the old ways of "unity, harmony, and mutuality."[66] Some traditionalists also saw the Western Reserve as an opportunity to revive orthodox Calvinism in the West at a time when it was increasingly under attack by liberals in New England.[67] This was most obvious in the case of the migrants who formed covenanted communities. In a self-conscious reenactment of their Puritan ancestors, bands of New Englanders, usually from the same town, established new towns in New Connecticut such as Oberlin, Tallmadge, and Hudson. Covenanting members agreed to follow strict regulations governing social, familial, and religious duties. In Hudson, for example, members were forbidden to attend "to any part of the business of making sugar or cheese" on the Sabbath, and in Oberlin they were required to eat "only plain and wholesome food."[68]

But the Yankee town proprietors' and missionaries' dream of reviving old New England in the Western Reserve was frustrated by challenges both internal and external to the Yankee migrant community. As David French explains, the social discipline and Calvinist orthodoxy of the Western Reserve's covenanted towns soon dissolved in the face of "the leveling tendencies of economic expansion on the frontier, the pressing claims of other Protestant sects, the challenge of noncovenanted frontiersmen, and the growing power of Jacksonian politics in the region itself."[69] Communal bonds were further eroded by poor land sales, as most Connecticut Land Company proprietors found it necessary to sell lots to all comers, including those with no interest in covenanting.[70] The Connecticut Missionary Society also met mixed results in its effort to establish Calvinist churches, as its agents competed with "sectarians"—primarily Methodists, Baptists, and Universalists—who lured away their members and sometimes heckled them during services.[71] As was true across the United States in the early national period, the Calvinists of the Connecticut Missionary Society could not match the popular appeal of the "sectarians." Ironically, the missionary society confronted its gravest challenge on the Western Reserve with the founding in 1833 of the Oberlin Colony and Collegiate Institute (as the college was initially called). As DeRogatis points out, the Oberlin colony was, in many respects, precisely the kind of settlement the missionary society had called for: a covenanted community that explicitly sought to revive Puritan ways of living, worshipping, and town planning. But fierce debates over the liberal theology and revival techniques taught at the Collegiate Institute ultimately split apart the Congregationalist and Presbyterian members of the Connecticut Missionary Society, ending the Plan of Union under which it had operated for thirty-six years.[72]

While contending, on the one hand, with the resistance of their fellow Yankees, the town proprietors and missionaries of the Western Reserve had to wrestle with an increasingly diverse population on the other. The Connecticut Missionary Society may have promoted the Western Reserve as a zone of homogeneous Yankee settlement, but the reality was otherwise. In its early decades, New Connecticut attracted migrants not only from the Mid-Atlantic and South (including a few African Americans) but also from abroad. By the 1830s Ravenna and Akron had substantial Irish neighborhoods; Deerfield, Rootstown, and Randolph had significant German populations; and Cleveland was home to the Western Reserve's most diverse population, including Irish, English, Canadians, Scots, Welsh, Manx, and Jews from the Germanies and the Austro-Hungarian empire. The Western Reserve would continue to attract immigrants after the Civil War, not only in its larger cities but also in smaller lakeshore towns like Lorain, Fairport, Ashtabula, and Conneaut, where they were worked in the mills and on the railroads and docks.[73] By 1880 the Western Reserve had a larger immigrant population than any other part of Ohio.[74]

The town proprietors and missionaries of the early nineteenth century may have failed in their efforts to revive Puritan New England in New Connecticut, but their successors—the preservationists of the Gilded Age—paid little notice. The latter persisted in romanticizing the Western Reserve as the one place where the faith, values, and bloodlines of the Puritans still lived. Indeed, they seemed to cling tighter to the fantasy with each passing decade. As accelerating changes in New England left them longing for the way things had been before the coming of factories, cities, and immigrants, they found refuge in an idyll of the Western Reserve.

James A. Garfield was probably the one person most responsible for introducing Gilded Age audiences to a nostalgic image of the Western Reserve. In an 1873 speech to the Geauga County Historical Society, that proud son of the Western Reserve declared, "There are townships on this Western Reserve which are more thoroughly New England in character and spirit than most of the towns of the New England of today. Cut off as they were from the metropolitan life that has gradually been molding and changing the spirit of New England, they preserved here in the wilderness the characteristics of New England, as it was when they left it at the beginning of the century."[75] Over the following decades, preservationists would regularly cite Garfield on the differences between New England and the Western Reserve.[76] But what he had intended as a neutral observation became a value-laden comparison for the preservationists. They blamed the mother region for abandoning the "spirit of New England" so lovingly preserved in the villages of the Western Reserve.

Many preservationists believed the differences between New England and the Western Reserve were most visible in their respective populations. They celebrated the men and women of the Western Reserve as true Yankees in the best sense—idealistic, moral, plain-living republicans—who still lived by values that had long since been abandoned in New England. In a 1927 memoir, Yankee scion and Western Reserve native Lucien Price remembered Western Reserve Academy as a bastion of those values.[77] Founded in 1826, along with Western Reserve College, by Yankee migrant and town planner David Hudson, the academy had fallen on hard times when Price arrived in 1901, but he nevertheless remembered it fondly: "More like New England than New England itself."[78] At "Hardscrabble Hellas," the schoolboys kept warm by sleeping three to a bed and bathed by "standing ankle-deep in snow and slashing pails of icy water at each other from crown to heel, as sturdily as ever Homer's warriors."[79] The faculty was equally heroic, turning down offers of lucrative business careers to teach on meager salaries: "These four men were inheritors of that stalwart Hellenic tradition of the New England schoolmaster which began before Harvard College with Boston Latin School and Ezekiel Cheever, a heritage which was the intellectual backbone of the rustic republic."[80] Price acknowledged that the Western Reserve Academy he remembered bore little resemblance to its successor institution—after closing due to financial troubles in 1903, the school reopened thirteen years later and embarked on an ambitious building campaign, thanks to the largesse of coal magnate James W. Ellsworth. Nevertheless, Price cherished the academy's early days as the epitome of old New England values: "Those Connecticut pioneers founding their school in an oak forest are type and symbol of the age and race that sired us. When we were young and poor, our poverty and struggle bred men. We grow prosperous. And now what are we? This wealth—is it to be a bed of ease or an alpenstock? These machines—are we to use them or be used by them?" "Hardscrabble Hellas" stood as a powerful reproach to an era gone soft with "machines," "wealth," and "ease."[81]

Other preservationists also celebrated the Yankees of the Western Reserve as throwbacks to old New England. Many cited John Brown as the classic example of the Puritan-derived courage and idealism that still pervaded towns such as Hudson, the childhood home of Brown after his family migrated from Connecticut. In contrast, the preservationists believed Gilded Age New England was full of jaded snobs who lacked convictions and the courage to fight for them. Methodist minister D. A. Goodsell contrasted a "true New Englander" like John Brown with his overcivilized cousins back east, with their "Anglo-maniacal varnish of dudery, drawl, quizzing-glass, and bore."[82] Attorney, author, and politician Albert Gallatin Riddle dramatized several awkward encounters between those effete New Englanders and their rugged cousins from the Western Reserve.[83] In his biography of James A. Garfield, Riddle lauded his subject for always remaining "on the common ground of common men."[84] Yet, when Garfield went east for his education, he encountered urban class hierarchy and fashion: "At Williams, the air was warm and close with the styles, fashions, and conventionalisms,—stifling, with the artificialities and refinements of eastern life."[85] Those refinements do not translate well to the Western Reserve. In Riddle's novel *Bart Ridgeley* (1873), a young snob with "high Boston" notions gets set straight by a daughter of the Western Reserve. As a friend of the young lady reports, "He was telling her how this and that is done in Boston, and she in return told him how we do not do the same things here, and claimed that our way is the best."[86] There was no place for urban artificiality and exclusiveness in the democratic villages of the Western Reserve.

Many preservationists also drew invidious comparisons between the demographics of the two regions, romanticizing the Yankee purity of the Western Reserve over against the appalling ethnic diversity of New England. Some merely implied the contrast. Riddle, for example, presented the Western Reserve as a "segregated" society of Yankees, recalling his own experience of growing up there and never hearing "the brogue, nor a word of German." He hinted that that the ethnic homogeneity of the Western Reserve had helped it conserve Yankee cultural practices that were disappearing back east. In one essay he maintained that in the Western Reserve, one could still hear "words and usages lost in the older homes."[87] Although he was not explicit, Riddle seemed to blame New England's cultural losses on immigration. Later in that same essay, he reflected wistfully on the heroic generation of Yankee migrants who founded New Connecticut: "There never was a peasantry in the New England of that day."[88] One is left to assume that there is such a peasantry—a foreign-born one—in the New England of the present and that it is responsible for the disappearance of Yankee culture from the mother region.

Other preservationists openly contrasted the alleged homogeneity of the Western Reserve with the ethnic diversity of New England. Like Riddle, they ignored the Western Reserve's own diversity to paint it as a bittersweet reminder of what New England had been before the coming of the foreign born. Many believed the demographic differences between the two regions were most obvious in their respective villages.[89] To prove his thesis that the founders of a village permanently set its moral character, clergyman and best-selling author Josiah Strong (a Puritan scion who spent most of his childhood in Hudson) cited Tallmadge in the Western Reserve, which, he claimed, was still benefiting from its founding by home missionary David Bacon. Unfortunately, the same was not true back in the mother region, where immigrants were obliterating all traces of the founders, and "the glory is departing from many a New England village, because men, alien in blood, in religion, and in civilization, are taking possession of homes in which were once reared the descendants of the Pilgrims."[90] Others endorsed this contrast between the village populations of the Western Reserve and New England. Lucien Price memorialized turn-of-the-century Hudson as a "transplanted academic village" that "was what New England had been half a century before and would have remained but for the invention of machinery and the importation of Southern European mill hands."[91] Also speaking of Hudson, Leonard Woolsey Bacon declared, "At this day, if one wishes to find a typical Connecticut town of the old unmixed Puritan strain, he should look for it in the 'New Connecticut,' not in the Old."[92] For the preservationists, the arrival of immigrants had turned everything topsy-turvy, with New Connecticut representing New England's Puritan past and old Connecticut embodying its polyglot future.

Some preservationists attributed the supposed Yankee purity of the Western Reserve's villages to their physical remoteness, arguing that places like Hudson and Tallmadge were simply too far off the beaten track to attract immigrants. Others believed the key to the Western Reserve's alleged homogeneity lay in the exclusiveness of the Yankee migrants, who had inherited from their Puritan ancestors an attitude of aloofness or even hostility toward other groups. Cleveland judge Henry C. White maintained:

> In our habits of intercourse and manners we are unconsciously tempered with that seclusive reserve and conservatism which have come down to us from our ancestors, who had gained the spirit of clannish self-reliance from the hard experiences of exile life with strangers or cautious reticence among unfriendly countrymen.

White believed this "seclusive reserve" enabled the Yankee Westerners of the Reserve to keep alive those "grand gifts of Puritanism to our modern social life": morality, piety, individualism, and respect for character.[93] A. G. Riddle likewise saw the exclusiveness of the Western Reserve's Yankees as a valuable legacy from their Puritan ancestors, which allowed the former to preserve their forebears' piety and sense of purpose.[94] Riddle contrasted the persistence of the Puritan influence in the Western Reserve with its disappearance from southern Ohio. He believed the key to this regional difference lay in the New England migrants' relations with other groups. Whereas the Yankees were isolated on the Western Reserve, in southern Ohio they mingled with other peoples. As a result, "[W]hile New England early lost its distinctive influence in southern Ohio, it concentrated and augmented it on the northern border, which was so much condensed Puritan New England. It still remains essentially New England."[95]

Few people now believe that the Western Reserve was ever "essentially New England," particularly not by 1886 when Riddle published those words. But he was certainly not alone in clinging to the myth of a "Puritan" Western Reserve well into the Gilded Age. At a time when the days of the Yankees seemed numbered in the East, the preservationists were loath to give up their dream of a place where the Puritans still strode the land, and since its earliest days, New Connecticut had played that cherished role in the Yankee imaginary.

The Nationalists

The preservationists' fantasy of retreating from modernity into the western remnants of old New England was thoroughly rejected by the final group of writers I will discuss, the nationalists. The latter celebrated the Yankee Westerners—the group to which most of them belonged—not for preserving New England traditions but for improving on them. Most nationalists would have agreed with their most famous member, Frederick Jackson Turner, who declared, "I am especially convinced of the importance of the New Englander *after* he has left his native heath!"[96] The nationalists believed the Yankee Westerner differed from his cousin back east in several important respects. Whereas the latter was conservative, narrow-minded, and provincial, the former was liberal, broad-minded, and national. The nationalists traced these differences to two distinct processes. First was the decision to migrate, which supposedly selected the most adventurous and progressive Yankees to go west. Second was the experience of living in the West, which allegedly surrounded Yankee Westerners with an array of broadening influences, including challenging living conditions, inspiring scenery, and above all a diverse and sometimes contentious array of ethnic groups. The nationalists maintained that the results of these two liberalizing processes were visible in the Yankee Westerners' economic, social, and political views, which consistently were more progressive than those of their New England cousins. Most nationalists thought the differences extended right to the core of the two groups' identities: whereas the Yankees of New England remained narrowly provincial, those of the West soon adopted an expansive American identity. Yet the nationalists believed those differences were shrinking, thanks to the Yankee Westerners' influence on their New England cousins. Having fled New England because of its intolerance and conservatism, the Yankee Westerners were sending back a "reflex tide" to remake the mother region in their own liberal image.[97]

Some of the nationalists' main ideas (e.g., the opposition between a liberal, nationalist West and a conservative, provincial East, the belief that the West powerfully influences the East, and the emphasis on environmental influences on human behavior) are strongly associated with Turner, who famously promoted them in his landmark essay "The Significance of the Frontier in American History" (1893). Yet it was not the early Turner of frontier fame but the later, lesser-known Turner of "sectional" (i.e., regional) history who explored how life in the Old Northwest had shaped his fellow Yankee Westerners.[98] In essays such as "The Middle West" (1901), "Middle

Western Pioneer Democracy" (1918), "Greater New England in the Middle of the Nineteenth Century" (1919), and "The Children of the Pioneers" (1926), Turner echoed what his nationalist predecessors had long been saying about the transformation of the Yankee in the Old Northwest.[99] These essays reflect their early twentieth-century context—most obviously in treating the Old Northwest as part of that young giant of American regions, the Middle West. (It was not until after the turn of the century that the Middle West emerged as a distinct region in scholarly and popular discourses, partly thanks to Turner himself.)[100] Yet they can also be read as the culmination of the ideas of Gilded Age nationalists such as historian B. A. Hinsdale, whose regional focus and specific arguments about the Yankee Westerner Turner frequently echoes.

The nationalists relied on several different, but closely related, metaphors to describe the transformation of the Yankee in the Old Northwest, including "softened," "liberalized," and "enlarged." But the most popular metaphor by far was "broadened," which was used to convey the full range of traits—economic, spiritual, and political—that distinguished the Yankee Westerners from their counterparts back east. Some nationalists invoked the broadening metaphor to gesture generally to the worldview of the Western Yankee, as when George Julian praised the Yankee settlers of the Western Reserve for developing "a broader and better type of humanity than that of New England itself"—a view of the Reserve's Yankees that would surely have raised eyebrows among the preservationists.[101] Other nationalists used the broadening metaphor to laud specific institutional innovations of the Yankee Westerners, as when Hinsdale praised the "broadening and liberalizing influence" of their educational policies.[102] In either case the point was to draw an invidious distinction between the liberalism, flexibility, and open-mindedness of the Yankee Westerners and the narrowness, rigidity, and conservatism of their New England cousins. Whether they had in mind the Yankee Westerner's business enterprises, religious beliefs, or educational and political reforms, the nationalists agreed that it was his breadth that distinguished him from his cousin back east.

Some nationalists associated the Yankee Westerner's broadening with the scale and ambition of his business schemes. They believed in the West the Yankee had finally found a land commensurate with his legendary talent for bold, risk-taking capitalism. In a book promoting the newly completed Union Pacific Railroad, *Springfield Republican* editor Samuel Bowles marveled at what the West had done for the migrant: "[H]ere the Yankee has broadened and softened; and what he can do, what he has done here, with a richer soil, a broader area, a larger hope, and surer realization, is worth the scrutiny of every American and every student of America."[103] The migrants from New England's "sterile hillsides" seemed to have had died and gone to heaven: "Stop and see if you recognize them in their new robes."[104] Turner also saw a heavenly match between the Yankee's boundless enterprise and the rich economic potential of the West:

> the men who became captains of industry in the West had vision and idealism respondent to the undeveloped spaces, the unexploited wilderness, and the tremendous opportunities which opened to their imagination as well as to their will power. With faith they stretched railroad lines out onto the open prairie in advance of settlement.[105]

Turner believed the enterprise of the Yankee Westerner had a broadening effect on business back in the mother region: "Thereafter the New England banker, railroad promoter, merchant, and manufacturer . . . lifted his eyes to a farther horizon and followed with his vision the extending frontier of New England's western sons; he was tempted to build more largely, to see farther."[106] Despite the New England Yankees' well-deserved reputation for capitalist innovation, Turner believed they were taking lessons from their western kinsmen.

In romanticizing the "faith" and "idealism" of people like John Rockefeller and Henry Ford, Turner deliberately sought to refute the stereotype of the Yankee Westerner as a greedy materialist. According to the nationalists, not only did the Yankee Westerner have a spiritual side but it was far more liberal than the crabbed faith of his eastern kin. They maintained that in his new western home the Yankee had jettisoned his dogmatism and distrust of other sects. Moreover, some nationalists thought the Yankee Westerner's doctrinal liberalism had already cast a broadening influence on religious culture back in the mother region.

The nationalists acknowledged that some Yankees had left New England to escape the moral surveillance of church and community, but they insisted that many more had gone west in search of a more open and accepting religious environment. A number of nationalists believed those migrants had found their Mecca in the Western Reserve. Rejecting the preservationists' portrayal of the Western Reserve as the last bastion of Puritanism, these nationalists presented it as a haven of theological liberalism and sectarian diversity. They saw the settlers of the Western Reserve as fugitives from the Standing Order, the alliance of Congregational ministers and Federalist politicians that had dominated political and religious life in early national New England. As Reserve native B. A. Hinsdale put it, "[T]hese people had not been long in their new home before they began to feel the throbbings of a new life, and they soon began to do things that in their old home they would never have dreamed of doing."[107] Those bold new things included the Yankee migrants' support for an array of Protestant sects and their abandonment of Congregationalist dogma.[108] As scholars have shown, on the Western Reserve, as elsewhere, liberalism and sectarianism were strenuously opposed by New England–based organizations such as the Connecticut Missionary Society.[109] Yet the nationalists believed the influence ran just as strong, if not stronger, in the other direction. As Turner put it:

> [I]t must be remembered that the West itself deeply affected and even shaped these spiritual forces by the influence of its own society and ideals, and that many a New England missionary of Puritan civilization became so changed by his removal as to find New England itself no longer a congenial home. There was giving as well as taking on the part of Greater New England in the West.[110]

As scholars have shown, this philosophy of "giving as well as taking" was particular evident at the Oberlin Institute, which from its founding, boldly offered seminary training to eastern students—this at a time when most New Englanders viewed the Old Northwest as anything but a center of theological wisdom.[111]

Most nationalists thought the same broadening breeze that blew through the Yankee Westerners' faith also inspired their social and political life. Comparing the Yankee Westerners with their New England kinsmen on issues such as slavery, education, and political reform, the nationalists consistently found the former more progressive and democratic. They rejected the popular stereotype of New England as a hotbed of radicals, deeming it instead a land of conservatism and social hierarchy, which had to look elsewhere for new ideas and the initiative to act on them. Fortunately, the nationalists contended, progressive thinking and reform movements were in ample supply along the Yankee Runway. They credited the Yankee Westerners with exerting a powerful liberalizing influence on the ideologies and institutions of their New England cousins.

The debate over slavery was probably the nationalists' favorite example of the Yankee Westerners' liberalizing influence on New England. Despite the mother region's reputation for militant abolitionism, the nationalists portrayed it as lagging far behind the Old Northwest on the issue. They argued that, thanks to the Northwest Ordinance of 1787, the Old Northwest was antislavery from the start, whereas New England had to overcome a long history of slaveholding and slave trading that persisted into the nineteenth century. Although some nationalists acknowledged the presence of proslavery elements in the Old Northwest, most nevertheless saw the region as the heart of the abolitionist movement. They celebrated the antislavery views of Yankee Westerners such as Joshua Giddings, Ben Wade, and the Oberlin students, though some expressed discomfort at the revolutionary violence of John Brown.[112] Many nationalists credited the Old Northwest with radiating a potent antislavery influence throughout the East, including New England. Albert Bushnell Hart praised the younger region for acting as the conscience of the eastern states on the issue: "The influence of Ohio, and Indiana, and Illinois helped to hold Connecticut, and New York and Pennsylvania and New Jersey to their schemes of gradual emancipation."[113] Hinsdale told a similar story, citing an 1860 speech in which William Henry Seward declared it providential that "these new States of the Northwest" had matured in time "to rally the free States of the Atlantic coast, to call them back to their ancient principles, to nerve them to sustain them in the contest at the Capitol, and to send their noble and true sons and daughters" to Bleeding Kansas.[114] The nationalists insisted that the Old Northwest had also injected antislavery views into the nation's politics through the Free Soil and Republican parties.[115] After celebrating his region's crucial contributions to the Republican Party—which included all its successful presidential candidates to date—Hinsdale boldly declared, "The Northwest decided the constitutional contest between freedom and slavery."[116]

Many nationalists thought education was another area where the Yankee Westerners had liberalized the views of their eastern cousins. Hinsdale (himself a former school superintendent) wrote that "no better example of the broadening and liberalizing influence of the Northwest can be given."[117] While the nationalists conceded the pioneering role that New England had played on the issue, they believed it had also learned much from the younger region. Hinsdale clarified just how much in a catalog of the foremost contributions of the northwestern states to educational progress, including "[t]he flexibility of their educational systems and their adaptation to existing conditions," "the prominence that they have accorded to the State University," and "the readiness with which the coeducation of the sexes has been taken up and developed."[118] (Significantly, Hinsdale did not mention another "first": the policy at Oberlin College of admitting students without respect to race.)

While conceding, "It is impossible to say how far these things have reacted upon the older part of the country," Albert Bushnell Hart credited the West with inspiring New England's state universities and its tentative embrace of coeducation.[119] Hinsdale was more emphatic: "We have heard a great deal about what the East has done for the West, as respects education and other matters; the time has come for drawing attention to what the West has done for the East."[120] Other nationalists supported him by citing the "reflex tide" of Yankee Westerners now serving on the faculties of eastern colleges and universities, Yale in particular.[121]

The nationalists maintained that the broadening influence of the Yankee Westerners also "reacted on" their cousins back east in the case of political reform. They claimed that political reforms typically began in the democratic West and gradually worked their way back to the more conservative East (a theory that has been rejected by recent scholars).[122] Their favorite example of this process was white manhood suffrage, but they also cited the election of judges, the rotation of political offices, and the limitation of executive power. Hart described white manhood suffrage as a firestorm originating in the West: "This flame of popular government swept backward across the mountains, and within about forty years from the planting of Ohio had practically overrun every New England State."[123] Hinsdale maintained that it was no accident that the colonization of the Old Northwest occurred in the same years as the "establishment of the American Republic" and "the increased energy of the democratizing movement."[124] Turner suggested that New England's entrance "upon a freer, political and social era" after the War of 1812 was at least partly due to the influence of the Yankee Westerners.[125]

The nationalists also credited the Yankee Westerner with teaching his eastern kinsman to think of himself as an American first and a Yankee afterward. They believed the Yankee Westerner had acquired his own nationalist views through the experience of migration, which transformed him from a chauvinistic, self-righteous provincial into a fervent champion of union. Hinsdale contrasted the "narrowness and jealousy" of the New Englanders who opposed the Louisiana Purchase with the selflessness of their northwestern descendants, who fought to preserve the Union during the Civil War.[126] The Reverend Rufus Clark similarly juxtaposed the intense provincialism of the late eighteenth-century New Englanders against the nationalism of their cousins who settled the Old Northwest: "Crossing the Hudson and Delaware and Ohio, they were no longer New Englanders, but Americans. They were divested of their tribal traits and of their state pride." Clark argued that those migrants and their children would become the glue that held the nation together. He paid special tribute to the first group of New Englanders to settle in the Old Northwest, the Ohio Company of Associates. Noting (with some inaccuracy) that the group's boat was called the *Union Gallery,* Clark enthused, "No inscription could have more appropriately been borne by the barge that carried that noble band of pioneers to the territory, that has so much to do in reconciling and uniting opposing sections of an infant Republic."[127] Minister (and Yankee Westerner) Henry M. Storrs believed the Americanization of the Yankee in the West was part of a larger nationalizing process that included the assimilation of immigrants and the reconciliation of North and South after the Civil War: "The local type is softening its rigid and exclusive lines. The New Englander, forgetting that he was born east of the Hudson, merges into the greater whole. . . . North and South, East and West, Atlantic shore and Pacific slope, are fast becoming vibrant with one common life—'the American throb.'"[128] Storrs believed the national impulse was particularly strong in the Old Northwest, quoting an eastern professor who confessed, "I never felt the American throb until I came this side the Alleghanies [*sic*] and entered Ohio."[129]

Other nationalists argued that the American throb of the Yankee Westerners was also being felt back in New England. Clark maintained that along with their "effect upon the settlements," the Yankee migrants had "an equally marked effect . . . upon the states from which they came in the broadening of their views and the breaking up of their selfishness."[130] He contended that the settlement of the Old Northwest forced the states of New England to start thinking and acting in national terms, most notably by ceding to the federal government their western territories (he ignored Connecticut's retention of the Western Reserve). Turner claimed that the Yankee Westerners had the same nationalizing effect across a whole range of New England experience: "[B]y the middle of the century, the history of New England's domestic commerce and manufacture and her political life in the nation shows an enlarged outlook and a more national attitude as the result of her new relationships with other sections." From the transcendentalists to the businessmen who founded express companies, all of New England was learning to think nationally from the Yankee Westerners.[131]

Yet exactly how was it that the Old Northwest changed Yankee provincials into broad-minded Americans? In answer to this question, the nationalists identified two distinct processes. First was the decision of whether to migrate in the first place, which supposedly selected only the most adventurous, progressive, and open-minded Yankees to go west. Second was the experience of living in the Old Northwest, which allegedly surrounded the migrant with such broadening influences as a challenging pioneer life, an inspiring natural landscape, and most important, a diverse and sometimes unruly array of ethnic groups. While some nationalists emphasized one of these processes over the other, most believed both had a hand in shaping the Yankee Westerner. As Alfred Mathews put it, "Ancestry and environment, the world-old powerful pair of formative causes, were at work."[132]

Most nationalists saw the Yankee migrants as a select group, the product of a winnowing process that sent west only the best New Englanders. They based this notion on the Puritans' historical self-construction as a chosen people, selected by God for their errand into the wilderness. Some nationalists quoted the 1668 election sermon in which Puritan minister William Stoughton famously declared, "God sifted a whole Nation that he might send choice Grain over into this Wilderness."[133] The nationalists believed a similar sifting process had been repeated on these shores each time the Puritans and their descendants moved west. Thus, Alfred Mathews reasoned, "If Massachusetts 'was sown with selected grain,' as has been truthfully enough claimed, Connecticut was sown with twice-winnowed grain."[134] As a proud son of the Western Reserve, Mathews further believed that New Connecticut was sown with thrice-winnowed grain.[135] But precisely which traits were being selected for? On this question the nationalists disagreed. Some argued that it was the most moral of the Yankees who went west. Mathews, for example, claimed that the ban on slavery in the Northwest Ordinance attracted "the more morally advanced" from New England and other places.[136] Yet elsewhere he suggested that migration had chosen Yankees with more worldly traits. Thus, the "broader-minded men" followed Thomas Hooker to Connecticut, and "the hardiest, the most resolute, and most enterprising of their race" left Connecticut for the Western Reserve.[137] Other commentators agreed that migration sent west the most liberal, energetic, and risk-taking Yankees. Turner claimed that the migrants were the "adventurous spirits of New England," "less contented, less conservative," and "less satisfied with the old order than were their neighbors in the East. They were the young men with initiative, with discontent."[138] By the time they got to the West, these rebels had already rejected many of the pieties of their native region.

Most nationalists believed the same traits that predisposed Yankees to migrate in the first place were reinforced by the "forest-change"—the Shakespearean pun is Turner's—that they underwent in their new homes.[139] They argued that life in the Old Northwest subjected migrants to an array of influences that broadened their minds, boosted their spirits, and fired their imaginations, freeing them from the lingering effects of a conservative, tradition-bound New England. Some nationalists emphasized the benefits the Yankee migrants had reaped from pioneering. They insisted that leaving civilized New England for the new lands had forced the migrants to give up old prejudices, learn new skills, and think more creatively. Turner quoted a letter from a pioneer to a friend back east warning him not to come

> if you can't stand seeing your old New England ideas, ways of doing, and living and in fact, all of the good old Yankee fashions knocked out of shape. . . . But if you can bear grief with a smile, can put up with a scale of accommodations ranging from the soft side of a plank before the fire (and perhaps three in a bed at that) down through the middling and inferior grades; if you are never at a loss for ways to do the most unpracticable things without tools; if you can do all this and some more come on.[140]

At a time when the lack of civilized comforts in the West was commonly cited by New Englanders as a reason not to go there, some nationalists saw an upside to a land where beds and tools were still scarce.

Many nationalists believed the distinctive physical environment of the Old Northwest also exerted a broadening influence on the Yankee migrant. Contrary to present-day stereotypes, they depicted the Old Northwest as a land of natural sublimity—vast lakes, enormous forests, expansive prairies, and bracing winds—where the Yankee was inspired to abandon outworn creeds, chase big dreams, and try new things. Turner enthused, "The winds of the prairies swept away almost at once a mass of old habits and prepossessions."[141] Mathews claimed the vistas of the Western Reserve gave the Yankees "a broad outlook upon the boundless potentialities that lay in the pure, pristine wilderness to fire their imagination and serve them with incentive."[142] Whereas the monument-sprinkled landscapes of New England constantly confronted Yankees with thoughts of their heroic ancestors, the "pure, pristine wilderness" of the Old Northwest left them free to imagine a future in which they would be the heroes.

Most nationalists believed the chief broadening influence on the Yankees in the Old Northwest was the array of ethnic groups they encountered there. In some ways the nationalists resembled the Greater New Englanders, who also wrote about the Yankees' encounters with other groups in the Old Northwest. But, whereas the Greater New Englanders saw outsiders as putty in the hands of the Yankee migrants, the nationalists believed the influence ran both ways. Some nationalists stressed cultural exchanges between the Yankees and other peoples, describing the conflict and negotiation that took place over such issues as temperance and sabbatarianism. Other nationalists believed bloodlines, as well as cultures, were being mingled in the Old Northwest. Ignoring the region's many clustered ethnic settlements, these nationalists saw the region as one big melting pot, where intermarriage between the Yankees and other groups was creating a new American "race." But, whether they emphasized culture or biology as the key ground of encounter, the nationalists agreed that the Yankee Westerner's attitude toward other groups distinguished him from his eastern cousin: whereas the former was welcoming and egalitarian toward outsiders, the latter was exclusive and domineering. As a result, the nationalists warned, the eastern Yankee was rapidly being shouldered aside by immigrants, while his western kinsman was busy building a new nation with them.

Some nationalists saw the Old Northwest as an egalitarian marketplace of cultural traditions, where the Yankees engaged in "give-and-take" with other groups to their mutual benefit. In a travel essay on Michigan, Rollin Lynde Hartt recounted how French Canadian *habitants* taught the Yankee "mossbacks" to farm the rich, but hitherto neglected, swamplands near Alpena. In return the Yankees led the evolution of the area's economy from lumber to agriculture.[143] On a visit to Ohio, Hartt found a vibrant political culture that centered on meetings in the district schoolhouses: "Cavalier joined issue with Puritan, Knickerbocker with Pennsylvania Dutchman, Quaker with Kentuckian; no two men had the same point of view." Though contentious, such debates helped turn the state into "one vast college of civics."[144] Inspired by fond memories of growing up in Portage, Wisconsin, where Yankee migrants rubbed elbows with immigrants, Frederick Jackson Turner celebrated the Middle West as

> a new type of society in which all gave and all received and no element remained isolated. Society was plastic. In the midst of more or less antagonism between "bowie knife Southerners," "cow-milking Yankee Puritans," "beer-drinking Germans," "wild Irishmen," a process of mutual education, a giving and taking, was at work."[145]

Turner's former student Lois Kimball Mathews Rosenberry also emphasized the social plasticity that had resulted from all the "giving and taking" between the Yankees and other groups in the Old Northwest. She described how the New England migrant in Ohio "had been forced to compromise with his neighbor from Pennsylvania or Virginia whose ideas of institutions differed from those of the Puritan."[146] Similar compromises between the Yankees and other groups in Michigan had produced a state "which is more flexible in its character than those of New England."[147] That flexibility was particularly evident in the institutions of the West, which, according to Rosenberry, were more liberal than the ones the Yankee had left back east.[148]

Many nationalists believed the cultural transactions between the Yankee Westerners and other groups led to a more fundamental fusion of peoples through intermarriage. They agreed with Turner that the Middle West was "a good mixer," where people from warring European nations and rival US sections put aside their differences to form an expansive new American race: "All were accepted and intermingling components of a forming society, plastic and absorptive."[149] In invoking the melting pot, Turner apparently had in mind the heterogeneous frontier village he knew as a boy, rather than the many homogeneous communities that also dotted the region. He was obviously not thinking of the Old Northwest's many clustered rural ethnic settlements, where foreign-language institutions such as schools and churches helped immigrants preserve Old World ways, maintain group identities, and discourage assimilation among their children. As scholars have shown, those homogeneous communities were the products of chain migrations that saw entire Old World neighborhoods and even villages reassemble in new settlements on the prairies. The immigrants who formed those colonies could be less than welcoming toward their own countrymen when they hailed from other villages in the old country. Needless to say, they were generally even more suspicious of other nationalities, including "Americans."[150] Gesturing at one point toward those exclusive ethnic communities, Turner conceded that "assimilation" was slower "where different groups were compact and isolated from the others," but for the most part, he and the other nationalists gave clustered settlements short shrift, instead romanticizing the Old Northwest as a land of welcoming, multiethnic communities.[151]

According to the nationalists, the product of those communities was a new American race, formed from the blending of white Americans from New England, the Mid-Atlantic, and the South (with nonwhites generally going unmentioned) together with immigrants from northern and western Europe. Several nationalists claimed it was in Ohio that the new race first saw light. Alfred Mathews declared it the first all-American territory:

> Hers was the first territory to be representative of the entire people. Within her borders the hitherto racially different or long-separated

> consanguineous elements—in some instances estranged, in others emasculated or enervated through dearth of fresh blood—came into contiguity—finally to be blent into a homogeneous whole. . . . It would savor of extremism to go further and to say that these once widely dissevered and dissimilar elements coming together in a virgin land not only advanced an old, but founded a new race; and yet, what were those elementary fragments in the old States but colonies of English Puritans and Cavaliers and Quakers, of Scotch-Irish and Germans? And, in a certain sense, were not the Ohioans truly the first Americans?[152]

Some nationalists believed that the Ohio melting pot had even engulfed the Yankees of the Western Reserve. "[T]hey are all talking about the Western Reserve," one newcomer reportedly quipped, "Darned if I see any!"[153] Hosea Paul argued that it was precisely their "contact with and . . . admixture with other elements" that saved the Yankees of the Western Reserve from "provincialism." At a time when the preservationists celebrated the Yankees of the Western Reserve for their "seclusive reserve," Paul found them impressively "cosmopolitan."[154]

Several nationalists celebrated the ethnic mingling of the Old Northwest over against the rigidity and exclusiveness that prevailed in New England. Alfred Mathews may have had that opposition in mind when he contrasted the mixed-blood Ohioans with an unnamed people or peoples "emasculated or enervated through dearth of fresh blood," which many readers would have taken as a reference to the New England Yankees. Hartt made the contrast explicit when he juxtaposed the hybrid vigor of the Ohioans against the decadent purity of the Yankees. He described the Buckeye State's early population as "a selection of daring, masterful spirits from all America. . . . [I]t was a mingling of widely varied peoples. Hence a stock endowed with indomitable energy." These vigorous, mixed-blood Ohioans struck Hartt as the antithesis of the inbred rural Yankees he had previously attacked in the *Atlantic Monthly:* "The Glenns of Sweet Auburn, in whose veins flows a salmon-hued, homogeneous fluid, are for sitting on their thumbs and waiting for the future to come. Not so the Ohioans."[155] Turner also believed the Yankees fared far better in the "plastic and absorptive" society of the Middle West than in exclusive, hierarchical New England.[156] He recalled how

> Puritan New England, which . . . drew to its shores an army of cheap labor, governed these people for a time by a ruling class like an upper

> stratum between which and the lower strata there was no assimilation. There was no such evolution into an assimilated commonwealth as is seen in Middle Western agricultural States, where immigrant and old native stock came in together and built up a homogeneous society on the principle of give and take.[157]

Nor were the prospects for building such a society in New England any brighter now that immigrants were assuming political control. Having lorded it over the foreign born for decades, it was now the Yankees' turn to be dominated.

Indeed, the nationalists viewed the New England Yankee's ethnic insularity as the one conservative tendency that remained impervious to influence from his more progressive Western cousins. The nationalists believed that influence had liberalized the eastern Yankee's ideas about religion, education, and politics, but not his fundamental hostility toward other ethnic groups. As a result the nationalists sometimes sounded quite pessimistic as they contemplated the Yankee's future in an immigrant-dominated New England. Turner, for example, observed:

> now the Northeastern coast finds its destiny, politically and economically, passing away from the descendants of the Puritans. It is the little Jewish boy, the Greek or the Sicilian, who takes the traveler through historic streets, now the home of these newer people to the Old North Church or to Paul Revere's house, or to Tea Wharf, and tells you in his strange patois the story of revolution against oppression.[158]

There is a hint of wistfulness here that recalls the Brahmins' anxieties about the immigrant takeover of their region. But, as usual, it is only a hint. For Turner, as for other Yankee Westerners, the relations between immigrants and the Puritan descendants that really mattered were the ones taking place in the West. It was there, they firmly believed, not in the historic streets of the mother region, that the destiny of the Yankees would finally be decided.

Coda

"The Pilgrims Were Illegal Aliens"

If Julian West, the Brahmin time traveler of *Looking Backward: 2000–1887* (1888), had awakened not in the utopia of Edward Bellamy's novel but in the real Boston of today, he would doubtless be surprised by a number of things. He would certainly be impressed by the physical transformation of the city: Boston is obviously much cleaner, taller, and better smelling than it was when he went to sleep in 1887. A confirmed admirer of the female form, he might be even more impressed by the physical transformation of the city's women. Coming from an era in which New England females were notorious for their poor health and scrawny bodies, he doubtless would be pleased by the sight of the biking, jogging, rollerblading female Bostonians of today, who—like their fictitious counterparts in Bellamy's utopia—radiate an aura "of health and abounding physical vitality too often lacking" in their "sickly" Gilded Age predecessors.[1]

But, while much has changed in the Hub and New England generally since 1887, much remains the same. One similarity that might well strike the Brahmin Rip Van Winkle is the uncertain and oftentimes contradictory relation of immigrants to New England regional identity. Sometimes it seems that everywhere one looks—whether it be historic sites, public monuments, or popular culture—one sees immigrants and their histories being scripted into the region's dominant narratives of itself. The message from those narratives seems clear: New England history is immigrant history, New England values are immigrant values, and New England was built by immigrants. Yet, in an age of resurgent nativism, it also is not surprising to find people—in New England and elsewhere—invoking the culture, history, and heroes of the region in their attacks on immigrants. Regionalism has long provided both the friends and foes of the foreign born with a storehouse of emotionally charged symbols and myths. That storehouse is arguably richer in New England than anyplace else, so its prominence in recent debates over immigration is to be expected.

In many ways, immigrants are far more integrated into New England's self-presentation now than they were in Julian West's day. If Bellamy's hero were to perambulate Boston today, he would be repeatedly struck by evidence of their incorporation into the region's historical narratives and iconography. Strolling through the city's public spaces, he would see the heroic Puritan statuary erected by his contemporaries matched by more recent memorials to Irish American politicians and Irish famine victims. Wandering through the city's residential districts, he would glimpse preservationists carefully restoring three-decker houses, surely a baffling sight for a man whose Brahmin contemporaries were still doubtful of the need to preserve their own ancestral homes, much less immigrant tenements.[2] (West plans to sell his own ancestral mansion, which is "very elegant in an old-fashioned way," but occupies a neighborhood that has been invaded by factories and tenements.)[3] Venturing into the North End, he would likely be disoriented to discover that once-notorious immigrant slum now transformed into Boston's Little Italy, a busy tourist destination with a historic appeal to rival the popular Puritan sites nearby. If he stopped to ask about the green and white jerseys adorning so many in the crowd, he would be confronted with yet another reminder of the region's long-standing identification with the foreign born: the Boston Celtics, an organization whose name was already redolent of both immigrant and basketball history when it was adopted in 1946 and which, along with the city's other professional sports franchises, now stands among the foremost symbols of regional pride for many New Englanders. For a Brahmin like Julian West, the thought of a professional sports team symbolizing the region would be baffling—the sporting ideal for men of his class was the gentleman amateur, not the crass professional (Bellamy tellingly banishes the latter from his utopia)—and West's bafflement would turn to amazement when he learned that the team plays in a league filled with foreign-born players and bears the name of the once-hated Irish.[4] Times have changed.

Or have they? If he spent enough time in contemporary New England, Julian West would likely run across signs that all is not well between immigrants and his native region. Like other parts of the United States, New England has experienced a rise in anti-immigrant sentiment in recent years, and, as elsewhere, that nativism has often been expressed in regionalist terms. One of the most obvious examples of this is the Minuteman Project, a group founded by Jim Gilchrist and Chris Simcox. The Minuteman Project is not an indigenous product of New England. Although Gilchrist was born in Rhode Island—the grandson of German and Greek immigrants—and returned there for high school and college, he was living in California in 2004 when he and Simcox launched the organization, which is best known for the volunteer patrols of the Arizona/Mexico border that it staged in the spring of 2005.[5] In its southwestern guise, the Minuteman Project conjures up a classic postmodern stew of ill-assorted historical and regional associations: Lexington and Concord give way to Cochise County, redcoats shade into "illegal immigrant invaders," and citizen-soldier heroes metamorphose into paramilitary border patrollers.[6] These bizarre juxtapositions inevitably dilute the regional resonance of the Minuteman Project's historical symbols, making them less evocative of New England per se than of vague ideological themes like nativism, patriotism, and nationalism.

But some of the modern-day Minutemen take quite seriously their ties to New England and its history. That is true of Gilchrist himself, who showed up at the first Minuteman Project demonstration carrying two flags, one a Revolutionary era stars and stripes and the other the flag of his birth state, Rhode Island.[7] Gilchrist would later underscore his New England roots on his first visit to Daniel Chester French's Minute Man statue in Concord. Gazing up at the figure, Gilchrist mused, "I feel connected. . . . What they created stays with us 230 years later—I would hope. A nation governed under the rule of law, and not at the whim of the mob—of tens of millions of illegal aliens."[8] At a time when most opponents of "illegal" immigration harp on the themes of crime, national security, and strained public services, there is something almost archaic in Gilchrist's warnings about the dangers of undocumented immigrants to the original minutemen's republican legacy. He could be a Brahmin restrictionist preaching about the threat the foreign born allegedly pose to the town meeting or a Yankee civic reformer bemoaning the rise of the immigrant political machine. But, given the regional context of his remarks, Gilchrist's republican rhetoric seems politically savvy. He plays powerfully to a New England audience and establishes his own credentials as a native son by celebrating the region's proud legacy of self-government over against the threat of the foreign born.

Regionalism has also been effectively deployed by immigrants and their supporters, and sometimes in ways that might seem familiar to a Gilded Age time traveler like Julian West (who occasionally views himself as an immigrant of sorts).[9] For example, friends of the foreign born have taken to comparing today's undocumented immigrants to the Pilgrims. Placards at pro-immigration rallies and antinativist editorials in the press sport phrases like "The Pilgrims were illegal aliens" and "The Pilgrims didn't have papers."[10] The popular animated television series *The Simpsons* has also taken up the cry. One "chalkboard gag" (i.e., the comic punishment scene that often accompanies the show's opening credits) features wise-acre protagonist Bart writing over and over the words, "THE PILGRIMS WERE NOT ILLEGAL ALIENS."[11] Such slogans echo the references to Irish and French Canadian "Pilgrims" that circulated in the Gilded Age, updated to account for the tightening of the nation's immigration laws: these days Pilgrims are being compared not just to immigrants but to illegal immigrants. The implication, one assumes, is that the Pilgrims violated the unwritten laws of the Native American communities of what is now New England in the same manner in which today's undocumented immigrants break US statutes. Such criticism of the Pilgrims' relations with the Indians was rare in the Gilded Age. Yet, even with that difference, the basic aim of the comparison remains the same: to remind Americans that the colonists they revere in many ways resemble the contemporary newcomers they so often revile. In New England, as we have seen, such comparisons have also served to contest nativists' claims of ownership over the region. In the Gilded Age, lauding Hibernian or French Canadian immigrants as Pilgrims was a way to underscore their contributions to the region and their right to a say in its future. Today calling the Pilgrims illegal immigrants serves the similar purpose of reminding New Englanders and other Americans of the contributions undocumented people have made to the region and the nation as a whole, contributions that have earned them a pathway to citizenship.

Thus, while much has changed since the Gilded Age in the debate over immigration, one thing has not: parties on all sides of the question continue to invoke Pilgrims, minutemen, and other ghosts of the New England past. There is no reason to expect that practice to go away. Regionalism—particularly New England regionalism—will likely continue to supply many of the symbols, narratives, and heroes through which Americans make sense of this complex and emotionally fraught issue. Confronted with the vexing question of who gets to be an American, they will follow past generations in looking to New England for an answer.

Notes

INTRODUCTION

1. Arthur W. Calhoun, *A Social History of the American Family from Colonial Times to the Present* (Cleveland: Arthur H. Clark, 1918), 2:17–18, 20–21.

2. William DeWitt Hyde, "Impending Paganism in New England," *Forum* 13 (June 1892): 528.

3. For scholarship on nineteenth-century conceptions of the white races, see especially Matthew Frye Jacobson, *Whiteness of a Different Color: European Immigrants and the Alchemy of Race* (Cambridge, MA: Harvard University Press, 1998); David R. Roediger, *The Wages of Whiteness: Race and the Making of the American Working Class* (London: Verso, 1991); Thomas F. Gossett, *Race: The History of an Idea in America*, new ed. (New York: Oxford University Press, 1997); Stuart Anderson, *Race and Rapprochement: Anglo-Saxonism and Anglo-American Relations, 1895–1904* (East Brunswick, NJ: Fairleigh Dickinson University Press, 1981); Reginald Horsman, *Race and Manifest Destiny: The Origins of American Racial Anglo-Saxonism* (Cambridge, MA: Harvard University Press, 1981).

4. Quoted in James M. McPherson, *Is Blood Thicker Than Water? Crises of Nationalism in the Modern World* (New York: Vintage, 1998), 47.

5. For the Cavalier-Norman thesis, see ibid., 43–51; James C. Cobb, *Away Down South: A History of Southern Identity* (New York: Oxford University Press, 2005), 22–26, 43–45; Rollin G. Osterweis, *Romanticism and Nationalism in the Old South* (New Haven, CT: Yale University Press, 1949), 47–48; Ritchie Devon Watson Jr., *Normans and Saxons: Southern Race Mythology and the Intellectual History of the American Civil War* (Baton Rouge: Louisiana State University Press, 2008).

6. See, for example, Thomas Nelson Page, *The Old South: Essays Social and Political* (New York: C. Scribner's Sons, 1892), 5, 14, 22, 101; and a speech by Senator Benjamin Tillman, *Congressional Record*, 57th Cong., 2nd sess., February 24, 1903, 2566.

7. See Edward L. Ayers, *The Promise of the New South: Life after Reconstruction* (New York: Oxford University Press, 1992), 199; Hasia R. Diner, *Erin's Daughters in America: Irish Immigrant Women in the Nineteenth Century* (Baltimore: Johns Hopkins University Press, 1983), 80–82; and "Female Help," *New England Farmer*, May 1857, 247.

8. See Dona Brown, *Inventing New England: Regional Tourism in the Nineteenth Century* (Washington, DC: Smithsonian Institution Press, 1995), 9, 108–9, 117–18, 139–40, 146, 192–94, 201, 204, 215–16.

9. See, for example, Roger B. Stein, "Gilded Age Pilgrims," in *Picturing Old New England: Image and Memory*, ed. William H. Truettner and Roger B. Stein (New Haven, CT: Yale University Press, 1999), 43, 51, 57, 59, 60; and in the same volume William H. Truettner and Thomas Andrew Denenberg, "The Discreet Charm of the Colonial," 91–92; and William H. Truettner, "Small-Town America," 122.

10. Barbara Miller Solomon, *Ancestors and Immigrants: A Changing New England Tradition* (Cambridge, MA: Harvard University Press, 1956), 84–86.

11. Joseph A. Conforti, *Imagining New England: Explorations of Regional Identity from the Pilgrims to the Mid–Twentieth Century* (Chapel Hill: University of North Carolina Press, 2001), 248–62.

12. James M. Lindgren, *Preserving Historic New England: Preservation, Progressivism, and the Remaking of Memory* (New York: Oxford University Press, 1995), 5.

13. Quoted in ibid., 37.

14. For a classic statement of this theory, see Kathleen Neils Conzen, David A. Gerber, Ewa Morawska, George E. Pozzetta, and Rudolph J. Vecoli, "The Invention of Ethnicity: A Perspective from the U.S.A.," *Journal of American Ethnic History* 12, no. 1 (1992): 12, 22–23.

CHAPTER 1

1. Henry Cabot Lodge, *Certain Accepted Heroes and Other Essays in Literature and Politics* (New York: Harper & Bros., 1897), 97.

2. Ibid., 98. For a similar comparison of the expansionist and assimilative capacities of the Anglo-Saxon race and the English language, see Josiah Strong, *The New Era; or, The Coming Kingdom* (New York: Baker & Taylor, 1893), 60. For a discussion of turn-of-the-century academics who made similar racialized comparisons, see Gavin Jones, *Strange Talk: The Politics of Dialect Literature in Gilded Age America* (Berkeley: University of California Press, 1999), 22–23.

3. Lodge, *Certain Accepted Heroes*, 97, 98.

4. For the backgrounds of the Brahmin Anglo-Saxonists, see Barbara Miller Solomon, *Ancestors and Immigrants: A Changing New England Tradition* (Cambridge, MA: Harvard University Press, 1956); Edward N. Saveth, *American Historians and European Immigrants, 1875–1925* (New York: Russell & Russell, 1965), chaps. 1–2; and Stuart Anderson, *Race and Rapprochement: Anglo-Saxonism and Anglo-American Relations, 1895–1904* (East Brunswick, NJ: Fairleigh Dickinson University, 1981), 37–45.

5. Barrett Wendell to Colonel Robert Thomson, December 17, 1893, in *Barrett Wendell and His Letters*, ed. M. A. De Wolfe Howe (Boston: Atlantic Monthly Press, 1924), 108.

6. Barrett Wendell, *Stelligeri, and Other Essays Concerning America* (New York: C. Scribner's Sons, 1893), 28.

7. For the Anglo-Saxonists' fear of decay, see especially Sarah Lyons Watts, *Rough Rider in the White House: Theodore Roosevelt and the Politics of Desire* (Chicago: Univer-

sity of Chicago Press, 2003), 22–25, 30–78; and Gail Bederman, *Manliness and Civilization: A Cultural History of Gender and Race in the United States, 1880–1917* (Chicago: University of Chicago Press, 1995), 185–87.

8. "The Celtic Element in Massachusetts," *Boston Pilot,* April 27, 1872, 4.

9. See, for example, Henry Adams, *The Education of Henry Adams: An Autobiography* (Boston: Houghton Mifflin, 2000), 6; Barrett Wendell to Robert Thomson, December 17, 1893, in Howe, *Barrett Wendell and His Letters,*108–9; William Dean Howells, *Suburban Sketches* (Boston: J. R. Osgood, 1877), 68–72, 79–80; and W. D. Howells, *The Minister's Charge; or, The Apprenticeship of Lemuel Barker* (Bloomington: Indiana University Press, 1978), 287–88.

10. On Roosevelt's view of the conquest of America as a recapitulation of the invasion of Britain by the ancient Germans, see Thomas G. Dyer, *Theodore Roosevelt and the Idea of Race* (Baton Rouge: Louisiana State University Press, 1980), 59; and Bederman, *Manliness and Civilization,* 179.

11. Some geneticists now argue that the Teutonic invaders intermingled with the original inhabitants of Britain rather than wiping them out. See Nicholas Wade, "A United Kingdom? Maybe," *New York Times,* March 6, 2007, D1, 4. Thanks to Alan Lessoff for this reference.

12. Theodore Roosevelt, *The Winning of the West: An Account of the Exploration and Settlement of Our Country from the Alleghanies to the Pacific* (New York: Charles Scribner's Sons, 1924), 1:3–21. Following British historian Edward A. Freeman, many US Anglo-Saxonists rejected the term *Anglo-Saxon* as historically inaccurate. They preferred terms such as *English-speaking peoples, English-speaking races, English folk,* and *English race.* See Solomon, *Ancestors and Immigrants,* 68; and John Fiske, *American Political Ideas Viewed from the Standpoint of Universal History* (Boston: Houghton Mifflin, 1911), 95–97.

13. Watts, *Rough Rider,* 156–57; Bederman, *Manliness and Civilization,* 180–84. See also Kim Townsend, *Manhood at Harvard: William James and Others* (New York: W. W. Norton, 1996), 264.

14. Owen Wister, "The Evolution of the Cow-Puncher," *Harper's New Monthly Magazine* 91 (Sept. 1895): 610.

15. Ben Merchant Vorpahl, *My Dear Wister: The Frederic Remington–Owen Wister Letters* (Palo Alto, CA: American West, 1972), 62–64, 75–76.

16. Remington to Wister, ca. September or October, 1894, in Vorpahl, *My Dear Wister,* 47.

17. Theodore Roosevelt, "Social Evolution," in *The Works of Theodore Roosevelt,* memorial ed. (New York: Charles Scribner's Sons, 1924), 14:111.

18. On Roosevelt's attitudes toward race suicide, see especially Dyer, *Theodore Roosevelt,* chap. 7; Bederman, *Manliness and Civilization,* 196–206; and Watts, *Rough Rider,* 82–86, 112–15.

19. For examples of Roosevelt's attacks on Yankee reproductive practices, see "The Law of Civilization and Decay," in *Works of Theodore Roosevelt,* 14:135; "Twisted Eugenics," in *Works of Theodore Roosevelt,* 14:173; "A Letter from President Roosevelt on Race Suicide," *Review of Reviews* 35 (May 1907): 550; and Dyer, *Theodore Roosevelt,* 146–48.

20. Theodore Roosevelt, "Race Decadence," in *Works of Theodore Roosevelt,* 14:154.

21. Ibid., 14:158.

22. For the Virginian's racial background, see Owen Wister, *The Virginian: A Horseman of the Plains* (New York: Harper & Row, 1965), 244.

23. Ibid., 329.

24. Ibid., 227. Wister similarly contrasts a bluff westerner with his genteel New England brother in "How Lin McLean Went East," *Harper's New Monthly Magazine* 86 (Dec. 1892): 135–47.

25. Nicholas Murray Butler, *Across the Busy Years: Recollections and Reflections* (New York: C. Scribner's Sons, 1939), 1:288; on Lodge's disdain for the West, see William C. Widenor, *Henry Cabot Lodge and the Search for an American Foreign Policy* (Berkeley: University of California Press, 1980), 87.

26. For the Teutonic origins theory and its popularity among the Brahmins, see especially Solomon, *Ancestors and Immigrants,* 60–69; Saveth, *American Historians and European Immigrants,* chaps. 1–2; Anderson, *Race and Rapprochement,* 37–45; and Gossett, *Race,* chap. 5.

27. Edward Augustus Freeman, *Comparative Politics. . . . ,* 2nd ed. (New York: Macmillan, 1896), 86–87.

28. Ibid., 30–31.

29. For the attacks on Teutonist theory, see John Higham, "Herbert Baxter Adams and the Study of Local History," *American Historical Review* 89, no. 5 (1984): 1236; John Higham, *History: Professional Scholarship in America* (Baltimore: Johns Hopkins University Press, 1983), 161–62; Saveth, *American Historians and European Immigrants,* 26–31; Peter Novick, *That Noble Dream: The "Objectivity Question" and the American Historical Profession* (Cambridge: Cambridge University Press, 1988), 87–88; and Dorothy Ross, "Historical Consciousness in Nineteenth-Century America," *American Historical Review* 89, no. 4 (1984): 927–28.

30. Prescott F. Hall, quoted in Solomon, *Ancestors and Immigrants,* 111. For further proof of the persistence of Teutonist ideas among turn-of-the-century Anglo-Saxonists, see Solomon, *Ancestors and Immigrants,* 139, 198.

31. Indeed, John Fiske thought the coming of the Puritans was more significant, given that they repeated "in a new environment and on a far grander scale the work which their forefathers had wrought in Britain." See John Fiske, *The Beginnings of New England; or, The Puritan Theocracy in Its Relation to Civil and Religious Liberty* (Boston: Houghton Mifflin, 1889), 49.

32. For examples of Teutonist scholarship on the New England village community, see Herbert B. Adams, "The Germanic Origins of New England Towns," *Johns Hopkins University Studies in Historical and Political Science,* 1st ser., no. 2 (1882): 5–38; James K. Hosmer, *A Short History of Anglo-Saxon Freedom: The Polity of the English-Speaking Race. . . .* (New York: C. Scribner's Sons, 1890), 110–22, 127–29; and Fiske, *American Political Ideas,* 28–37.

33. Hosmer, *Short History of Anglo-Saxon Freedom,* 278.

34. Ibid., 122–25; Fiske, *American Political Ideas,* 26.

35. Kenneth A. Lockridge and Alan Kreider, "The Evolution of Massachusetts Town Government, 1640 to 1740," *William and Mary Quarterly,* 3rd ser., 23, no. 4 (1966): 549–74.

36. David Grayson Allen, *In English Ways: The Movement of Societies and the Transferal of English Local Law and Custom to Massachusetts Bay in the Seventeenth Century* (Chapel Hill: University of North Carolina Press, 1981), 4, 38, 54.

37. Hosmer, *Short History of Anglo-Saxon Freedom,* 214.

38. Henry Cabot Lodge and Theodore Roosevelt, *Hero Tales from American History* (New York: Century, 1917), 258, 275–76.

39. Fiske wrote the three lectures when he was invited to speak at the Royal Institute in London and repeated them many times in America. The final lecture, "'Manifest Destiny,'" was by far the most popular of the three. Fiske delivered it fifty times in Britain and the United States. See Milton Berman, *John Fiske: The Evolution of a Popularizer* (Cambridge, MA: Harvard University Press, 1961), 139.

40. Fiske, *American Political Ideas,* 107.

41. Ibid., 124.

42. Ibid., 135.

43. Ibid., 107.

44. Ibid., 133.

45. Ibid., 97.

46. Ibid., 48. Fiske's racial pride in the successes of the British Empire was shared by other Brahmin Anglo-Saxonists, including James K. Hosmer. On the interimperial ties between turn-of-the-century US and British Anglo-Saxonists, see Paul A. Kramer, "Empires, Exceptions, and Anglo-Saxons: Race and Rule between the British and United States Empires, 1880–1910," *Journal of American History* 88, no. 4 (2002): 1315–53.

47. Fiske, *American Political Ideas,* 11–17.

48. Ibid., 11–12.

49. Ibid., 17.

50. Ibid., 18.

51. Ibid.

52. Hosmer, *Short History of Anglo-Saxon Freedom,* 311.

53. Ibid., 354.

54. Ibid., 117–18, 213–17, 285–88.

55. Ibid., 277–78.

56. Ibid., 318.

57. Ibid., 313. Hosmer slightly misquotes the original, which reads, "[I]n such a nation there commonly is a certain element which is more than an element, something which is its real kernel, its real essence, something which attracts and absorbs all other elements, so that the other elements are not co-ordinate elements but mere infusions into a whole which is already in being." See Edward A. Freeman, *Four Oxford Lectures. . . .* (London: Macmillan, 1888), 80.

58. Hosmer, *Short History of Anglo-Saxon Freedom,* 325–26.

59. Ibid., 325.

60. Ibid., 324.

61. On the IRL, see Solomon, *Ancestors and Immigrants;* John Higham, *Strangers in the Land: Patterns of American Nativism, 1860–1925* (New Brunswick, NJ: Rutgers University Press, 2002), 102–8, 112, 152, 162–63, http://hdl.handle.net/2027/heb.00398; and Dale T. Knobel, *"America for the Americans": The Nativist Movement in the United States* (New York: Twayne, 1996), 219–23.

62. Francis A. Walker, "Restriction of Immigration," *Atlantic Monthly* 77 (June 1896): 828.

63. Ibid., 828.

64. See, for example, Henry Cabot Lodge, "A Million Immigrants a Year," *Century Magazine* 67 (Jan. 1904): 466–67; Henry Cabot Lodge, "The Question of Immigration," printed speech, April 25, 1892, Immigration Restriction League Papers, Houghton Library, Harvard University.

65. *Congressional Record,* 54th Cong., 1st sess., March 16, 1896, 2820.

66. See Lodge's speech in *The Proceedings at the Celebration by the Pilgrim Society, at Plymouth, August 1st, 1889, of the Completion of the National Monument to the Pilgrims* (Plymouth, MA: Avery & Doten, 1889), 133.

67. Henry Cabot Lodge, *A Short History of the English Colonies in America* (New York: Harper & Bros., 1881), 406–7, 473, 475.

68. Henry Cabot Lodge, *Boston* (New York: Longmans, Green, 1891), 205.

69. Henry Cabot Lodge, "True Americanism," *Harvard Graduates' Magazine* 3 (Sept. 1894): 19, 20.

70. Henry Cabot Lodge, *Early Memories* (New York: Charles Scribner's Sons, 1913), 203–4.

71. Ibid., 205.

72. Ibid., 19. See Edward Saveth's discussion of this passage in *American Historians and European Immigrants,* 54.

73. Theodore Roosevelt, "True Americanism" in *The Works of Theodore Roosevelt,* ed. Hermann Hagedorn (New York: C. Scribner's Sons, 1926), 13:23.

74. Dyer, *Theodore Roosevelt,* 129–35.

75. Wister, "Evolution of the Cow-Puncher," 603–4.

76. The Virginian identifies one gang of railroad workers as "I-talians," but they turn out to be Chinese. See Wister, *The Virginian,* 119.

77. Watts, *Rough Rider,* 59–60; Vorpahl, *My Dear Wister,* 40–41.

78. Frederic Remington, "Chicago under the Mob," *Harper's Weekly* 38 (July 21, 1894): 681.

79. Ibid., 680.

CHAPTER 2

1. For literary scholars who explore the nativist sources of regionalism, see Richard H. Brodhead, *Cultures of Letters: Scenes of Reading and Writing in Nineteenth-Century America* (Chicago: University of Chicago Press, 1993), 134–37; and Nancy Glazener, *Reading for Realism: The History of a U.S. Literary Institution, 1850–1910* (Durham, NC: Duke University Press, 1997), 194–95. By contrast, Stephanie Foote argues that nineteenth-century literary regionalism assumes that "at the core of every representation of the native was a foreigner." See her *Regional Fictions: Culture and Identity in Nineteenth-Century American Literature* (Madison: University of Wisconsin Press, 2001), 13.

2. For a scholar who sees nativism as the motivator of most, if not all, regionalist movements, see Roberto Maria Dainotto, "'All the Regions Do Smilingly Revolt': The Literature of Place and Region," *Critical Inquiry* 22, no. 3 (1996): 486–505.

3. Dona Brown, *Inventing New England: Regional Tourism in the Nineteenth Century* (Washington, DC: Smithsonian Institution Press, 1995); Joseph A. Con-

forti, *Imagining New England: Explorations of Regional Identity from the Pilgrims to the Mid–Twentieth Century* (Chapel Hill: University of North Carolina Press, 2001); John Seelye, *Memory's Nation: The Place of Plymouth Rock* (Chapel Hill: University of North Carolina Press, 1998).

4. For examples of regional approaches to Irish Americans, see Timothy J. Meagher, *Inventing Irish America: Generation, Class, and Ethnic Identity in a New England City, 1880–1928* (Notre Dame, IN: University of Notre Dame Press, 2001); Edward J. O'Day, "The 'Second Colonization of New England' Revisited: Irish Immigration before the Famine," in *New Perspectives on the Irish Diaspora,* ed. Charles Fanning (Carbondale: Southern Illinois University Press, 2000), 93–114; and Cheryl Temple Herr, *Critical Regionalism and Cultural Studies: From Ireland to the American Midwest* (Gainesville: University of Florida Press, 1996).

5. *Journal of the American-Irish Historical Society* 1 (1898): 8.

6. Ibid., 74.

7. For the history of the ethnic historical societies, see John J. Appel, *Immigrant Historical Societies in the United States, 1880–1950* (New York: Arno, 1980); Kenneth J. Moynihan, "History as a Weapon for Social Advancement: Group History as Told by Jewish, Irish, and Black Americans, 1892–1950" (PhD diss., Clark University, 1973); and John Higham, "The Ethnic Historical Society in Changing Times," *Journal of American Ethnic History* 13, no. 2 (1994): 30–44. See also John J. Bukowczyk, "'Harness for Prosperity the Values of the Nation': Fifty Years of the Polish American Historical Association and *Polish American Studies,*" *Polish American Studies* 50, no. 2 (1993): 5–100.

8. Orm Øverland, *Immigrant Minds, American Identities: Making the United States Home, 1870–1930* (Urbana: University of Illinois Press, 2000), 19.

9. Higham, "Ethnic Historical Society," 31–34.

10. Ibid., 33, emphasis in original.

11. Moynihan, "History as a Weapon," 33.

12. Signs of the New England Societies' influence on the ethnic historical societies include the commentators from the 1890s who explicitly compared the New England Societies to the Scotch-Irish Society. See Appel, *Immigrant Historical Societies,* 87.

13. John J. Appel, "The New England Origins of the American Irish Historical Society," *New England Quarterly* 33, no. 4 (1960): 463–66.

14. James Bernard Cullen, *The Story of the Irish in Boston. . . .* (Boston: J. B. Cullen, 1889), v.

15. Appel, "New England Origins," 465.

16. "A Valuable Hint," *Boston Pilot,* December 1, 1894, 1; editorial, June 22, 1895, 4.

17. *Journal of the American-Irish Historical Society* 1 (1898): 2.

18. See, for example, John C. Linehan, "Early Irish-American Settlers," *Boston Pilot,* October 26, 1889, 1–3, and July 19, 1890, 1, 2; Thomas Hamilton Murray, "The Irish Soldiers in King Philip's War, Who Served under the 'Great Commanders,' 1675–6," *Rosary Magazine* 8 (Mar. 1896): 268–87; and "David O'Kelly, the Irishman," *Boston Pilot,* March 16, 1895, 1–2.

19. Appel, "New England Origins," 473. See also Appel, *Immigrant Historical Societies,* 150.

20. For the backgrounds of the AIHS founders, see Moynihan, "History as a Weapon for Social Advancement," 18–19.

21. Helena Nordhoff Gargan called the AIHS Smith's brainchild in Helena Nordhoff Gargan, ed., *Thomas J. Gargan: A Memorial* (Boston: G. H. Ellis, 1910), 51.

22. Joseph Smith, "Statistics and Prejudices," *Boston Pilot,* August 12, 1893, 1.

23. See, for example, Edward N. Saveth, *American Historians and European Immigrants, 1875–1925* (New York: Russell & Russell, 1965), 32–42, 51–64.

24. On the long tradition of national regionalism in New England, see Conforti, *Imagining New England,* 82, 91, 95–96.

25. Joseph Smith, "Some Ways in Which History Is Falsified," *Journal of the American-Irish Historical Society* 1 (1898): 87–88.

26. Ibid., 87.

27. Thomas Hamilton Murray, "The Passing of New England," *Boston Pilot,* April 8, 1893, 1.

28. There were exceptions. Founding member Robert Ellis Thompson complained that the region had been overemphasized in the work of some American historians. See Appel, *Immigrant Historical Societies,* 111.

29. Murray, "Passing of New England," 1.

30. Ibid.

31. Ibid., 8.

32. Kerby A. Miller, *Emigrants and Exiles: Ireland and the Irish Exodus to North America* (New York: Oxford University Press, 1985), 413.

33. Murray, "Passing of New England," 8.

34. James F. Brennan, "The Irish Pioneers and Founders of Peterborough, New Hampshire," *Journal of the American-Irish Historical Society* 2 (1899): 150.

35. John C. Linehan, "John Sullivan and the Capture of the Powder at Newcastle," *Journal of the American-Irish Historical Society* 1 (1898): 35. See Moynihan's discussion in "History as a Weapon for Social Advancement," 18–19.

36. Rev. S. Banks Nelson, "Address," *Journal of the American-Irish Historical Society* 2 (1899): 109.

37. See Barbara Miller Solomon, *Ancestors and Immigrants: A Changing New England Tradition* (Cambridge, MA: Harvard University Press, 1956), 85–86, for the Brahmins' efforts to assimilate immigrant youth by immersing them in New England history.

38. As Cheryl Herr has demonstrated, a shared "legacy of oppression" has similarly prompted commentators to draw comparisons between Ireland and the American Middle West. See Herr, *Critical Regionalism and Cultural Studies,* 28.

39. Murray, "Passing of New England," 8.

40. Fiske, *Beginnings of New England,* 144–53.

41. Appel, "New England Origins," 472.

42. "The American-Irish Historical Society," *Boston Pilot,* January 30, 1897, 1.

43. Ibid., 5.

44. Brennan, "Irish Pioneers," 150.

45. See, for example, John C. Linehan, "Some Pre-Revolutionary Irishmen," *Journal of the American-Irish Historical Society* 2 (1899): 82; and John C. Linehan, "Early New Hampshire Irish: Some Pre-Revolutionary Dennises, Corneliuses, Patricks and Michaels," *Journal of the American-Irish Historical Society* 3 (1900): 123–24.

46. Fiske, *Beginnings of New England,* 140; see also Lodge, *Short History,* 407.

47. Fiske, *Beginnings of New England,* 18.

48. Lodge, *Short History,* 414.

49. Smith, "Some Ways," 84–85.

50. Miller, *Emigrants and Exiles,* 156–67.

51. Samuel Swett Green, *The Scotch-Irish in America* (Worcester, MA: C. Hamilton, 1895), 25–28; Appel, *Immigrant Historical Societies,* 85.

52. Appel, *Immigrant Historical Societies,* 79, 101.

53. Green, *Scotch-Irish in America,* 6; Appel, *Immigrant Historical Societies,* 80, 90, 93.

54. John C. Linehan, *The Irish Scots and the "Scotch-Irish."* . . . (Concord, NH: American-Irish Historical Society, 1902), 6–7.

55. Ibid., 67.

56. "Mr. Lodge Counts Again," *Boston Pilot,* July 9, 1892, 4, emphasis in original.

57. Linehan, "Some Pre-Revolutionary Irishmen," 82.

58. Rev. John J. McCoy, "The Irish Element in the Second Massachusetts Volunteers in the Recent War (with Spain)," *Journal of the American-Irish Historical Society* 2 (1899): 86.

59. Thomas Addis Emmet, "Irish Emigration during the Seventeenth and Eighteenth Centuries," *Journal of the American-Irish Historical Society* 2 (1899): 65.

60. Linehan, *Irish Scots,* 66–67.

61. Thomas Hamilton Murray, "From Dawn to Revolution," *Donahoe's Magazine,* January 1889, 15.

62. For the celebration of the Pilgrims and Puritans in the 1880s and 1890s, see Conforti, *Imagining New England,* 221–25; and Seelye, *Memory's Nation,* chaps. 19–23.

63. Murray, "From Dawn to Revolution," 15. The AIHS would continue to struggle against the influence of Henry Cabot Lodge after his death in 1924, particularly during debates over the National Origins quotas established by the Johnson-Reed Act (1924). See Appel, *Immigrant Historical Societies,* 161; Marion R. Casey, "Ireland, New York, and the Irish Image in American Popular Culture, 1890–1960" (PhD diss., New York University, 1998), 146–49.

64. On the causes of the French Canadian emigration, see Yves Roby, *The Franco-Americans of New England: Dreams and Realities,* trans. Mary Ricard (Sillery, Quebec: Septentrion, 2004), 12–17.

65. Ibid., 40–41.

66. Robert G. LeBlanc, "The Francophone 'Conquest' of New England: Geopolitical Conceptions and Imperial Ambition of French-Canadian Nationalists in the Nineteenth Century," *American Review of Canadian Studies* 15, no. 3 (1985): 288–89.

67. On the colonization and repatriation movements, see ibid., 289; and Roby, *Franco-Americans of New England,* 38–40.

68. Roby, *Franco-Americans of New England,* 39.

69. Ibid., 42.

70. É. Hamon, *Les Canadiens-Français de la Nouvelle-Angleterre* (Quebec: N. S. Hardy, 1891), 34. All quotations from this text were translated by Michèle Schoenfeld. See also the quote from Ferdinand Gagnon in Roby, *Franco-Americans of New England,* 42.

71. LeBlanc "Francophone 'Conquest,'" 290.

72. On the reassessment of emigration by the *Canadien* elites, see ibid., 290–93.

73. See Charles Thibault, *Le double avènement de l'Homme-Dieu ou les deux unités politiques et religieuses des peoples* (Montreal, 1887), 34. All quotations from this text were translated by Michèle Schoenfeld. See also Roby, *Franco-Americans of New England,* 43.

74. Roby, *Franco-Americans of New England,* 43. See also Joseph-Adolphe Chapleau, "Discours de Sir Adolphe Chapleau," in *Orateurs canadiens-français aux États-Unis: Conférences et discours,* ed. Georges Bellerive (Quebec: Imprimerie H. Chasse, 1908), 152.

75. Roby, *Franco-Americans of New England,* 46.

76. Speech delivered by Chapleau at the national banquet, June 27, 1884, in *Noces d'or de la Saint-Jean-Baptiste: Compte-rendu officiel des fêtes de 1884 à Montréal,* ed. Pierre-Philippe Charette (Montreal: Journal le Monde, 1884), 177. All quotations from this text were translated by Michèle Schoenfeld. See also Roby, *Franco-Americans of New England,* 47.

77. Chapleau, "Discours," 155. See also Roby, *Franco-Americans of New England,* 48.

78. Edmond de Nevers, *L'avenir du peuple canadien-français* (Paris, 1893), 429–31. All quotations from this text were translated by Michèle Schoenfeld.

79. Ibid., 435, quoted in Roby, *Franco-Americans of New England,* 48.

80. Thibault, *Le double avènement de l'Homme-Dieu,* 34.

81. George Austin Bowen, "Existing Forces in Agriculture," in *Twenty-Third Annual Report of the Secretary of the Connecticut Board of Agriculture* (Hartford, CT: Case, Lockwood & Brainard, 1889), 103.

82. Ibid., 103–4.

83. LeBlanc "Francophone 'Conquest,'" 294.

84. Ronald A. Petrin, *French Canadians in Massachusetts Politics, 1885–1915: Ethnicity and Political Pragmatism* (Philadelphia: Balch Institute Press, 1990), 31, 57.

85. Hamon, *Les Canadiens-Français de la Nouvelle-Angleterre,* 150.

86. Ibid., 149–50.

87. Petrin, *French Canadians,* 29. See also LeBlanc, "Francophone 'Conquest,'" 298.

88. See Roby, *Franco-Americans of New England,* 32.

89. Hamon, *Les Canadiens-Français de la Nouvelle-Angleterre,* 147.

90. See LeBlanc, "Francophone 'Conquest,'" 297–98.

91. Brown, *Inventing New England,* 139–40.

92. For commentary on *Les Canadiens-Français de la Nouvelle-Angleterre,* see "Recent Speculation in Canada," *Andover Review* 16 (Sept. 1891), http://search.proquest.com/docview/124353173?accountid'14663; Henry Loomis Nelson, "French Canadians in New England," *Harper's Monthly* 87 (July 1893): 180–87; and William MacDonald, "The French Canadians in New England," *Quarterly Journal of Economics* 12, no. 3 (1898): 245–79.

93. Hamon, *Les Canadiens-Français de la Nouvelle-Angleterre,* 32.

94. LeBlanc, "Francophone 'Conquest,'" 298.

95. Hamon, *Les Canadiens-Français de la Nouvelle-Angleterre,* 33, 125–28.

96. Ibid., 120.

97. Ibid., 144. Compare Charles Thibault's attack on Yankee family limitation in *Le double avènement de l'Homme-Dieu,* 34.

98. Hamon, *Les Canadiens-Français de la Nouvelle-Angleterre,* 143–44.

99. See FlorenceMae Waldron, "'I've Never Dreamed It Was Necessary to *Marry!*': Women and Work in New England French Canadian Communities, 1870–1930," *Journal of American Ethnic History* 24, no. 2 (2005): 35, 53.

100. See Leon F. Bouvier, "The Spacing of Births among French-Canadian Families: An Historical Approach," *Canadian Review of Sociology and Anthropology* 5, no. 1 (1968): 24.

101. Hamon, *Les Canadiens-Français de la Nouvelle-Angleterre,* 152.

102. Ibid., 129.

103. On the attitudes of the *Canadiens* in Quebec toward annexation, see LeBlanc, "Francophone 'Conquest,'" 299–300.

104. Hamon, *Les Canadiens-Français de la Nouvelle-Angleterre,* 129–30.

105. Ibid., 131.

106. For other French Canadians who predicted that the dissolution of the United States might produce a *Canadien* state, see Roby, *Franco-Americans of New England,* 50; and LeBlanc, "Francophone 'Conquest,'" 300–301.

107. Hamon, *Les Canadiens-Français de la Nouvelle-Angleterre,* 131.

108. The tract is mentioned in MacDonald, "French Canadians," 245.

109. See the discussion of Smyth's review in LeBlanc, "Francophone 'Conquest,'" 302–3.

110. Egbert C. Smyth, "The French-Canadians in New England," *Proceedings of the American Antiquarian Society,* n.s., 7 (1891): 322–23.

111. Ibid., 323.

112. Ibid., 329–36. The quote is on p. 330.

113. Ibid., 322.

114. Ibid., 336.

115. Solomon, *Ancestors and Immigrants,* 178–91.

116. Solomon argues that the pluralism of sociologist Emily Balch sets her apart from her fellow Brahmin antirestrictionists, who were more protective of New England culture. See ibid., 188–91; and Emily Greene Balch, *Our Slavic Fellow Citizens* (New York: Charities Publication Committee, 1910). Although the latter work does not discuss the relation of immigrants to New England culture, it repeatedly affirms the contributions of the foreign born to US culture generally. See, for example, pp. 370–72, 405–6, 412.

117. Solomon, *Ancestors and Immigrants,* 191.

118. Edward E. Hale, *Letters on Irish Emigration* (Boston: Phillips, Sampson, 1852), 56.

119. Ibid., 53, 61–62.

120. Ibid., 32, 33.

121. Ibid., 36.

122. Ibid., 35.

123. Ibid., 36.

124. Ibid., 54.

125. Mrs. C. A. Hopkinson, "The Poor in Cities," *Atlantic Monthly* 22 (July 1868): 55.

126. Ibid., 55–56.

127. Ibid., 55.

128. Albert L. Bartlett, "The Transformation of New England," *Forum* 7 (Aug. 1889): 634–44.
129. William DeWitt Hyde, "The Transformation of New England: Is It Decay or Development?," *Forum* 15 (Mar. 1893): 110.
130. Ibid., 109.
131. Ibid., 112.
132. Ibid., 111.
133. Ibid.
134. Ibid., 112.
135. Ibid., 109.
136. Ibid., 110.
137. Ibid., 112.
138. Ibid., 111, 108.
139. Ibid., 111.
140. Henry Childs Merwin, "The Irish in American Life," *Atlantic Monthly* 78 (Mar. 1896): 299.
141. Ibid., 301.
142. Merwin even ventured that America's greatest writer "will come of mixed New England and Irish stock, and will be a product of the West." See ibid., 300.
143. Ibid., 299–300.
144. Ibid., 301.
145. "Discours prononce par le lieutenant gouverneur Pothier a Biddeford, Me.," *L'Avenir national,* January 22, 1898, 2. All quotations from this text were translated by Michèle Schoenfeld. See also Roby, *The Franco-Americans of New England,* 64.
146. "The Old Guard," *Boston Pilot,* August 12, 1893, 6.
147. Godfroy S. Dupré, "Discours," in Félix Gatineau, *Historique des conventions générales des canadiens-français aux Etats-Unis, 1865–1901* (Woonsocket, RI: L'Union Saint-Jean-Baptiste d'Amérique, 1927), 420. All quotations from this text were translated by Michèle Schoenfeld. See also Roby, *The Franco-Americans of New England,* 68.
148. On the French Canadian elites' changing attitude toward naturalization, see Petrin, *French Canadians,* 49–52.
149. Dupré, "Discours," 421. J. Roch Magnan likewise repudiated the idea of "an independent nation inside of this Republic." See his "Notre position aux Etats-Unis," in Félix Gatineau, *Historique des conventions générales des canadiens-français aux Etats-Unis, 1865–1901* (Woonsocket, RI: L'Union Saint-Jean-Baptiste d'Amérique, 1927), 319. All quotations from this text were translated by Michèle Schoenfeld.
150. Dupré, "Discours," 422.
151. T. J. Corbett, "New England a Misnomer," *Donahoe's Magazine* 21 (June 1889): 549, emphasis in original.
152. Ibid., 552–53.
153. Ibid., 556.
154. Merwin cites Lodge in "Irish in American Life," 299.
155. I have discussed McNeirny as a regional pluralist, but he was also a founding member of the AIHS. See *Journal of the American-Irish Historical Society* 1 (1898): 6.
156. Seelye, *Memory's Nation,* 542–43.
157. In addition to Seelye, *Memory's Nation,* see Conforti, *Imagining New England,* 171–96.

158. Quoted in Seelye, *Memory's Nation,* 540.

159. On Breckinridge's background, see ibid., 543.

160. Ibid., 547.

161. Pilgrim Society, *The Proceedings at the Celebration by the Pilgrim Society, at Plymouth, August 1st, 1889, of the Completion of the National Monument to the Pilgrims* (Plymouth, MA: Avery & Doten, 1889), 102.

162. Ibid., 134.

163. John Boyle O'Reilly, "Mayflower," *Boston Globe,* September 12, 1886, 1.

164. "That Monument Dedicated," *Boston Post,* August 2, 1889, 2.

165. Francis R. Walsh, "Who Spoke for Boston's Irish? The *Boston Pilot* in the Nineteenth Century," *Journal of Ethnic Studies* 10, no. 3 (1982): 30–31.

166. *Boston Pilot,* April 27, 1872, quoted in Walsh, "Who Spoke for Boston's Irish?," 30.

167. "Catholicity on Plymouth Rock," *Boston Pilot,* July 19, 1879, 4.

168. See the editorials praising O'Reilly's poem in *Boston Post,* August 2, 1889, 4; *Springfield Republican,* August 2, 1889, 4; *Boston Daily Advertiser,* August 3, 1889, 4; and *Boston Evening Traveller,* August 2, 1889, 2.

169. Pilgrim Society, *Proceedings,* 112.

170. Ibid., 110–11.

171. Ibid., 112.

172. Ibid., 113.

173. Ibid., 114.

174. Ibid., 115.

175. Ibid., 114.

176. Ibid., 115.

177. Seelye, *Memory's Nation,* 521, 530–31, 613–16, 620, 622–28, 638.

178. Mary Antin, *They Who Knock at Our Gates: A Complete Gospel of Immigration* (Boston: Houghton, Mifflin, 1914), 40.

179. Seelye, *Memory's Nation,* 627, 626.

180. Antin, *They Who Knock,* 38, 50.

181. See the discussion of Dunne's "Immigration" in Seelye, *Memory's Nation,* 628.

182. Finley Peter Dunne, "Immigration," in *Observations by Mr. Dooley* (New York: Greenwood, 1969), 51, 52. For Dunne's marriage to Margaret Abbott, see Elmer Ellis, *Mr. Dooley's America: A Life of Finley Peter Dunne* (Hamden, CT: Archon, 1969), 179.

183. Dunne, "Immigration," 53.

184. Ibid., 53–54.

185. Seelye, *Memory's Nation,* 528.

CHAPTER 3

1. Carroll Smith-Rosenberg and Charles E. Rosenberg, "The Female Animal: Medical and Biological Views of Woman and Her Role in Nineteenth-Century America," in *Women and Health in America: Historical Readings,* ed. Judith Walzer Leavitt, 2nd ed. (Madison: University of Wisconsin Press, 1999), 122.

2. Quoted in Antonello Gerbi, *The Dispute of the New World: The History of a Polemic, 1750–1900,* trans. Jeremy Moyle, rev. ed. (Pittsburgh: University of Pittsburgh Press, 1973), 6.

3. Ibid., 27.

4. Pehr Kalm, *The America of 1750: Peter Kalm's Travels in North America,* ed. Adolph B. Benson (New York: Dover, 1966), 1:56. See also the discussion of Kalm in Gilbert Chinard, "Eighteenth Century Theories on America as a Human Habitat," *Proceedings of the American Philosophical Society* 91, no. 1 (1947): 33–34.

5. Quoted in Lee Alan Dugatkin, *Mr. Jefferson and the Giant Moose: Natural History in Early America* (Chicago: University of Chicago Press, 2009), 44.

6. Abbé Raynal, *A Philosophical and Political History of the Settlements and Trade of the Europeans in the East and West Indies,* trans. J. O. Justamond (Dublin: John Exshaw and Luke White, 1784), 5:443. For a discussion of Raynal's theory about the Salem witch trials, see Dugatkin, *Mr. Jefferson,* 42.

7. Quoted in Gerbi, *Dispute,* 99.

8. See Dugatkin, *Mr. Jefferson.*

9. Jedidiah Morse, *The History of America in Two Books. . . . ,* 3rd ed. (Philadelphia: Thomas Dobson, 1798), 1:76. For a discussion of Morse's response to the degeneration theory, see Dugatkin, *Mr. Jefferson and the Giant Moose,* 117–18.

10. David Humphreys et al., *The Anarchiad: A New England Poem, 1786–1787,* ed. Luther G. Riggs (Gainesville, FL: Scholars' Facsimiles & Reprints, 1967), 74–75.

11. Ibid., 75. For a discussion of the Wits' response to the degeneration thesis, see Dugatkin, *Mr. Jefferson,* 119–20.

12. On Raynal's retraction of his attack on the Creoles, see Chinard, "Eighteenth Century Theories," 37–38; and Dugatkin, *Mr. Jefferson,* 44–46.

13. On the European travelers' commentary about the premature aging of American women, see Lois W. Banner, *American Beauty* (Los Angeles: Figueroa, 2005), 86–87.

14. Frederick Marryat, *A Diary in America: With Remarks on Its Institutions,* ed. Sydney Jackman (New York: Knopf, 1962), 419.

15. Isabella Lucy Bird, *The Englishwoman in America* (Madison: University of Wisconsin Press, 1966), 362. Thomas Hamilton likewise insisted that "beauty in this climate is not durable. . . . At one or two-and-twenty the bloom of an American lady is gone. . . . At thirty the whole fabric is in decay." See Thomas Hamilton, *Men and Manners in America* (Edinburgh: W. Blackwood, 1833), 1:33.

16. Frederick von Raumer, *America and the American People,* trans. William W. Turner (New York: J. & H. G. Langley, 1846), 498–99.

17. On the difference between British and American beauty standards, see Banner, *American Beauty,* 71–72, 86.

18. See Harriet Martineau, *Society in America* (New York: Saunders and Otley, 1837), 2:263; and Archibald Prentice, *A Tour in the United States with Two Lectures on Emigration,* 3rd ed. (London: John Johnson, 1849), 109.

19. Frances Trollope, *Domestic Manners of the Americans,* 4th ed. (London: Whittaker, Treacher, 1832), 2:136.

20. Hamilton, *Men and Manners,* 2:15, emphasis in original.

21. Bird, *The Englishwoman in America,* 362.

22. For complaints about the excessive dryness of the American climate, see Charles Lyell, *A Second Visit to North America,* 3rd ed. (London: J. Murray, 1855), 1:154–55; and James Hunt, "On the Acclimatisation of Europeans in the United States of America," *Anthropological Review* 8, no. 29 (1870): 111–13, 129, 133, 134.

23. Martineau, *Society in America,* 2:264.

24. Alfred Bunn complained of the "extremes of climate" in New England and New York in *Old England and New England, in a Series of Views Taken on the Spot* (London: R. Bentley, 1853), 2:222.

25. Fredrika Bremer, *The Homes of the New World; Impressions of America,* trans. Mary Howitt (New York: Harper & Bros., 1858), 1:199.

26. Harriet Martineau, *Retrospect of Western Travel* (London: Saunders and Otley, 1838), 2:169–70.

27. Charles Wentworth Dilke, *Greater Britain: A Record of Travel in English-Speaking Countries during 1866 and 1867* (London: Macmillan, 1868), 1:54, 55.

28. Lyell, *Second Visit,* 1:153.

29. Emerson to Elizabeth Hoar, December 28, 1847, in *A Memoir of Ralph Waldo Emerson,* ed. James Elliot Cabot (London: Macmillan, 1887), 2:132.

30. Ralph Waldo Emerson, *English Traits,* ed. Howard Mumford Jones (Cambridge, MA: Belknap, 1966), 41.

31. Oliver Wendell Holmes, *The Autocrat of the Breakfast-Table: Every Man His Own Boswell* (Boston: Houghton, Mifflin, 1892), 171.

32. Ibid., 170.

33. Ibid., 43.

34. Ibid., 237.

35. Ibid., 238.

36. Nathaniel Hawthorne, *Our Old Home: A Series of English Sketches,* ed. William Charvat, Roy Harvey Pearce, Claude M. Simpson, Matthew J. Bruccoli, Fredson Bowers, and L. Neal Smith (Columbus: Ohio State University Press, 1970), 48–49.

37. Ibid., 48.

38. Ibid., 49.

39. Ibid., 319.

40. Ibid., 320.

41. Ibid., 64.

42. For the theory that the survival of the Anglo-Saxons in America depended on steady reinforcements from England, see Robert Knox, *The Races of Man: A Fragment* (Philadelphia: Lea & Blanchard, 1850), 55–57.

43. Hawthorne, *Our Old Home,* 334.

44. Ibid.

45. Nathaniel Hawthorne, *The Scarlet Letter* (New York: Oxford University Press, 2007), 42.

46. Barbara Welter, "The Cult of True Womanhood, 1820–1860," *American Quarterly* 18, no. 2, pt. 1 (1966): 152.

47. Lois Banner discusses the relationship between True Womanhood and the ethereal, "steel-engraving" feminine ideal. See Banner, *American Beauty,* 80.

48. Amy Louise Reed, "Female Delicacy in the Sixties," *Century Magazine* 90 (Oct. 1915): 859.

49. Quoted in ibid., 860.

50. Quoted in Mary P. Ryan, *The Empire of the Mother: American Writing about Domesticity, 1830 to 1860* (New York: Institute for Research in History and the Haworth Press, 1982), 37.

51. Ibid., 55–57.

52. William Harper, "Harper on Slavery," in William Harper, Thomas R. Dew, James Henry Hammond, and William Gilmore Simms, *The Proslavery Argument. . . .* (Philadelphia: Lippincott, Grambo, 1853), 41. For a discussion of Harper's essay and other proslavery portrayals of slave mistresses and female slaves, see Diane Roberts, *The Myth of Aunt Jemima: Representations of Race and Region* (London: Routledge, 1994), 71. For a discussion of the opposed stereotypes of the pure mistress and her libidinous female slave, see Hazel V. Carby, *Reconstructing Womanhood: The Emergence of the Afro-American Woman Novelist* (New York: Oxford University Press, 1987), 26–34.

53. Harper, "Harper on Slavery," 40–43, 66.

54. Nathaniel Hawthorne, "An Ontario Steam-Boat," in *Hawthorne's American Travel Sketches,* ed. Alfred Weber, Beth L. Lueck, and Dennis Berthold (Hanover, NH: University Press of New England, 1989), 49.

55. Nathaniel Hawthorne, "Sketches from Memory. By a Pedestrian. No. II," in *Hawthorne's American Travel Sketches,* ed. Alfred Weber, Beth L. Lueck, and Dennis Berthold (Hanover, NH: University Press of New England, 1989), 44.

56. Hawthorne, "Ontario Steam-Boat," 52, 54.

57. Nathaniel Hawthorne, *The American Notebooks,* ed. Claude M. Simpson (Columbus: Ohio State University Press, 1972), 63, 50, 48. For a discussion of these passages, see Monika Elbert, "Nathaniel Hawthorne, *The Concord Freeman,* and the Irish 'Other,'" *Eire-Ireland* 29, no. 3 (1994): 69–70.

58. Hawthorne, *American Notebooks,* 40.

59. W. D. Howells, *Suburban Sketches* (Boston: J. R. Osgood, 1877), 66.

60. Ibid., 65–66.

61. Ibid., 79.

62. Ibid., 66.

63. Ibid., 194.

64. Ibid.

65. Ibid., 190, 118.

66. Ibid., 68.

67. Ibid., 96.

68. Nathaniel Hawthorne, *The Blithedale Romance* (Boston: Bedford, 1996), 172.

69. Ibid., 174.

70. Henry Morgan, *Ned Nevins, the News Boy; or, Street Life in Boston* (Boston: Lee and Shepard, 1867), 109.

71. Ibid, 111.

72. There is one "benevolent," brogue-speaking old lady in the room, who sympathizes with Sophia. See ibid., 112.

73. Sarah E. Henshaw, "The Kitchen," *Lippincott's Magazine* 2 (Sept. 1868): 316; E. Elcourt, "The Persecuted Woman," *Lippincott's Magazine* 5 (Jan. 1870): 27.

74. Abby Sage Richardson, "A Plea for Chinese Labor," *Scribner's Monthly* 2 (July 1871): 287.

75. Maureen Murphy, "Bridget and Biddy: Images of the Irish Servant Girl in *Puck* Cartoons, 1880–1890," in *New Perspectives on the Irish Diaspora,* ed. Charles Fanning (Carbondale: Southern Illinois University Press, 2000), 163–64, 168–69.

76. Virginia F. Townsend, "Our Irish Girls," Home-Life and Character, *Arthur's Illustrated Home Magazine* 43 (Nov. 1875): 668.

77. Faye E. Dudden, *Serving Women: Household Service in Nineteenth-Century America* (Middletown, CT: Wesleyan University Press, 1983), 47–60.

78. Elcourt, "Persecuted Woman," 29.

79. Ibid., 29–30.

80. Townsend, "Our Irish Girls," 668.

81. Richardson, "Plea for Chinese Labor," 286.

82. Ibid., 287.

83. In 1870 there were only 368 Chinese in the US living outside the West. See Roger Daniels, *Coming to America: A History of Immigration and Ethnicity in American Life,* 2nd ed. (New York: Perennial, 2002), 240.

84. Smith-Rosenberg and Rosenberg, "Female Animal," 122.

85. For feminists who warned of the health risks of excessive domestic labor, see Antoinette L. Brown Blackwell, "The Relation of Woman's Work in the House to the Work Outside," *Woman's Journal,* November 8, 1873, 360; Eliza Bisbee Duffey, *No Sex in Education; or, An Equal Chance for Both Girls and Boys. . . .* (Philadelphia: J. M. Stoddart, 1874), 62–63.

86. For statistics on the Yankee birthrate, see Daniel Scott Smith, "'All in Some Degree Related to Each Other': A Demographic and Comparative Resolution of the Anomaly of New England Kinship," *American Historical Review* 94, no. 1 (1989): 69.

87. See, for example, John Ellis, *Deterioration of the Puritan Stock and Its Causes* (New York: Printed by the author, 1884), 7–8.

88. Nathan Allen, "The New England Family," *New Englander,* n.s., 5 (Mar. 1882): 144.

89. For Allen's role in establishing the Department of Physical Culture at Amherst, see Theodore M. Brown and Elizabeth Fee, "Nathan Allen: Social Reformer and Health Advocate," *American Journal of Public Health* 93, no. 5 (2003): 722, http://www.ncbi.nlm.nih.gov/pmc/articles/PMC1447826/.

90. Nathan Allen, *The Law of Human Increase; or, Population Based on Physiology and Psychology* (New York: Moorhead, Simpson & Bond, 1868), 23.

91. Nathan Allen, "Changes in New England Population," *Popular Science Monthly* 23 (Aug. 1883): 444.

92. Allen, "New England Family," 153.

93. Allen, "Changes in New England," 442.

94. Allen, *Law of Human Increase,* 22.

95. Ibid., 36.

96. Nathan Allen," Female Education," *Congregationalist and Boston Recorder,* December 26, 1867, 270.

97. Christopher Crowfield [Harriet Beecher Stowe], *The Chimney-Corner* (Boston: Ticknor and Fields, 1868), 126–27. See also R. R. Bowker, "*In Re* Bridget.—The Defense," *Old and New* 4 (Oct. 1871): 497, http://search.proquest.com/docview/137128547?accountid=14663.

98. Allen, *Law of Human Increase,* 24.

99. For Gilded Age theories of physiological development, see Smith-Rosenberg and Rosenberg, "Female Animal," 115–16; Rosalind Rosenberg, *Beyond Separate Spheres: Intellectual Roots of Modern Feminism* (New Haven, CT: Yale University Press, 1982), 9–10; and Sue Zschoche, "Dr. Clarke Revisited: Science, True Womanhood,

and Female Collegiate Education," *History of Education Quarterly* 29, no. 4 (1989): 550–51.

100. Smith-Rosenberg and Rosenberg, "Female Animal," 115.

101. Allen, *Law of Human Increase,* 37–38.

102. Ibid., 38–39.

103. Allen, "New England Family," 154–55.

104. For the antebellum critique of fashion, see William Leach, *True Love and Perfect Union: The Feminist Reform of Sex and Society* (New York: Basic Books, 1980), 243–51; Banner, *American Beauty,* 134–38.

105. Ellis, *Deterioration of the Puritan,* 9, 15.

106. John Ellis, *Personal Experience of a Physician. . . .* (Philadelphia: Hahnemann, 1892), 58. For similar sentiments, see Ellis, *Deterioration of the Puritan,* 9. Ellis was a native of Massachusetts. After practicing medicine for over three decades in Massachusetts, Michigan, and New York, he retired from it in 1873 to pursue a business career. See Ellis, *Personal Experience,* 3–15.

107. Ellis, *Deterioration of the Puritan,* 7.

108. Ibid., 10–11.

109. Ibid., 15.

110. See Elizabeth Ewen, *Immigrant Women in the Land of Dollars: Life and Culture on the Lower East Side, 1890–1925* (New York: Monthly Review Press, 1985), 25–27, 67–71; and Kathy Lee Peiss, *Cheap Amusements: Working Women and Leisure in Turn-of-the-Century New York* (Philadelphia: Temple University Press, 1986), 62–67.

111. Allen, *Law of Human Increase,* 27.

112. Ellis, *Deterioration of the Puritan,* 9–10.

113. Janet Farrell Brodie, *Contraception and Abortion in Nineteenth-Century America* (Ithaca, NY: Cornell University Press, 1994), 254.

114. Ibid., 256–57.

115. James C. Mohr, *Abortion in America: The Origins and Evolution of National Policy, 1800–1900* (New York: Oxford University Press, 1978), 189.

116. Quoted in Brodie, *Contraception and Abortion,* 271.

117. Horatio Robinson Storer, *Why Not? A Book for Every Woman* (Boston: Lee and Shepard, 1866), 55–56. See also the discussion in Brodie, *Contraception and Abortion,* 271.

118. Quoted in Brodie, *Contraception and Abortion,* 271.

119. Nathan Allen and Edward Clarke both broke with the physician crusaders over the question of whether the declining birthrate among Yankee women was primarily a result of abortion and contraception, as opposed to physiological causes. See Edward H. Clarke, *Sex in Education; or, A Fair Chance for the Girls* (Boston: J. R. Osgood, 1873), 140–41; W. B. Clarke, "Dr. Allen's Statistics," *Congregationalist and Boston Recorder,* March 4, 1869, 71; and Nathan Allen, "Vital Statistics," *Congregationalist and Boston Recorder,* April 8, 1869, 111.

120. Ellis, *Deterioration of the Puritan,* 11.

121. Allen, "New England Family," 156.

122. Ellis, *Deterioration of the Puritan,* 11–12.

123. Allen, "New England Family," 155.

124. Ibid., 151; Nathan Allen, "Comparative Decrease of Children," *Congregationalist and Boston Recorder,* February 4, 1869, 39.

125. Ellis, *Deterioration of the Puritan,* 12.

126. Allen, "New England Family," 158.

127. Ellis, *Deterioration of the Puritan,* 18–19.

128. Allen, *Law of Human Increase,* 51.

129. Allen, "New England Family," 156.

130. See Mohr, *Abortion in America,* 166–67.

131. For the role of German immigrants, including those in Boston, as providers and procurers of abortions, see ibid., 91–93.

132. Ellis, *Deterioration of the Puritan,* 13.

133. The phrase comes from Clarke, *Sex in Education,* 134.

134. On the warnings about the physical risks of female education, see Jane H. Hunter, *How Young Ladies Became Girls: The Victorian Origins of American Girlhood* (New Haven, CT: Yale University Press, 2002), 213.

135. Allen, "Female Education," 270.

136. S. Weir Mitchell, *Wear and Tear; or, Hints for the Overworked,* 4th ed. (Philadelphia: J. B. Lippincott, 1871), 29, 36. Physician T. S. Clouston also identified New England as a place where inappropriate female education was leading to health problems. See T. S. Clouston, "Female Education from a Medical Point of View," *Popular Science Monthly* 24 (Jan. 1884): 332–33.

137. John Todd, *Woman's Rights* (Boston: Lee and Shepard, 1867), 25.

138. For the feminist response to Todd's *Woman's Rights,* see especially Gail Hamilton, *Woman's Wrongs: A Counter-Irritant* (Boston: Ticknor and Fields, 1868).

139. Prior to the appearance of *Sex in Education,* Clarke had a reputation for cautiously supporting women's advancement. In 1869 he had condemned male medical students in Philadelphia for driving female students out of the classroom with tobacco quids and tinfoil. See Rosenberg, *Beyond Separate Spheres,* 5; Mary Roth Walsh, *"Doctors Wanted, No Women Need Apply": Sexual Barriers in the Medical Profession, 1835–1975* (New Haven, CT: Yale University Press, 1977), 120–22.

140. For the furor around Clarke's book, see Zschoche, "Dr. Clarke Revisited," 545–69; and Walsh, *Doctors Wanted,* 124, 127–31. In 1873–74 reviews of Clarke's book appeared in many newspapers and periodicals, the *Woman's Journal* in particular. In 1874 four books were published critiquing various aspects of *Sex in Education:* George F. Comfort and Anna Manning Comfort, *Woman's Education and Woman's Health. Chiefly in Reply to "Sex in Education"* (Syracuse, NY: T. W. Durston, 1874); Julia Ward Howe, ed., *Sex* and *Education: A Reply to Dr. E. H. Clarke's "Sex in Education"* (Boston: Roberts Brothers, 1874); Anna C. Brackett, ed., *The Education of American Girls: Considered in a Series of Essays* (New York: G. P. Putnam's Sons, 1874); and Duffey, *No Sex in Education.* In 1874 Clarke published a companion volume to *Sex in Education* that significantly revised his earlier recommendations about female education. See note 146; and Edward H. Clarke, *The Building of a Brain* (Boston: J. R. Osgood, 1874).

141. See the testimonies by Sarah Dix Hamlin, Mary O. Nutting, Adelia A. F. Johnston, and Alida C. Avery in Brackett, *Education of American Girls,* 307–61; and "Testimony from Colleges," in Howe, *Sex* and *Education,* 191–203.

142. M. Carey Thomas, "Present Tendencies in Women's College and University Education," *Publications of the Association of Collegiate Alumnae,* 3rd ser., (Feb. 1908): 49. See also Zschoche, "Dr. Clarke Revisited," 547.

143. Zschoche, "Dr. Clarke Revisited," 548–50.

144. Clarke, *Sex in Education,* 12.

145. Ibid., 37, 59.

146. Ibid., 41–42, 154–58. In his companion volume to *Sex in Education,* Clarke significantly revised his guidelines, now recommending that all female students remit exercise and socializing during menstruation, but not their studies, except in cases in which the student's health was weak or the institution required excessive schoolwork. See Clarke, *Building of a Brain,* 61–63.

147. Clarke, *Sex in Education,* 18.

148. Ibid., 40.

149. Ibid., 99–103.

150. Ibid., 66.

151. Ibid., 71, 78, 69, 82.

152. Ibid., 69, 72.

153. Ibid., 20–21. For another passage where Clarke singles out New England females as victims of inappropriate education, see *Sex in Education,* 31.

154. Clarke, *Sex in Education,* 21.

155. Ibid., 27–28.

156. Ibid., 90.

157. Ibid., 138–40.

158. Ibid., 170–72, 175–77.

159. Ibid., 63.

160. For a similar prediction, see Regina Markell Morantz, "Making Women Modern: Middle Class Women and Health Reform in 19th-Century America," *Journal of Social History* 10, no. 4 (1977): 506, n. 39.

161. For the response to Nathan Allen outside New England, see, for example, Editorial, *Raleigh News and Observer,* July 25, 1883; "Are the Yankees Dying Out?," *San Francisco Daily Evening Bulletin,* December 4, 1866; Arthur W. Calhoun, *A Social History of the American Family: From Colonial Times to the Present* (Cleveland: Arthur H. Clarke, 1919), 3:230–31; and Charles Cowley, *Our Divorce Courts. . . .* (Lowell, MA: Penhallow, 1879), 44, 50.

162. See, for example, "Where Do the Paupers and Criminals Come From?," *Boston Pilot,* July 15, 1876, 4; "Important Figures," *Boston Pilot,* June 2, 1877, 4; and "The Foreign Element in New England," *Boston Pilot,* Sept. 15, 1877, 4.

163. For Yankee feminists who warned of the dangers of late hours, tight lacing, and rich food, see Julia Ward Howe's introduction and the untitled essays by Mrs. Horace Mann, Caroline H. Dall, and Mercy B. Jackson in Howe, *Sex* and *Education,* 10–11, 69–70, 95, 97, 106–7, 156–57. For feminists who condemned the fashionable for relying on abortion and contraceptive devices, see Leach, *True Love,* 84.

164. For the various groups that attacked fashion in the antebellum era, see Leach, *True Love,* 243–51; and Banner, *American Beauty,* 134–38.

165. Higginson offered a qualified endorsement of Clarke's conclusions in "Sex in Education Again," *Woman's Journal,* December 6, 1873, 385. As coeditor of the *Woman's Journal,* Higginson published numerous responses to *Sex in Education,* the vast majority quite critical. For Yankee feminists who rejected Clarke's view about the special vulnerability of females, see Howe's introduction to *Sex* and *Education,* 9; and Mercy B. Jackson, "Sex in Education," *Woman's Journal,* February 14, 1874, 56.

166. See, for example, the untitled essay by Dall in Howe, *Sex* and *Education,* 94; and T. W. H., "Sex in Education," *Woman's Journal,* November 8, 1873, 353.

167. For the studies that attempted to test Clarke's claims, see Zschoche, "Dr. Clarke Revisited," 561–66; and Walsh, *Doctors Wanted,* 130–31.

168. For background on the Association of Collegiate Alumnae and *Health Statistics of Women College Graduates,* see Zschoche, "Dr. Clarke Revisited," 561–63; Rosenberg, *Beyond Separate Spheres,* 18–24; and Marion Talbot and Lois Kimball Mathews Rosenberry, *The History of the American Association of University Women, 1881–1931* (Boston: Houghton, Mifflin, 1931), 116–24.

169. Carroll D. Wright, "Health Statistics of Female College Graduates," in Association of Collegiate Alumnae, *Health Statistics of Women College Graduates. . . .* (Boston: Wright & Potter, 1885), 77.

170. For feminists who advocated education as the key to female health, see Howe's introduction and the untitled essays by Thomas Wentworth Higginson, Mrs. Horace Mann, Ada Shepard Badger, Caroline H. Dall, "C.," and Elizabeth Stuart Phelps in Howe, *Sex* and *Education,* 20, 41–42, 60, 67–68, 80–83, 98, 121, 134.

171. Alida C. Avery to Edward H. Clarke, November 4, 1873, in Howe, *Sex* and *Education,* 194. See also the testimony by Adelia A. F. Johnson and Alida C. Avery in Brackett, *Education of American Girls,* 333, 356.

172. Ada Shepard Badger, untitled essay, in Howe, *Sex* and *Education,* 83.

173. Ibid., 77.

174. Dall, untitled essay, in Howe, *Sex* and *Education,* 97. For Dall's efforts to defend coeducation and higher education for women from the attacks of conservatives, see Leach, *True Love,* 282–83.

175. Caroline H. Dall, "The Other Side," in Brackett, *Education of American Girls,* 151. Anna C. Brackett likewise asked, "[W]ere the 'old times' so much better than the present?" See "Sex in Education," in Brackett, *Education of American Girls,* 376.

176. Thomas Wentworth Higginson, *Common Sense about Women* (Boston: Lee and Shepard, 1882), 25.

177. Ibid., 27. Eliza Bisbee Duffey agreed that the health of American women had improved since "those good old days of our grandmothers and great-grandmothers." She insisted, "The men and women of to-day are healthier and longer lived than any of their progenitors." Duffey, *No Sex in Education,* 32.

178. Higginson, *Common Sense about Women,* 26.

179. Annie G. Howes, "Report of the Committee on Health Statistics," in Association of Collegiate Alumnae, *Health Statistics,* 7. Eliza Bisbee Duffey likewise asked, "May it not be those notable grandmothers of ours whom we must thank for the present degeneracy of the race?" She speculated that if her own mother—"New England born and bred"—had worked less and studied more, she herself might not be so nervous. Duffey, *No Sex in Education,* 62–63.

180. Dall, untitled essay, in Howe, *Sex* and *Education,* 95–97.

181. T. W. H., "Dr. Allen's Alarms," *Woman's Journal,* July 28, 1883, 233.

182. Clarke, *Sex in Education,* 168.

183. Dall, "The Other Side," 153. Dall complained that in the past year she had been forced to fire three consumptive Irish servants, who had refused her suggestions to take better care of their health.

184. T. W. H., "Sex in Education," 353.

185. T. W. H., "Dikes and Defenses," *Woman's Journal,* May 17, 1884, 157.

186. Higginson, *Common Sense about Women,* 25.

187. T. W. H., "Dr. Allen's Alarms," 233. For Jarvis's argument, see Edward Jarvis, "Immigration," *Atlantic Monthly* 29 (Apr. 1872): 463. For a similar argument about the effect of Irish mortality on the group's total population, see "Yankee and Irish," *Independent* 35 (Aug. 2, 1883): 17.

188. T. W. H., "Dr. Allen's Alarms," 233.

189. T. W. H., "Dikes and Defenses," 157.

190. T. W. H., "Dr. Allen's Alarms," 233.

191. T. W. H., "The Physique of Irish-Americans," *Woman's Journal,* June 21, 1884, 197.

192. For Higginson's complaints about the antifeminism of Roman Catholics, see T. W. H., "Sex in Education," 353. For evidence of Higginson's support among Catholics, see editorial, *Boston Pilot,* October 3, 1885, 4.

193. Charles E. Buckingham et al., *The Sanitary Condition of Boston* (Boston: Rockwell and Churchill, 1875), 66–67.

194. Ibid., 77.

195. Ibid., 18. The *Pilot* responded to the Sanitary Commission's report by calling on Irish American physicians to look into its claims: "Are the statements true? and [*sic*] if so, why?" See *Boston Pilot,* February 5, 1876, 4.

196. Frederick A. Bushee, "Ethnic Factors in the Population of Boston," *Publications of the American Economic Association* 4, no. 2 (1903): 51.

197. Miriam King and Steven Ruggles, "American Immigration, Fertility, and Race Suicide at the Turn of the Century," *Journal of Interdisciplinary History* 20, no. 3 (1990): 353.

198. Bushee, "Ethnic Factors," 51.

199. In Sarah Orne Jewett's story "Between Mass and Vespers" (1893), the narrator observes that the young second-generation Irishwomen "were not so fair and fresh-colored" as their mothers, "having been brought up less wholesomely and too much indoors." See Sarah Orne Jewett, *The Irish Stories of Sarah Orne Jewett,* ed. Jack Morgan and Louis A. Renza (Carbondale: Southern Illinois University Press, 1996), 53.

200. W. D. Howells, *The Shadow of a Dream and An Imperative Duty* (Bloomington: Indiana University Press, 1970), 4.

201. Howells, *Suburban Sketches,* 68.

CHAPTER 4

1. Rollin Lynde Hartt, "Our Rural Degeneracy," *Boston Evening Transcript,* May 17, 1899. For Hartt's criticism of the hill country, see his "A New England Hill Town: I. Its Condition," *Atlantic Monthly* 83 (Apr. 1899): 561–74; and "A New England Hill Town: II. Its Revival," *Atlantic Monthly 83* (May 1899): 712–20.

2. See, for example, Hartt, "New England Hill Town: I and II"; Philip Morgan, "The Problems of Rural New England," *Atlantic Monthly* 79 (May 1897): 577–87; and Alvan F. Sanborn, "The Future of Rural New England," *Atlantic Monthly* 80 (July 1897): 74–83. For more such commentary, see the bibliography in Harold Fisher Wil-

son, *The Hill Country of Northern New England: Its Social and Economic History, 1790–1930* (New York: AMS, 1967), 403–37.

3. Josiah Strong, *The New Era; or, The Coming Kingdom* (New York: Baker & Taylor, 1893), 173–74; Hartt, "New England Hill Town: I," 574.

4. Michael M. Bell, "Did New England Go Downhill?," *Geographical Review* 79, no. 4 (1989): 450–66; Paul Glenn Munyon, *A Reassessment of New England Agriculture in the Last Thirty Years of the Nineteenth Century: New Hampshire, a Case Study* (New York: Arno, 1978), 193.

5. John Donald Black, *The Rural Economy of New England: A Regional Study* (Cambridge, MA: Harvard University Press, 1950), 142–49.

6. Hal S. Barron, *Those Who Stayed Behind: Rural Society in Nineteenth-Century New England* (New York: Cambridge University Press, 1984), 52, 55.

7. Ibid., 88.

8. Ibid., 112–31. The quote is from p. 112.

9. Albert Gardner Robinson, "Notes of a Returned New Englander," *Independent* 54 (July 31, 1902): 1832.

10. I do not accept the theory, advanced by Hal Barron and Dona Brown, that the crucial line of division in the commentary on rural New England was the one between rural and urban writers. The traditionalists and progressive farmers both numbered urban and rural dwellers among their members, and it is often impossible to tell from the commentary alone whether a given writer was from the city or countryside. See Barron, *Those Who Stayed Behind,* 31–36; and Dona Brown, *Inventing New England: Regional Tourism in the Nineteenth Century* (Washington, DC: Smithsonian Institution Press, 1995), 151–54.

11. My traditionalists shared the same agrarian republican ideology as the rural Vermonters whom Paul Searls calls "uphillers," but whereas Searls's uphillers were exclusively small farmers from rural districts, my traditionalists are much more diverse, including large and small farmers, as well as politicians, journalists, and urban reformers. For the backgrounds and ideologies of the uphillers, see Paul M. Searls, *Two Vermonts: Geography and Identity, 1865–1910* (Hanover, NH: University Press of New England, 2006), 25–28, 30, 72–73, 87–88, 91–93, 157.

12. For a discussion of the enthusiasm of Vermont "downhillers" for progressive farming, see ibid., 36–37, 43, 86–87.

13. William H. Brewer, "How It Has Come about That the American Farmers and Especially Those of New England Are Treated with Disrespect by the Writers in Our Newspapers," *New Englander and Yale Review* 52 (May 1890): 421. By arguing that New England's agricultural commentators fell into two distinct camps, I dissent from Hal Barron and Dona Brown, who conceive of the region's agricultural spokesmen as a single group that held self-contradictory attitudes toward consumption and profit maximization. See Barron, *Those Who Stayed Behind,* 36; and Brown, *Inventing New England,* 147–49.

14. On early nineteenth-century farm labor, see Christopher Clark, *The Roots of Rural Capitalism: Western Massachusetts, 1780–1860* (Ithaca, NY: Cornell University Press, 1990), 105–11. For hired girls, see Faye E. Dudden, *Serving Women: Household Service in Nineteenth-Century America* (Middletown, CT: Wesleyan University Press, 1983), 4–6, 12–43; David E. Schob, *Hired Hands and Plowboys: Farm Labor in the Midwest, 1815–60* (Urbana: University of Illinois Press, 1975), 191–208; and Catherine E.

Kelly, *In the New England Fashion: Reshaping Women's Lives in the Nineteenth Century* (Ithaca, NY: Cornell University Press, 1999), 27–35.

15. Clark, *Roots of Rural Capitalism,* 304.

16. On the changes in the ethnicity, class background, and status of the farm labor work force in the nineteenth century, see ibid., 304–9; Schob, *Hired Hands and Plowboys,* 250–72; Sally Ann McMurry, *Transforming Rural Life: Dairying Families and Agricultural Change, 1820–1885* (Baltimore: Johns Hopkins University Press, 1995), 65–71; LaWanda F. Cox, "The American Agricultural Wage Earner, 1865–1900: The Emergence of a Modern Labor Problem," *Agricultural History* 22, no. 2 (1948): 95–114; *U.S. Industrial Commission Report,* 57th Cong., 1st sess., House Document 179, 1900–1902, 10:87, 243, 255–56, 402–3, 929; Massachusetts Bureau of Statistics of Labor, *Report* (Boston: Wright & Potter, 1871), 155, 160; Massachusetts Bureau of Statistics of Labor, *Third Annual Report* (Boston: Wright & Potter, 1872), 33–34; and Massachusetts Bureau of Statistics of Labor, *Ninth Annual Report* (Boston: Rand, Avery, 1878), 171–80.

17. For state-by-state statistics of the ethnic backgrounds of New England's agricultural laborers, see U.S. Bureau of the Census, *Occupations at the Twelfth Census* (Washington, DC: Government Printing Office, 1904), 239, 291, 301, 333, 379, 401. Smaller groups included the Italians who worked the market gardens of eastern Massachusetts and the Portuguese who labored on the farms of eastern Rhode Island.

18. W. A. Kilbourn, "The Employment of Farm Labor," in *Thirty-Ninth Annual Report of the Secretary of the Massachusetts Board of Agriculture. . . .* (Boston: Wright & Potter, 1892), 415.

19. *U.S. Industrial Commission Report,* 57th Cong., 1st sess., House Document 180, 1900–1902, 11:89, quoted in Cox, "American Agricultural Wage Earner," 100.

20. L. P. Chamberlain, "Farm Labor in New England," in *Seventeenth Annual Report of the Secretary of the Connecticut Board of Agriculture, 1883–84* (Hartford, CT: Case, Lockwood & Brainard, 1884), 105, quoted in Cox, "American Agricultural Wage Earner," 101.

21. Hiram R. Roberts, "Will Farming Pay," in *Second Annual Report of the Board of Agriculture* (Manchester, NH: James M. Campbell, 1872), 354; F. L. Scott, "Farm Life As It Was, As It Is, and As It Should Be," in *Fifteenth Annual Report of the Secretary of the Connecticut Board of Agriculture, 1881–82* (Hartford, CT: Case, Lockwood & Brainard, 1882), 282.

22. Joseph Rood, "Connecticut Farming," in *Twentieth Annual Report of the Secretary of the Connecticut Board of Agriculture, 1886* (Hartford, CT: Case, Lockwood & Brainard, 1886), 93–94.

23. Roberts, "Will Farming Pay," 353–54.

24. Scott, "Farm Life," 285–86. Scott was a successful farmer from Bethlehem, Connecticut, and a frequent contributor to the agricultural press. For his biography, see J. A. Spalding, *Illustrated Popular Biography of Connecticut* (Hartford, CT: Case, Lockwood & Brainard, 1891), 133–34.

25. D. M. Camp, "Some Hindrances to Success," in *Tenth Vermont Agricultural Report. . . .* (Burlington, VT: Free Press, 1888), 190. Camp was the editor of the *Newport Express* and *Newport Standard.*

26. Ibid., 190–91; Roberts, "Will Farming Pay," 353–54.

27. Camp, "Some Hindrances to Success," 190–91; Scott, "Farm Life," 275–98.

28. Camp, "Some Hindrances to Success," 191.

29. Scott, "Farm Life," 281, emphasis in original.

30. Ibid., 276.

31. For a recommendation that rural females exercise, see R. S. Hinman, "Connecticut Farm Life, Past, Present, and Future," in *Twenty-First Annual Report of the Secretary of the Connecticut Board of Agriculture, 1887* (Hartford, CT: Case, Lockwood & Brainard, 1887), 260–61.

32. Scott, "Farm Life," 298, emphasis in original.

33. James Russell Lowell, *Literary and Political Addresses* (Cambridge, MA: Riverside, 1904), 23.

34. John D. Long, George B. Loring, Rev. Samuel W. Dike, and Rev. George A. Jackson, "The Future of the New England Country," *New England Magazine*, n.s., 9 (Jan. 1891): 662. New Hampshire governor Frank W. Rollins similarly argued that the immigrants were more willing to "work longer hours" than the natives in "The Renaissance of New England," *Independent* 53 (Jan. 10, 1901): 70.

35. Geoffrey Champlin, "The Decline of New England," Notes and Comments, *North American Review* 146 (June 1888): 588.

36. For invidious comparisons of Yankee and immigrant farm laborers, see Schob, *Hired Hands and Plowboys*, 254; R., "Female Help," *New England Farmer*, May 1857, 247–48; and "The Hired Girl upon the Farm," *Ohio Cultivator*, August 1, 1854, 10, http://search.proquest.com/docview/137213126?accountid'14663.

37. R., "Female Help," 247. Other writers confirmed that Yankee farmers' children increasingly viewed farm labor as degrading "immigrant work." See Thomas W. Ward, "Let the Poor Lands Go," *New England Farmer*, November 1856, 523; and Michael McNerney, "The Irish and Farming," *New England Farmer*, August 1870, 362.

38. R., "Female Help," 247.

39. Warren Brown, "Farm Labor," in *Fourth Annual Report of the Board of Agriculture. . . .* (Concord, NH: Edward A. Jenks, 1874), 309–10.

40. Ibid., 311, 312.

41. Ibid., 310.

42. J. A. Nash, "Wanted—Less Land or More Labor," *New England Farmer*, December 1856, 539. The Reverend Nash was Professor of Agriculture at Amherst College in 1852–56, although a historian of the college describes his position as "nominal." See W. S. Tyler, *History of Amherst College during Its First Half Century, 1821–1871* (Springfield, MA: Clark W. Bryan, 1873), 421.

43. See, for example, William Clift, "How to Make Farming Profitable," in *Sixteenth Annual Report of the Secretary of the Massachusetts Board of Agriculture. . . .* (Boston: Wright & Potter, 1869), 151; and Searls, *Two Vermonts*, 71.

44. George S. Philbrick, "Concentration of Thought and Action," in *Fifteenth Annual Report of the Board of Agriculture. . . .* (Manchester, NH: John B. Clarke, 1886), 194; G. A. Bowen, "Opportunities of New England Agriculture," in *Twentieth Annual Report of the Secretary of the Connecticut Board of Agriculture, 1886* (Hartford, CT: Case, Lockwood & Brainard, 1886), 97.

45. J. W. Sanborn, "Comparison of Eastern and Western Farming," in *Forty-Second Annual Report of the Secretary of the Massachusetts State Board of Agriculture. . . .* (Boston: Wright & Potter, 1895), 168. A native of Gilmanton, New Hampshire, Jeremiah Wilson Sanborn served as farm superintendent at the New Hampshire College of Agriculture and the Mechanic Arts in 1876–82, as dean of the agricultural faculty at the University of Missouri in 1882–89, and as president of the Utah Agriculture College in 1889–94. See Alfred Charles True, *A History of Agricultural Experimentation and*

Research in the United States, 1607–1925. . . . (Washington, DC: Government Printing Office, 1937), 116.

46. The popular song "A Little Farm Well Tilled," by the prolific British composer James Hook, was well known to Gilded Age Americans. See the discussion of the conflict between Vermont "uphillers" and "downhillers" over the rural ideal of "small farms, well tilled," in Searls, *Two Vermonts,* 87–88, 157.

47. Joseph B. Walker, "The Progress of New England Agriculture during the Last Thirty Years," *New Englander and Yale Review* 47 (Oct. 1887): 243. Along with his interests in farming and banking, Concord, New Hampshire, resident Joseph Burbeen Walker was for many years the president of the New Hampshire Board of Agriculture. See "Hon. Joseph B. Walker," *Granite Monthly* 45 (Feb. 1913): 60–61. For critiques of Hook's song by other progressive farmers, see Nash, "Wanted—Less Land," 540; and S. L. Goodale, "The Changes in Farming; Which Have Taken Place, and Which Should Be Made," in *Seventeenth Annual Report of the Secretary of the Maine Board of Agriculture. . . .* (Augusta, ME: Sprague, Owen & Nash, 1873), 352.

48. Joseph B. Walker, "The Hay Crop," in *Sixth Annual Report of the Board of Agriculture. . . .* (Concord, NH: Edward A. Jenks, 1876), 255.

49. See, for example, Goodale, "Changes in Farming," 353–54; and Clift, "How to Make Farming Profitable," 151.

50. James O. Adams, "The Better Culture," in *Fourth Annual Report of the Board of Agriculture. . . .* (Concord, NH: Edward A. Jenks, 1874), 232, emphasis in original; "Concentration of Capital," in *Massachusetts Ploughman and New England Journal of Agriculture* 58 (Jan. 14, 1899): 4, http://search.proquest.com/docview/136369116?accountid'14663.

51. Henry E. Alvord, "The Farmer and His Family," in *Sixteenth Annual Report of the Secretary of the Connecticut Board of Agriculture, 1882–83* (Hartford, CT: Case, Lockwood & Brainard, 1883), 183.

52. Brewer, "How It Has Come About," 410–21.

53. J. W. Sanborn, "A Change in Farm System Demanded," in *Sixth Report upon Vermont Agriculture. . . .* (Montpelier, VT: Freeman, 1880), 145.

54. On machinery as a marker of class divisions between large and small farmers, see Sally Ann McMurry, *Families and Farmhouses in Nineteenth-Century America: Vernacular Design and Social Change* (New York: Oxford University Press, 1988), 90.

55. Sanborn, "Comparison of Eastern and Western Farming," 176–77.

56. "No More Abandoned Farms," *Nation* 69 (Sept. 7, 1899): 185, emphasis in original. For similar sentiments, see Goodale, "Changes in Farming," 352.

57. "No More Abandoned Farms," 185. William Clift likewise called for urban capitalists to buy New England's farms and hire college-educated managers to run them in "How to Make Farming Profitable," 149.

58. Cables may well be C. H. Cables of Thomaston, Connecticut.

59. For employment agencies, see Frank J. Sheridan, *Italian, Slavic, and Hungarian Unskilled Immigrant Laborers in the United States,* in U.S. Department of Commerce and Labor, *Bulletin,* no. 72 (Washington, DC, 1907), 414–22.

60. Mr. Cables, comment, in *Twenty-First Annual Report of the Secretary of the Connecticut Board of Agriculture, 1887* (Hartford, CT: Case, Lockwood & Brainard, 1887), 310–11.

61. For progressive farmers who advocated housing and/or boarding laborers separately from the farmer's family, see Mr. Sedgwick, comment, in *Seventeenth Annual Report of the Secretary of the Connecticut Board of Agriculture, 1883–84* (Hartford, CT: Case, Lockwood & Brainard, 1884), 126; and J. H. Putnam, "The Depopulation of Our Rural Districts: Cause, and Some Suggestions in Regard to a Remedy," in *Fifth Report of the Vermont Board of Agriculture, for the Year 1878* (Montpelier, VT: J. & J. M. Poland, 1878), 137. Lillian Mayne unapologetically called for feeding the "help" at a separate table and treating them as menials: "Servants in the city have no idea of dining with the family, nor should they in the country." See Lillian Mayne, "Farmers' Families and 'Help,'" *Cultivator and Country Gentleman,* February 19, 1885, 156.

62. McMurry, *Families and Farmhouses,* 106–7; McMurry, *Transforming Rural Life,* 196–97.

63. McMurry, *Families and Farmhouses,* 108–9.

64. According to a report from Maine, farmers generally housed native-born employees with their families, but not foreign-born ones. See the testimony by S. W. Harris and B. Walker McKeen in *U.S. Industrial Commission Report,* 57th Cong., 1st sess., House Document 180, 1900–1902, 11:87–88.

65. L. P. Chamberlain, "Farm Labor in New England," in *Seventeenth Annual Report of the Secretary of the Connecticut Board of Agriculture, 1883–84* (Hartford, CT: Case, Lockwood & Brainard, 1884), 105–6. Chamberlain directed the model farm at the State Reform School in Meriden. See *Reports of the Board of Trustees of the Connecticut School for Boys at Meriden, Conn.* (Meriden, CT: Press of Connecticut School for Boys, 1909), 2:612–15.

66. Mr. Hyde, comment, in *Seventeenth Annual Report of the Secretary of the Connecticut Board of Agriculture, 1883–84* (Hartford, CT: Case, Lockwood & Brainard, 1884), 121. Hyde is likely E. H. Hyde, a board member from Stafford.

67. Mr. Sedgwick, comment, in *Seventeenth Annual Report of the Secretary of the Connecticut Board of Agriculture, 1883–84* (Hartford, CT: Case, Lockwood & Brainard, 1884), 126. Sedgwick is likely Harry Sedgwick, president of the Litchfield Agricultural Society for 1883–84.

68. For attacks on immigrant laborers by progressive farmers, see the testimony of Charles S. Murkland and William P. Brooks in *U.S. Industrial Commission Report,* 57th Cong., 1st sess., House Document 180, 1900–1902, 11:88–89; Albert Chapman, "Farm Accounts," in *Fifth Report of the Vermont Board of Agriculture, for the Year 1878* (Montpelier, VT: J. & J. M. Poland, 1878), 143; Adams, "Better Culture," 229; and Bowen, "Opportunities of New England," 100.

69. Joel Benton, "The Decadence of Farming," *Popular Science Monthly* 36 (Nov. 1889): 31. For similar sentiments, see Charles C. Nott, "A Good Farm for Nothing," *Nation* 49 (Nov. 21, 1889): 406–8.

70. Chapman, "Farm Accounts," 145; Putnam, "Depopulation," 135; Adams, "Better Culture," 239–40.

71. McMurry, *Families and Farmhouses,* 88–100.

72. Adams, "Better Culture," 230; Sara J. Smith, "Shall We Have the 'New Education' for Our Farmers' Daughters?," in *Twentieth Annual Report of the Secretary of the Connecticut Board of Agriculture, 1886* (Hartford, CT: Case, Lockwood & Brainard, 1886), 72–74; G. A. Bowen, "The Health of the Farmer and His Family," in *Seventeenth*

Annual Report of the Secretary of the Connecticut Board of Agriculture, 1883–84 (Hartford, CT: Case, Lockwood & Brainard, 1884), 142–43. On the prevalence of insanity among farmwives, see J. W. Lees, "Reconstructive Energy Needed," in *Eighth Annual Report of the Board of Agriculture for the Year 1878* (Manchester, NH: John B. Clarke, 1879), 254.

73. Sanborn, "Change in Farm System," 144–45.

74. For the progressive farmers' attacks on the immigrants' labor practices, see Benton, "Decadence of Farming," 31; and Lees, "Reconstructive Energy Needed," 255–56.

75. Bowen, "Opportunities of New England,"106–7. T. D. Curtis of Utica, Vermont, told the same humorous story to ridicule inefficient agricultural practices at an 1871 Vermont Dairymen's Association meeting. See Searls, *Two Vermonts,* 192–93.

76. Kathleen Neils Conzen, "Immigrants in Nineteenth-Century Agricultural History," in *Agriculture and National Development: Views on the Nineteenth Century,* ed. Lou Ferleger (Ames: Iowa State University Press, 1990), 316.

77. Ibid., 317–18.

78. Balch, *Our Slavic Fellow Citizens,* 341. With some chagrin, New England descendant M. F. Greeley declared the immigrant agriculturalists of Minnesota better progressive farmers than the natives. See *U.S. Industrial Commission Report,* 57th Cong., 1st sess., House Document 179, 1900–1902, 10:929.

79. The *Boston Globe* claimed that in the 1880s farmers Charles Parsons of Northampton and Francis Clapp of South Deerfield brought the first Poles from New York City to do agricultural and domestic labor in the Connecticut River valley. See "Poles Prosper Where Yankees Failed," *Boston Globe,* June 29, 1902, 41.

80. For nativist attacks on the Connecticut River valley Poles, see Edward Kirk Titus, "The Pole in the Land of the Puritan," *New England Magazine,* n.s., 29 (Oct. 1903): 163; "Poles and Puritans," *Hampshire Gazette and Northampton Courier,* April 26, 1910, 8.

81. Elizabeth Stearns Tyler, "The Poles in the Connecticut Valley," Sketches, *Smith College Monthly* 16 (June 1909): 581.

82. Ibid., 584.

83. "Aliens in New England," *Greenfield (MA) Gazette and Courier,* December 7, 1912, http://americancenturies.mass.edu/collection/itempage.jsp?itemid'15822&img'0&level'advanced&transcription'1.

84. Clarence Deming, "Broken Shadows on the New England Farm," *Independent* 55 (Apr. 30, 1903): 1018.

85. Ibid., 1019.

86. Ibid., 1020.

87. For rural consumerism in the Gilded Age, see Hal S. Barron, *Mixed Harvest: The Second Great Transformation in the Rural North, 1870–1930* (Chapel Hill: University of North Carolina Press, 1997), 155–76; and McMurry, *Families and Farmhouses,* 153–56.

88. Danby, Vermont, farmer Bradford Sumner Congdon warned that there was "much to fear . . . from the increasing luxuriousness and wealth of the people. Our fathers, living in log huts, dressed in home spun, founded this government." Quoted in Searls, *Two Vermonts,* 30.

89. Friend Taylor, comment, in *Seventeenth Annual Report of the Secretary of the*

Maine Board of Agriculture, for the Year 1872 (Augusta, ME: Sprague, Owen & Nash, 1873), 356. For the lecture to which Taylor was responding, see Goodale, "Changes in Farming," 334–54.

90. Taylor, comment, 356.

91. On the Yankee farmer's speculative tendencies, see *U.S. Industrial Commission Report,* 57th Cong., 1st sess., House Document 179, 1900–1902, 10:335.

92. Camp, "Some Hindrances to Success," 192. See also Joseph Rood, "Connecticut Farming," in *Twentieth Annual Report of the Secretary of the Connecticut Board of Agriculture, 1886* (Hartford, CT: Case, Lockwood & Brainard, 1886), 92.

93. Roberts, "Will Farming Pay," 353.

94. D. W. H., "Does Intelligent Farming Pay in Massachusetts?," *New England Farmer,* December 1871, 643, http://search.proquest.com/docview/127826121?accountid'14663.

95. Scott, "Farm Life," 281, emphasis in original.

96. Ibid., 284.

97. Hinman, "Connecticut Farm Life," 255. On the defeminization of agriculture and the farmers' arrogation of traditional women's tasks, see McMurry, *Families and Farmhouses,* 94–95; and McMurry, *Transforming Rural Life,* 145–46. For the growing association of rural consumerism and women, see Barron, *Mixed Harvest,* 160–61.

98. Scott, "Farm Life," 295.

99. Ibid., 296.

100. Ibid., 276, emphasis in original. See also E. R. Towle, "Farming, Past and Present," in *Ninth Vermont Agricultural Report. . . .* (Montpelier: Vermont Watchman & State Journal, 1886), 164; and Champlin, "Decline of New England," 588–89.

101. "Labor and Luxury," *New England Farmer,* June 1855, 269, emphasis in original.

102. Champlin, "Decline of New England," 588. On the rise of "farm vacations" in the 1890s, see Brown, *Inventing New England,* 142–67. New Hampshire physician W. H. H. Mason warned that the craze for fashionable dressing was causing the same health and reproductive problems among rural Yankee women as among their urban sisters. Echoing the medical moralists discussed in chapter 3, Mason insisted that fashion was undermining the reproductive capacity of Yankee women, leaving it up to the immigrants to bear the nation's children. See W. H. H. Mason, "Hygiene on the Farm," in *Fifth Annual Report of the Board of Agriculture for the Year Ending June 1, 1875* (Concord, NH: Charles C. Pearson, 1875), 209–10.

103. Alvan F. Sanborn, "The Future of Rural New England," *Atlantic Monthly* 80 (July 1897): 79. The Reverend Julius Ward similarly argued, "The attempt to imitate city habits in houses, in dress, and in other appointments, by people in the country, however well intended, is a great mistake." See Rev. Julius H. Ward, "The Revival of Our Country Towns," *New England Magazine,* n.s., 7 (Nov. 1889): 247.

104. Sanborn, "Future of Rural New England," 79.

105. Quoted in Brown, *Inventing New England,* 151.

106. John F. French, "Farming—Present and Prospective," in *Third Annual Report of the Board of Agriculture. . . .* (Nashua, NH: Orren C. Moore, 1873), 204–5.

107. Scott, "Farm Life," 284.

108. Sanborn, "Future of Rural New England," 83.

109. Frank W. Rollins, "The Renaissance of New England," *Independent* 53 (Jan. 10, 1901): 70. In an illustrated book on rural New England, artist and writer Clifton Johnson similarly observed that "thrift seems to dwell rather with recent comers from across the water than with the older families. . . . The scions of the old families are looser in their methods and more reckless and showy, and far less given to vigorous work." Clifton Johnson, *The New England Country* (Boston: Lee and Shepard, 1893), 45–46.

110. Amos N. Currier, "The Decline of Rural New England," *Popular Science Monthly* 38 (Jan. 1891): 386.

111. Titus, "Pole in the Land," 163.

112. Ibid., 163–64.

113. Ibid., 166.

114. "Poles and Puritans," 8.

115. The author of books on Cuba and Puerto Rico, Robinson had recently returned to his native New England after being away for much of the previous two decades. See Albert Gardner Robinson, "Notes of a Returned New Englander," *Independent* 54 (July 31, 1902): 1831.

116. Ibid., 1832.

117. "No More Abandoned Farms," 184. For similar sentiments, see Robinson, "Notes of a Returned New Englander," 1832.

118. Charles A. Mills, "The Laws of Competition as Affecting the Massachusetts Farmer," in *Thirty-Ninth Annual Report of the Secretary of the Massachusetts Board of Agriculture. . . .* (Boston: Wright & Potter, 1892), 407. Likewise, see Nash, "Wanted—Less Land," 540; M. V. B. Hathaway, "Education, Its Advantage to the Farmer," in *Fifth Report of the Vermont Board of Agriculture for the Year 1878* (Montpelier, VT: J. & J. M. Poland, 1878), 353, 356; and Philbrick, "Concentration of Thought," 197.

119. Sanborn, "Change in Farm System," 124.

120. Philbrick, "Concentration of Thought," 197.

121. On the advantages of New England, see Nahum J. Bachelder, "New England Agriculture," in *Twenty-Second Annual Report of the Board of Agriculture. . . .* (Concord, NH: Edward N. Pearson, 1893), 269; and Brewer, "How It Has Come About," 420.

122. Chapman, "Farm Accounts," 145; Philbrick, "Concentration of Thought," 197.

123. Educator A. E. Winship insisted, "It is one of the best signs of the times that a man must be able to live relatively as well on a Massachusetts farm as he could hope to live in the city, or he will not stay there." A. E. Winship, "Are the Massachusetts Country Towns Degenerating?," *New England Magazine,* n.s., 22 (Aug. 1900): 656. The secretary of the Massachusetts Board of Agriculture declared, "It is our endeavor to keep the rural homes equal to those of the same class of citizens in our villages, with all conveniences and comforts found there." "Testimony of Hon. J. W. Stockwell," in *U.S. Industrial Commission Report,* 57th Cong., 1st sess., House Document 179, 1900–1902, 10:884.

124. For a call for closer relations between countryside and city, see J. M. Hubbard, "The Rural Neighborhood," in *Twenty-Fifth Annual Report of the Secretary of the Connecticut Board of Agriculture, 1891* (Hartford, CT: Case, Lockwood & Brainard, 1891), 86–87.

125. Charles S. Phelps, "Is There a Decadence of New England Agriculture?," *New*

England Magazine, n.s., 25 (Nov. 1901): 382. Phelps was Professor of Agricultural Science at the Connecticut Agricultural College at Storrs.

126. George Austin Bowen, "Existing Forces in Agriculture," in *Twenty-Third Annual Report of the Secretary of the Connecticut Board of Agriculture, 1889* (Hartford, CT: Case, Lockwood & Brainard, 1889), 94, 92. A native of Woodstock, Connecticut, Bowen was a practicing physician with a strong interest in agriculture, serving on the boards of various state and local agricultural organizations. See William Harrison Taylor, *Taylor's Legislative History and Souvenir of Connecticut, 1897–1912* (Putnam, CT: William Harrison Taylor, 1903), 4:56.

127. Mills, "Laws of Competition," 407. For a similar portrayal of the Western immigrant as the enemy of the Yankee farmer, see Nott, "Good Farm for Nothing," 406–8. For other attacks on the low living standards of the immigrant farmers, see Balch, *Our Slavic Fellow Citizens,* 342.

128. Brewer, "How It Has Come About," 420. In 1864 Brewer became the first Chair of Agriculture in the Sheffield Scientific School at Yale.

129. William H. Brewer, *The Brighter Side of New England Agriculture. . . .* (Manchester, NH: J. B. Clarke, 1890), 22; William H. Brewer, "The Past and Future of Connecticut Agriculture," in *Twenty-Fourth Annual Report of the Secretary of the Connecticut Board of Agriculture, 1890* (Hartford, CT: Case, Lockwood & Brainard, 1891), 166.

130. Brewer, "Past and Future," 163.

131. William H. Brewer, "Is It True That Farming Is 'Declining' in New England?," *New Englander and Yale Review* 52 (April 1890): 337.

132. Reversing the argument of the Yankee progressive farmers, some of their western counterparts thought their own high standard living was threatened by the cheap-living immigrant farmers of New England. See the testimony of Eugene Davenport, in *U.S. Industrial Commission Report,* 57th Cong., 1st sess., House Document 179, 1900–1902, 10:263.

133. Lees, "Reconstructive Energy Needed," 251, 255–56. Lees was a Congregational minister from Lee, New Hampshire.

134. Benton, "Decadence of Farming," 31.

135. Lees, "Reconstructive Energy Needed," 255–56; Benton, "Decadence of Farming," 30–35.

136. Nott, "Good Farm for Nothing," 407.

137. J. G. Crawford, "How to Make Farming Profitable," in *Eighth Annual Report of the Board of Agriculture for the Year 1878* (Manchester, NH: John B. Clarke, 1879), 441–42.

138. "Poles Prosper," 41.

139. Eugene Barry, "The Prairie Farmer," *New England Magazine,* n.s., 8 (June 1890): 388.

140. Horace G. Wadlin, *Abandoned Farms in Massachusetts,* in *Twenty-First Annual Report of the Massachusetts Bureau of Statistics of Labor* (Boston: Wright & Potter, 1891), 251. See the discussion of Wadlin's pamphlet in "The Editors' Table," *New England Magazine,* n.s., 10 (July 1899): 675–77.

141. Wadlin, *Abandoned Farms in Massachusetts,* 252.

142. Ibid., 254.

143. Ibid., 255.

144. "Rev. John Todd's Address," *New England Farmer,* December 2, 1835, 161.

145. John D. Vose, *Barnum's New Year's Address* (New York, 1851), 10, emphasis in original.

146. Ralph Waldo Emerson, "Self-Reliance," in *Essays: First and Second Series* (New York: Vintage, 1990), 45, emphasis in original.

147. Quoted in Richard Lyle Power, *Planting Corn Belt Culture: The Impress of the Upland Southerner and Yankee in the Old Northwest* (Indianapolis: Indiana Historical Society, 1953), 45.

148. Charles McDaniel, "Advantages of Eastern over Western Farming," in *Eighteenth Annual Report of the Board of Agriculture. . . .* (Manchester, NH: John B. Clarke, 1889), 59.

149. Ibid. For a biographical sketch of McDaniel, see Henry H. Metcalf, *New Hampshire Agriculture: Personal and Farm Sketches* (Concord, NH: Republican Press, 1897), 129–32. McDaniel's encounter with the western agriculturalist likely occurred during an 1885 trip to California. See D. Hamilton Hurd, ed., *History of Cheshire and Sullivan Counties, New Hampshire* (Philadelphia: J. W. Lewis, 1886), 365.

150. McDaniel, "Advantages of Eastern over Western Farming," 58.

151. For similar sentiments, see Herbert Wendell Gleason, "The Old Farm 'Revisited,'" *New England Magazine*, n.s., 22 (Aug. 1900): 672.

152. Ibid., 678, emphasis in original. Born 1855 in Malden, Massachusetts, Gleason served in 1883–99 as a Congregational minister before going on to a successful career as a nature photographer.

153. Ibid., 677–79. For the origins of Old Home Week, see Brown, *Inventing New England,* 135–42. For recommendations on developing home ties in rural youth, see D. W. H., "Does Intelligent Farming Pay"; Mrs. J. M. Wright, "On Keeping Our Boys at Home," in *Sixth Report upon Vermont Agriculture. . . .* (Montpelier, VT: Freeman, 1880), 106–9; Mrs. Alonzo Towle, "Possibilities," in *Twenty-First Annual Report of the Board of Agriculture. . . .* (Concord, NH: Ira C. Evans, 1893), 52–60; and Mrs. C. W. Emery, "Home Attractions," in *Eighteenth Annual Report of the Board of Agriculture. . . .* (Manchester, NH: John B. Clarke, 1889), 84–93.

154. Gleason, "Old Farm," 678–79.

155. Ibid., 678. The quote comes from James Bryce, *The American Commonwealth* (Chicago: C. H. Sergel, 1891), 2:722.

156. Currier, "Decline of Rural New England," 387, 385–86. Born 1832 in Canaan, New Hampshire, Currier was Professor of Ancient Languages at the Central University of Iowa in 1857–67 and the State University of Iowa (where he also held several administrative positions) in 1867–1907.

157. Joseph Schafer, "The Yankee and the Teuton in Wisconsin," *Wisconsin Magazine of History* 6 (Dec. 1922): 143.

158. Ibid., 144. For similar sentiments, see Joseph Schafer, *Four Wisconsin Counties: Prairie and Forest* (Madison: State Historical Society of Wisconsin, 1927), 103–4, 118–19, 123; and Ellis Baker Usher, *Wisconsin: Its Story and Biography, 1848–1913* (Chicago: Lewis, 1914), 3:502.

159. Schafer, "Yankee and the Teuton," 130–45.

160. For farming communities where Yankees were more persistent than some immigrant groups, see Allan G. Bogue, *From Prairie to Corn Belt: Farming on the Illinois and Iowa Prairies in the Nineteenth Century* (Chicago: University of Chicago

Press, 1963), 25–26; and Robert C. Ostergren, "Land and Family in Rural Immigrant Communities," *Annals of the Association of American Geographers* 71, no. 3 (1981): 406.

161. Conzen, "Immigrants in Nineteenth-Century Agricultural History," 319–20; Kathleen Neils Conzen, "Peasant Pioneers: Generational Succession among German Farmers in Frontier Minnesota," in *The Countryside in the Age of Capitalist Transformation: Essays in the Social History of Rural America,* ed., Steven Hahn and Jonathan Prude (Chapel Hill: University of North Carolina Press, 1985), 267–85; Ostergren, "Land and Family," 405–11.

162. Jon Gjerde, *From Peasants to Farmers: The Migration from Balestrand, Norway, to the Upper Middle West* (Cambridge: Cambridge University Press, 1985), 166.

163. Ibid., 140, 166.

164. See, for example, John A. Hawgood, *The Tragedy of German-America: The Germans in the United States of America during the Nineteenth Century—and After* (New York: G. P. Putnam's Sons, 1940), 30–34; and Carl Wittke, *The Irish in America* (New York: Russell, 1956), 65.

165. See, for example, Marcus Lee Hansen, *The Immigrant in American History,* ed. Arthur M. Schlesinger (Cambridge, MA: Harvard University Press, 1942), 53–76; and *U.S. Industrial Commission Report,* 57th Cong., 1st sess., House Document 179, 1900–1902, 10:323.

166. Mary Alden Hopkins, "Whom the Land Loves," *Atlantic Monthly* 129 (May 1922): 620, 622. See Van Wyck Brooks's praise for Hopkins's essay in *Sketches in Criticism* (New York: E. P. Dutton, 1932), 127–30.

167. "Decline of Agriculture in New England," *Philadelphia North American and United States Gazette,* March 6, 1873, 1. For a similar invidious comparison of Yankees and Germans, see "The Pennsylvania Germans," pt. 4: "Their Occupations," *Reformed Church Messenger,* March 11, 1868, 5, http://search.proquest.com/docview/137345830?accountid'14663.

168. The unnamed New Hampshire newspaper is quoted in "The Decline of New England," *New York Evangelist,* June 2, 1881, 4, http://search.proquest.com/docview/125364522?accountid'14663.

169. *New York Sun,* quoted in Editorial, *Boston Pilot,* August 21, 1886, 4.

170. "Abandoned Farms in Massachusetts," *Boston Pilot,* March 21, 1891, 4. For more comparisons of the advantages of farming in the West and East, see "Can a Laborer Better His Position?," *Boston Pilot,* August 25, 1877, 4; and "Go West!," *Boston Pilot,* August 2, 1879, 1, 8.

171. *New York Sun,* quoted in Editorial, *Boston Pilot,* August 21, 1886, 4.

172. J. F. Lawrence, "The New Departure," in *Second Annual Report of the Board of Agriculture. . . .* (Manchester, NH: James M. Campbell, 1872), 259, emphasis in original.

173. Nott, "Good Farm for Nothing," 408.

174. Putnam, "Depopulation," 134; for similar sentiments, see Bowen, "Existing Forces in Agriculture," 103.

175. William Waldo Hyde, "Address of Welcome," in *Twenty-Seventh Annual Report of the Secretary of the Connecticut Board of Agriculture, 1893* (Hartford, CT: Fowler & Miller, 1893), 44–45. For a similar comparison of the Yankee and immigrant farmers of Wisconsin, see Passaconoway, "A Trip to the West, No. 3," *New Hampshire Patriot and State Gazette,* September 5, 1850, 2.

176. See, for example, Goodale, "Changes in Farming," 336; T. H. Hoskins, "New England Agriculture," *Popular Science Monthly* 38 (Mar. 1891): 700. The drop in farmland classified as "improved" (from 54 percent in 1890 to 40 percent in 1900) suggests how rapidly New England's farmers were allowing marginal cropland to return to forest. See Bell, "Did New England Go Downhill?," 460.

177. Phelps, "Is There a Decadence?," 381.

178. William Clift, "New London County," in *Fourteenth Annual Report of the Secretary of the Connecticut Board of Agriculture, 1880–81* (Hartford, CT: Case, Lockwood & Brainard, 1881), 232–33.

179. Phelps, "Is There a Decadence?," 381; Clift, "How to Make Farming Profitable," 149.

180. J. H. Hale, "The Business Side of Agriculture," in *Forty-Sixth Annual Report of the Secretary of the Massachusetts State Board of Agriculture. . . .* (Boston: Wright & Potter, 1899), 85.

181. Ibid., 86, 92.

182. Nott, "Good Farm for Nothing." Compare George Austin Bowen's warning that if New England agriculture failed to keep up with the "restless spirit and tireless energy that characterizes the times. . . . its progressive men will leave it for other callings, and we shall see it passing into such hands as are carrying it on in other parts of the world, a debased, spiritless peasantry." See Bowen, "Existing Forces in Agriculture," 92.

183. Sanborn, "Comparison of Eastern and Western Farming," 161. For Sanborn's biography, see note 45.

184. Ibid., 167, 161, 170, 168.

185. Bowen, "Opportunities of New England," 97.

186. For evidence of his nativism, see Bowen, "Existing Forces in Agriculture," 103–4.

CHAPTER 5

1. The *Magazine of Western History* was founded in Cleveland in 1884 by William W. Williams. James Harrison Kennedy became editor in 1887 and moved the magazine to New York City in 1888, where it abandoned its western focus. See Frank Luther Mott, *A History of American Magazines, 1741–1930*, vol. 3: *1865–1885* (Cambridge, MA: Harvard University Press, 1967), 262.

2. Susan Gray puts the western boundary of the "Yankee West" in southeastern Minnesota. John C. Hudson offers both a narrow definition of "Yankeeland" that terminates in the central Dakotas and a broad definition that extends from central Kansas to the Canadian border. See Susan E. Gray, *The Yankee West: Community Life on the Michigan Frontier* (Chapel Hill: University of North Carolina Press, 1996), 1–2; and John C. Hudson, "Yankeeland in the Middle West," *Journal of Geography* 85, no. 5 (1986): 196.

3. The relations between New England and the Old Northwest call to mind Cheryl Herr's richly theorized discussion of the cross-regional ties between Ireland and the Midwest in her *Critical Regionalism and Cultural Studies: From Ireland to the*

American Midwest (Gainesville: University of Florida Press, 1996).

4. Nicole Etcheson, *The Emerging Midwest: Upland Southerners and the Political Culture of the Old Northwest, 1787–1861* (Bloomington: Indiana University Press, 1996), 2.

5. Ibid., 119.

6. Richard Lyle Power, *Planting Corn Belt Culture: The Impress of the Upland Southerner and Yankee in the Old Northwest* (Indianapolis: Indiana Historical Society, 1953), 16–20.

7. A. D. Jones, *Illinois and the West. . . .* (Boston: Weeks, Jordan, 1838), 157. See also Power, *Planting Corn Belt Culture,* 16.

8. See, for example, "Anniversary of the New Hampshire Home Missionary Society," *Independent* 1 (Sept. 13, 1849): 162, http://search.proquest.com/docview/90028971?accountid=14663.

9. H. D. Kitchel, "The New England Zone: The Social and Religious Relations of the East and West," *Congregational Quarterly* 3 (Oct. 1861): 341. See also Power, *Planting Corn Belt Culture,* 19–20.

10. Kitchel, "New England Zone," 342, emphasis in original.

11. Ibid.

12. Ibid., 346.

13. Ibid., 348.

14. T. W. Palmer, "New England at the West," *Independent* 40 (July 12, 1888): 2, http://search.proquest.com/docview/90384540?accountid=14663. He spoke at the Independence Day celebration in Woodstock, Connecticut. See "Independence Day," *Independent* 40 (July 12, 1888): 1, http://search.proquest.com/docview/90420771?accountid=14663. Palmer was born in 1830 in Detroit of Yankee migrant parents. He served in the US Senate in 1883-89. See M. Agnes Burton, "Thomas Witherell Palmer," in Michigan Historical Commission, *Michigan Historical Collections* (Lansing, MI: The Commission, 1915), 39:207–17; and "Thomas Witherell Palmer," in *Dictionary of American Biography,* ed. Dumas Malone (New York: Charles Scribner's Sons, 1934), 7:192–93.

15. Powell was born in Clinton, New York, of Yankee ancestry. He graduated from the Union Theological Seminary in 1858, and went on to serve in churches in New York, Michigan, Missouri, and Illinois. See "Edward Payson Powell," in *Dictionary of American Biography,* ed. Dumas Malone (New York: Scribner's, 1935), 8:144–45; and E. P. Powell, "Ye Old-Time Farmhouse," *Independent* 97 (Feb. 22, 1919): 262, http://search.proquest.com/docview/90597601?accountid=14663.

16. E. P. Powell, "New England in Michigan," *New England Magazine,* n.s., 13 (Dec. 1895): 427.

17. "The Decline of New England," *New York Evangelist,* June 2, 1881, 4.

18. E. P. Powell, "The Romance of Pioneering," *New England Magazine,* n.s., 21 (Nov. 1899): 352.

19. Palmer "New England," 2.

20. "Decline of New England," 4.

21. Ibid.

22. Ellis Baker Usher, *Wisconsin: Its Story and Biography, 1848–1913* (Chicago: Lewis, 1914), 1:17.

23. See Palmer, "New England," 2; and "Decline of New England," 4.

24. Palmer "New England," 2.

25. Powell saw Michigan as "New England amended and perfected;—as New England was Old England with less of Saxon brute force and more of Puritan conscience." See Powell, "New England in Michigan," 427.

26. Powell, "Romance of Pioneering," 346.

27. Ibid.

28. Ibid., 345–46. Powell further claimed the Yankee migrants "built New England farmhouses and villages, with whitewashed fences, raised New England beans and planted New England orchards." E. P. Powell, "New England in New York," *New England Magazine,* n.s., 19 (Oct. 1895): 147.

29. Palmer, "New England," 2.

30. William E. Gienapp, *The Origins of the Republican Party, 1852–1856* (New York: Oxford University Press, 1987), 429–31.

31. See Hudson, "Yankeeland," 195–20; Ihna Thayer Frary, *Early Homes of Ohio* (Richmond, VA: Garrett and Massie, 1936), 25, 27, 239; and Thomas J. Schlereth, *Cultural History and Material Culture: Everyday Life, Landscapes, Museums* (Ann Arbor: UMI Research Press, 1990), 197–213.

32. See Hudson, "Yankeeland," 197–99; and Power, *Planting Corn Belt Culture,* 97–100.

33. Etcheson, *Emerging Midwest,* 4.

34. Gienapp, *Origins of the Republican Party,* 428–31; Etcheson, *Emerging Midwest,* 78–90, 94–102.

35. Carl F. Kaestle, "The Development of Common School Systems in the States of the Old Northwest," in "*. . . Schools and the Means of Education Shall Forever Be Encouraged": A History of Education in the Old Northwest, 1787–1880,* ed. Paul H. Mattingly and Edward W. Stevens Jr. (Athens: Ohio University Libraries, 1987), 31–38; Carl F. Kaestle, *Pillars of the Republic: Common Schools and American Society, 1780–1860* (New York: Hill and Wang, 1983), 182–92.

36. Ian R. Tyrrell, *Sobering Up: From Temperance to Prohibition in Antebellum America, 1800–1860* (Westport, CT: Greenwood, 1979), 244; Etcheson, *Emerging Midwest,* 85–86.

37. Etcheson, *Emerging Midwest,* 87.

38. Ibid., 94–101.

39. Richard Jensen, *The Winning of the Midwest: Social and Political Conflict, 1888–1896* (Chicago: University of Chicago Press, 1971), 64–68; Paul Kleppner, *The Cross of Culture: A Social Analysis of Midwestern Politics, 1850–1900* (New York: Free Press, 1970), 73–75.

40. Theodore C. Blegen, *Norwegian Migration to America, 1825–1860* (Northfield, MN: Norwegian-American Historical Association, 1940), 2:223, quoted in Jensen, *Winning of the Midwest,* 81.

41. Kaestle, "Development of Common School Systems," 36–37; Kaestle, *Pillars of the Republic,* 192.

42. My summary of the conflict over the Bennett law is drawn from Jensen, *Winning of the Midwest,* 122–48; and Kleppner, *Cross of Culture,* 158–70. Born in 1836 in Stockbridge, New York, of New England-descended parents, William Dempster Hoard migrated to Wisconsin in 1857.

43. Jensen, *Winning of the Midwest,* 134.

44. Quoted in ibid., 129.

45. On the remaking of the Republican Party, see Andrew R. L. Cayton and Peter S. Onuf, *The Midwest and the Nation: Rethinking the History of an American Region* (Bloomington: Indiana University Press, 1990), 113–15; and Jensen, *Winning of the Midwest,* 175–77.

46. Jensen, *Winning of the Midwest,* 69–70.

47. See Gienapp, *Origins of the Republican Party,* 425; Jensen, *Winning of the Midwest,* 122.

48. Jensen, *Winning of the Midwest,* 120–21.

49. Melvin G. Holli, *Reform in Detroit: Hazen S. Pingree and Urban Politics* (New York: Oxford University Press, 1969), 18. See the discussion of Pingree in Cayton and Onuf, *Midwest and the Nation,* 115.

50. Ellis Baker Usher, "New England in Wisconsin," *New England Magazine,* n.s., 22 (June 1900): 451.

51. Ibid., 460. In the same essay, Usher argued that the Yankee "blazed the way for intellectual and material progress, and his descendants and the descendants of his foreign-born neighbors are following and must continue to follow in his broad pathway" (461).

52. See Kleppner, *Cross of Culture,* 165–67. For Usher's biography, see A. M. Thomson, *A Political History of Wisconsin,* 2nd ed. (Milwaukee: C. N. Casper, 1902), 357–58.

53. Palmer, "New England," 2.

54. U.S. Bureau of the Census, *The Seventh Census of the United States, 1850* (Washington, DC: Robert Armstrong, 1853), xxxvi.

55. Ellis B. Usher, *Puritan Principles and Influence: An Address Delivered by Ellis B. Usher at the Annual Dinner of the Congregational Club of Milwaukee, Commemorative of Forefathers' Day, Hotel Pfister, December 18, 1900* (Milwaukee, WI: [The Club?], 1900).

56. Usher, "New England in Wisconsin," 449.

57. S. Doc. 553, 50th Cong., 1st sess., December 12, 1887, 4. Many thanks to Mary Baumann of the US Senate historical office for providing me with a copy of this bill.

58. *Congressional Record,* 50th Cong., 1st sess., vol. 9, pt. 1, 653–57.

59. Palmer, "New England," 2.

60. On the growth of New England's center villages in the late eighteenth and early nineteenth centuries, see Joseph S. Wood, *The New England Village* (Baltimore: Johns Hopkins University Press, 1997), 119–34; and Joseph A. Conforti, *Imagining New England: Explorations of Regional Identity from the Pilgrims to the Mid–Twentieth Century* (Chapel Hill: University of North Carolina Press, 2001), 124–44.

61. Dona Brown, *Inventing New England: Regional Tourism in the Nineteenth Century* (Washington, DC: Smithsonian Institution Press, 1995), 140.

62. George Perry Morris, introduction to *Historic Towns of New England,* ed. Lyman P. Powell, 2nd ed. (New York: G. P. Putnam's Sons, 1898), 31.

63. Ibid., 32–33.

64. On the Connecticut Missionary Society and the Plan of Union, see James R. Rohrer, *Keepers of the Covenant: Frontier Missions and the Decline of Congregationalism, 1774–1818* (New York: Oxford University Press, 1995), 11–13; and Amy DeRogatis, *Moral Geography: Maps, Missionaries, and the American Frontier* (New York: Columbia University Press, 2003), 37.

65. DeRogatis, *Moral Geography*, 16–17, 20–21, 40–47.

66. Rohrer, *Keepers of the Covenant,* 98. See also pp. 21–22.

67. See David French, "Puritan Conservatism and the Frontier: The Elizur Wright Family on the Connecticut Western Reserve," *Old Northwest* 1 (1975): 88–89, 93.

68. Quoted in DeRogatis, *Moral Geography,* 112, 160.

69. French, "Puritan Conservatism and the Frontier," 89.

70. DeRogatis, *Moral Geography,* 45.

71. Rohrer, *Keepers of the Covenant,* 4, 134–37.

72. DeRogatis, *Moral Geography,* 157–66, 172–73. Over the following decades, the famous liberalism of Oberlin College—its abolitionism, Arminian theology, and nondiscriminatory admission policies (both woman and African Americans were admitted)—would help create a counterimage for the Western Reserve that clashed with its reputation for Puritan nostalgia. While many persisted in viewing the Western Reserve as a throwback to old New England, others increasingly saw it as a hotbed of the latest fads and reforms (aka "crankisms"). See Harriet Taylor Upton, *History of the Western Reserve* (Chicago: Lewis, 1910), 1:17–18.

73. George W. Knepper, "Early Migration to the Western Reserve," in *Ohio's Western Reserve: A Regional Reader,* ed. Harry F. Lupold and Gladys Haddad (Kent, OH: Kent State University Press, 1988), 35–36; Eric J. Cardinal, "Epilogue: New England and the Western Reserve in the Nineteenth Century—Some Suggestions," in Lupold and Haddad, *Ohio's Western Reserve,* 257.

74. Robert P. Swierenga, "The Settlement of the Old Northwest: Ethnic Pluralism in a Featureless Plain," *Journal of the Early Republic* 9, no. 1 (1989): 82–84.

75. James A. Garfield, "Discovery and Ownership of the Northwestern Territory, and Settlement of the Western Reserve," *Western Reserve and Northern Ohio Historical Society* 20 (1874): 10.

76. See, for example, Ellen D. Larned, "New Connecticut, or Western Reserve," *Connecticut Quarterly* 3, no. 1 (1897): 96–97.

77. Lucien Price, *Hardscrabble Hellas: An Ohio Academe* (Hudson, OH: Printed for Western Reserve Academy, 1929). The memoir was originally published as "Hardscrabble Hellas," *Atlantic Monthly* 139 (Feb. 1927): 153–66.

78. Price, *Hardscrabble Hellas,* 17.

79. Ibid., 21.

80. Ibid., 28.

81. Ibid., 49.

82. D. A. Goodsell, "The American in Literature," *Chautauquan* 7 (Oct. 1886): 23, http://search.proquest.com/docview/125220022?accountid=14663.

83. Born 1816 in Monson, Massachusetts, and raised on the Western Reserve, Riddle served in the Thirty-Seventh Congress (1861–63). He was also a prolific author of fiction, biography, and memoir.

84. A. G. Riddle, *The Life, Character, and Public Services of Jas. A. Garfield* (Philadelphia: William Flint, 1880), 392.

85. Ibid., 43.

86. [Albert Gallatin Riddle], *Bart Ridgeley; A Story of Northern Ohio* (Boston: Nichols and Hall, 1873), 118. See the discussion of this novel in Robert A. Wheeler, "The Literature of the Western Reserve," *Ohio History* 100 (1991): 110.

87. A. G. Riddle, "Rise of the Antislavery Sentiment on the Western Reserve," *Magazine of Western History* 6 (June 1887): 146.

88. Ibid., 150.

89. D. A. Goodsell, in contrast, believed the demographic differences between the two regions were most visible in Boston, which, "They tell me . . . is an Irish city. An old man told me the other Sunday that New England is best seen now in the Western Reserve." Goodsell, "The American in Literature," 23.

90. Josiah Strong, *Our Country,* ed. Jurgen Herbst (Cambridge, MA: Belknap, 1963), 188, 191.

91. Price, *Hardscrabble Hellas,* 17, quoted in Kenneth V. Lottich, *New England Transplanted. . . .* (Dallas: Royal, 1964), 109.

92. Leonard Woolsey Bacon, "John Brown," *New Englander and Yale Review* 45 (April 1886): 293.

93. Henry C. White, "The Western Puritan," *Magazine of Western History* 2 (Oct. 1885): 626, 630, http://search.proquest.com/docview/137847091?accountid=14663.

94. Riddle, "Rise of the Antislavery Sentiment," 148.

95. A. G. Riddle, *The Life of Benjamin F. Wade* (Cleveland: W. W. Williams, 1886), 46.

96. Turner to Max Farrand, May 14, 1903, in Wilbur R. Jacobs, *The Historical World of Frederick Jackson Turner, with Selections from His Correspondence* (New Haven, CT: Yale University Press, 1968), 202, emphasis in original.

97. Alfred Mathews, *Ohio and Her Western Reserve. . . .* (New York: D. Appleton, 1902), 200.

98. For Turner's transformation from a frontier to a regional historian, see Michael Steiner, "From Frontier to Region: Frederick Jackson Turner and the New Western History," *Pacific Historical Review* 64, no. 4 (1995): 479–501; and Michael C. Steiner, "Frederick Jackson Turner and Western Regionalism," in *Writing Western History: Essays on Major Western Historians,* ed. Richard W. Etulain (Albuquerque: University of New Mexico Press, 1991), 103–35. For Turner's background as a Yankee Westerner, see Wilbur R. Jacobs, *On Turner's Trail: 100 Years of Writing Western History* (Lawrence: University Press of Kansas, 1994), 17, 19–22.

99. For a discussion of Turner's essays on the Yankee in the West, see Gray, *Yankee West,* 6–9.

100. On the emergence of the Middle West as a region, see James R. Shortridge, *The Middle West: Its Meaning in American Culture* (Lawrence: University Press of Kansas, 1989), 1–26.

101. George W. Julian, *The Life of Joshua R. Giddings* (Chicago: A. C. McClurg, 1892), 14.

102. B. A. Hinsdale, *The Old Northwest: With a View of the Thirteen Colonies as Constituted by the Royal Charters* (New York: T. MacCoun, 1888), 404.

103. Samuel Bowles, *The Pacific Railroad—Open: How to Go, What to See* (Boston: Fields, Osgood, 1869), 22. For an earlier version of this work, see Samuel Bowles, "The Pacific Railroad—Open: How to Go, What to See," *Atlantic Monthly* 23 (Apr. 1869): 493–502; (May 1869): 617–25; (June 1869): 753–62.

104. Bowles, *Pacific Railroad,* 23.

105. Frederick Jackson Turner, "The Children of the Pioneers," in *The Significance of Sections in American History* (Gloucester, MA: P. Smith, 1959), 262.

106. Frederick J. Turner, "Greater New England in the Middle of the Nineteenth Century," *Proceedings of the American Antiquarian Society,* n.s., 29 (1919): 231.

107. Hinsdale, *Old Northwest,* 390. Hinsdale was born in 1837 in Wadsworth, Ohio, of New England–descended parents. See Burke A. Hinsdale, *History of the University of Michigan,* ed. Isaac N. Demmon (Ann Arbor: Published by the University, 1906), 278.

108. Hinsdale, *Old Northwest,* 391. For a similar description of the broadening of Yankee religious culture in the Western Reserve, see Mathews, *Ohio and Her Western Reserve,* 172–74.

109. See DeRogatis, *Moral Geography,* 39–40; and Rohrer, *Keepers of the Covenant,* 11–12, 21–22, 25, 47–51.

110. Turner, "Greater New England," 238–39.

111. Robert Samuel Fletcher, *A History of Oberlin College: From Its Foundation through the Civil War* (Oberlin, OH: Oberlin College, 1943), 1:119; DeRogatis, *Moral Geography,* 164–65.

112. See, for example, Mathews, *Ohio and Her Western Reserve,* 189.

113. Albert Bushnell Hart, "The Westernization of New England," *Ohio Archeological and Historical Publications* 17, no. 2 (1908): 273.

114. Hinsdale, *Old Northwest,* 413–14.

115. See, for example, Frederick Jackson Turner, "The Middle West," in *The Frontier in American History* (Huntington, NY: Robert E. Krieger, 1976), 141–42. Turner also quoted Seward's 1860 speech on the antislavery influence of the Old Northwest on the East.

116. Hinsdale, *Old Northwest,* 413.

117. Ibid., 404. In 1882–86 Hinsdale served as superintendent of the Cleveland public schools. See Hinsdale, *History of the University,* 278.

118. Hinsdale, *Old Northwest,* 404–5.

119. Hart, "Westernization of New England," 268.

120. Hinsdale, *Old Northwest,* 405.

121. Mathews, *Ohio and Her Western Reserve,* 200. See also Turner, "Greater New England," 231; and Hart, "Westernization of New England," 263.

122. See the challenges to this theory—as espoused by Turner—in Edward Pessen, *Jacksonian America: Society, Personality, and Politics,* rev. ed. (Urbana: University of Illinois Press, 1985), 152; and Alexander Keyssar, *The Right to Vote: The Contested History of Democracy in the United States* (New York: Basic Books, 2000), 34.

123. Hart, "Westernization of New England," 270.

124. Hinsdale, *Old Northwest,* 410.

125. Turner, "Greater New England," 229.

126. Hinsdale, *Old Northwest,* 414–15.

127. Rev. Rufus W. Clark, *New England in the Northwestern Territory: Address before the New England Society at the Russell House, Detroit, Michigan, April 14th, 1898* ([Detroit?]: [1898?]), 4. According to Stewart Holbrook, some of the associates called the boat the *Union Gallery,* but others called it the *Adventure* or the *Mayflower.* See Stewart H. Holbrook, *The Yankee Exodus: An Account of Migration from New England* (New York: Macmillan, 1950), 22.

128. Henry M. Storrs, "Address," *Ohio Archeological and Historical Quarterly* 2, no.

1 (1888): 101–2. The son of Charles B. Storrs, the first president of Western Reserve College, Henry M. Storrs was born in Ravenna, Ohio, in 1827.

129. Ibid., 100.

130. Clark, "New England," 4.

131. Turner, "Greater New England," 240–41. The quote is on p. 232.

132. Mathews, *Ohio and Her Western Reserve,* 170–71.

133. William Stoughton, "New-Englands True Interest," in *The Puritans: A Sourcebook of Their Writings,* ed. Perry Miller and Thomas H. Johnson (Mineola, NY: Dover, 2001), 246.

134. Mathews, *Ohio and Her Western Reserve,* 13.

135. The New England–descended Mathews was born in Painesville, Ohio, in 1871.

136. Mathews, *Ohio and Her Western Reserve,* xi.

137. Ibid., 15, 170.

138. Turner, "Middle West," 137; Frederick Jackson Turner, "The Problem of the West," in *The Frontier in American History* (Huntington, NY: Robert E. Krieger, 1976), 215; Frederick Jackson Turner, "Middle Western Pioneer Democracy," in *The Frontier in American History,* 347. For similar sentiments, see Turner, "Greater New England," 232; and Turner, "Children of the Pioneers," 258.

139. Turner, "Problem of the West," 216.

140. Turner, "Middle Western Pioneer Democracy," 348.

141. Ibid.

142. Mathews, *Ohio and Her Western Reserve,* 171.

143. Rollin Lynde Hartt, "Notes on a Michigan Lumber Town," *Atlantic Monthly* 85 (Jan. 1900): 108.

144. Rollin Lynde Hartt, "The Ohioans," *Atlantic Monthly* 84 (Nov. 1899): 689–90.

145. Turner, "Middle Western Pioneer Democracy," 349. See also Frederick Jackson Turner, "The West and American Ideals," in *The Frontier in American History* (Huntington, NY: Robert E. Krieger, 1976), 295. For Turner's memories of his childhood, see Jacobs, *On Turner's Trail,* 22–25.

146. Lois Kimball Mathews Rosenberry, *The Expansion of New England: The Spread of New England Settlement and Institutions to the Mississippi River, 1620–1865* (New York: Russell & Russell, 1962), 192.

147. Ibid., 224.

148. Ibid., 261–62.

149. Turner, "Middle Western Pioneer Democracy," 351.

150. On the clustered ethnic communities of the Old Northwest and the Midwest more generally, see Conzen, "Immigrants in Nineteenth-Century Agricultural History," 312–23; Gjerde, *From Peasants to Farmers,* 138–67; and Jon Gjerde, *The Minds of the West: Ethnocultural Evolution in the Rural Middle West, 1830–1917* (Chapel Hill: University of North Carolina Press, 1997), 79–131.

151. Turner, "Middle Western Pioneer Democracy," 349.

152. Mathews, *Ohio and Her Western Reserve,* 263–64.

153. Hartt, "Ohioans," 684.

154. White, "Western Puritan," 626; Hosea Paul, "The Land System of the Western Reserve," *New England Magazine,* n.s., 2 (Aug. 1890): 705–6.

155. Hartt, "Ohioans," 689. For Hartt's controversial essays on the decadence of hill country Yankees, see "A New England Hill Town: I. Its Condition," *Atlantic Monthly* 83 (Apr. 1899): 561–74; and "A New England Hill Town: II. Its Revival," *Atlantic Monthly 83* (May 1899): 712–20.

156. Turner, "Middle Western Pioneer Democracy," 351.

157. Turner, "West and American Ideals," 294–95. For similar discussions of the contrast between ethnic relations in the Midwest and New England, see Turner, "Middle Western Pioneer Democracy," 350–51; Turner, "Greater New England," 234; and Frederick Jackson Turner, *The United States, 1830–1850: The Nation and Its Sections* (Gloucester, MA: Peter Smith, 1958), 280.

158. Turner, "West and American Ideals," 295.

CODA

1. Edward Bellamy, *Looking Backward: 2000–1887,* ed. Daniel H. Borus (Boston: Bedford, 1995), 50, 155.

2. On the rise of preservationist sentiment among turn-of-the-century Brahmins, see James M. Lindgren, *Preserving Historic New England: Preservation, Progressivism, and the Remaking of Memory* (New York: Oxford University Press, 1995), esp. chap. 2.

3. Bellamy, *Looking Backward,* 40. See the discussion of this passage in Lindgren, *Preserving Historic New England,* 21.

4. For the absence of professional athletes from Bellamy's utopia, see *Looking Backward,* 126.

5. On the origins of the Minuteman Project, see Jim Gilchrist and Jerome R. Corsi, *Minutemen: The Battle to Secure America's Borders* (Los Angeles: World Ahead, 2006), xxi.

6. Ibid., 14.

7. Ibid., 8.

8. Yvonne Abraham, "Minuteman Project Founder Finds Inspiration in Concord," *Boston Globe,* December 14, 2006, http://global.factiva.com/en/du/headlines.asp?napc=p&exclude=Recurring|Republished&sortBy=r&searchLanguage=custom&searchLang=EN&dedupe=2&srchuiver=4&atx=%e2%80%9cMinuteman+Project+Founder+Finds+Inspiration+in+Concord%22&accountid=9UNI006500&namespace=16.

9. West fears that the Bostonians of 2000 will see him as a "strange uncanny being, a stranded creature of an unknown sea," who needs to become "naturalized." See Bellamy, *Looking Backward,* 175.

10. See, for example, Donovan Slack, "Activists Rally against Senate Immigration Crackdown," *Boston Globe,* May 29, 2010, http://www.boston.com/news/local/breaking_news/2010/05/activists_rally_1.html; and Tony Horwitz, "Immigration—and the Curse of the Black Legend," *New York Times,* July 9, 2006, http://www.nytimes.com/2006/07/09/opinion/09horwitz.html?pagewanted=all.

11. Matt Selman and Nancy Kruse, "Husbands and Knives," November 18, 2007, in Matt Groening and James L. Brooks, *The Simpsons,* Fox, Culver City, CA.

Index

Note: Pages in italics indicate illustrations.